120 Days

In Deep Hiding

Lest we forget

Robert E[...]

— 2004

S. Boston Ma

120 Days In Deep Hiding

Outwitting the Iraqis in Occupied Kuwait

Dr. Robert E. Morris
with
James W. Ryan

Copyright © 2002 by Dr. Robert E. Morris.

ISBN :   Softcover   1-4010-6584-8

All rights reserved. No part of this book may be reproduced or transmitted in any form or by any means, electronic or mechanical, including photocopying, recording, or by any information storage and retrieval system, without permission in writing from the copyright owner.

This book was printed in the United States of America.

To order additional copies of this book, contact:
Xlibris Corporation
1-888-795-4274
www.Xlibris.com
Orders@Xlibris.com

15021

Contents

About The Authors 11
Acknowledgements 13
Prologue 15
Chapter 1
   Kuwait Invaded 23
Chapter 2
   Battle for the Capital 33
Chapter 3
   Pillage and Rape 43
Chapter 4
   Iraqi Confrontations 54
Chapter 5
   Forays and Forages 63
Chapter 6
   Captured 75
Chapter 7
   Escape from Headquarters 84
Chapter 8
   Foiled Flight 92
Chapter 9
   A Dash for Saudi 103
Chapter 10
   Mired in the Desert 114
Chapter 11
   Swindled in the Sands 124
Chapter 12
   Death of a Major 131

Chapter 13
- *Regrouping* *139*

Chapter 14
- *Hanging Separately* *168*

Chapter 15
- *Terror Call* *175*

Chapter 16
- *Contacting the Media* *188*

Chapter 17
- *On My Own* *198*

Chapter 18
- *Close Call* *208*

Chapter 19
- *The Green Line* *214*

Chapter 20
- *Capture of the Hoyles* *221*

Chapter 21
- *Running Amok* *229*

Chapter 22
- *Loose Cannons* *239*

Chapter 23
- *Man of Action* *249*

Chapter 24
- *Thanksgiving* *255*

Chapter 25
- *Up to Baghdad* *259*

Chapter 26
- *Into the Lion's Lair* *270*

Chapter 27
- *Saddam's Surprise* *276*

Chapter 28
- *Free at Last* *283*

Epilogue 289

Chapter Notes 295

Addendum
- *The Boston Globe Letters* *299*

*To my dearest wife and best friend Jill;
to the best daughters in the world—Anna and Trish.*

*To Imad—a saint—who so demonstrated
that people from two opposing cultures can show love and
kindness, even in the worst of times*

Cast a cold eye on life, on death. Horseman, pass by.

W.B. Yeats

ABOUT THE AUTHORS

A native of South Boston, Massachusetts, Dr. Morris has traveled extensively in the past three decades to help bring health care to myriad populations.

A graduate of the College of the Holy Cross, Harvard, and the University of Maryland, he served for two years in the United States Navy as a Dental Officer—one of those years on combat assignment with the U.S. Marine Corps near DaNang, Vietnam. He was decorated by the U.S. Navy for his humanitarian efforts and professionalism in Vietnam.

After the Navy, he had a private practice in San Francisco, CA., and later worked on a federal research project in health services delivery at the University of Maryland.

In 1975, the United Nations recruited him as a consultant in training and education. As an advisor, he worked in over 13 countries in the Caribbean and South America over the next ten years. In 1985 he returned to the United States to attend the Harvard School of Public Health as a Kellogg Fellow. After receiving his Master of Public Health degree, he was recruited by the State of Kuwait to upgrade its oral health care programs. He was there on Aug. 2, 1990 when the Iraqi army invaded this tiny Arab country. After a series of remarkable escapades over some 120 days, he returned to the United States on a false passport.

After the Gulf War ended he returned to Kuwait where he led a team of experts in rebuilding the Oral Health Services of the National Health Care System. The programs of preventive care for children developed since then have been internationally recognized for their excellence.

His family returned to Kuwait in 1993.

Morris and his family returned to live in Boston at the end of 1999. Currently, he is in semi-retirement while still finding time for independent lecturing, consulting and scientific writing. His scientific articles have been published widely in international health journals. This is his first full-length book.

-o-

Boston native, James W. Ryan, has been involved in just about every facet of writing during the past four decades. He was an editor and correspondent for United Press International for 11 years before going into corporate public relations work. A prize-winning short story writer, military historian and travel writer, he is the author of 16 books and another 15 ghost written. He has been published in 12 countries, and three of his books have been optioned to film companies. A former Army paratrooper, he is a member of the Veterans of Foreign Wars and American Legion.

ACKNOWLEDGEMENTS

I wish to especially acknowledge and thank the following, all who in some way have affected me and this story: Jim Ryan who has stuck with me to finish this story, Jawad Behbehani who with his wife went beyond the call of duty in Kuwait, Senator John Kerry for not missing a beat when someone came to him for help, the Embassy of Ireland and its foreign office for keeping track of one of its own two generations removed, all my family members who prayed and worked to assure my return, George Gillespie who pushed the buttons in Washington, Mohammed Attai for unfailing generosity in Kuwait, all those who prayed, all those class members of the University of Maryland who were so generous.

PROLOGUE

December 10, 1990

If nothing else, Dr. Robert Morris was a stubborn man. In his mind, he would not be free of Iraqi President Saddam Hussein's clutches until the Pan Am jet took off from Germany's Frankfurt-am-Main airport. Perhaps by the time the aircraft was ten minutes into its flight for the States, he would be truly convinced that he was out of the reach of the Iraqis.

Only then would he experience a sense of euphoria. A sense that they had slipped out of the remaining surly bonds fashioned in Iraq. A sense that finally they were homeward bound—just in time for Christmas with family and friends.

"Even when we took off from Frankfurt, there was still some apprehension and fear that somehow or other, through some devious plan unbeknownst to us, Saddam Hussein still held us in thrall. At no time during our six-hour flight aboard the Iraqi jet the previous day from Baghdad did we do any celebrating. None of us wanted to give the Iraqis the slightest excuse to turn the plane around."

It was Monday, December 10, 1990, when the Americans boarded the Pan Am plane in Frankfurt. The Iraqis had held most of them for varying lengths of time as hostages. With a few others, Dr. Morris had been captured briefly but had escaped. After that, he never surrendered, opting instead to go into deep hiding from the conquerors of Kuwait for more than four months.

"I'm an American. I didn't want to be just another one of Saddam's hostages. We remained free from Saddam, but we were never free from the fear of capture, torture, and execution. Never free from such dark thoughts."

Inside the aircraft cabin, Dr. Morris would share four seats across with one of his best friends, George Daher, a professional landscaper from Pennsylvania. Slouched in his deep-cushioned seat, Dr. Morris appeared hollow-eyed and gaunt, his beard dishelved although he had managed to keep it trim during his ordeal. In evading the Iraqis for more than 130 days, he had lost 23 pounds, and his beard now contained far more gray hair than red.

Impatient and apprehensive, he longed for the 740,000-pound jet to lumber down the runway and head west. Perhaps then, he figured, he would believe he was out of the grasp of Saddam's hordes of lackeys and barbarians—the bastards who had plundered and raped the tiny Persian Gulf emirate at will since invading it on August 2, 1990.

Once again, all the awful memories flashed across the screen of his mind in a series of flesh-colored blips even though he struggled mentally to focus on other matters.

The thunderous explosion of the first Iraqi shell in the pre-dawn darkness—bursting just across Al-Hilali Street from his eighth-floor apartment. The approaching Republican Guard—Saddam's elite troops—and the firefights unfolding right below his window. The dead and dying sprawled in the city streets. The assault on the television station and other key government buildings. The daylong seizure of Kuwaitis, who had been left uninformed of the invasion.

He would never forget his own capture and escape from Iraqi military headquarters in the Sheraton Hotel. Going underground and the interminable months of secrecy. Incredibly exhausting. The failed attempts to escape across the desert. The establishment of the "group" within the huge apartment complex. The strict rules of conduct set up to foil the endless round-ups. Always the reports of the rape and murder of innocent civilians. The fears at every awakening moment of betrayal. The price on his head. The members of the group turning on each other. The threats of physical confrontations. The dramatic mood swings suffered by all. The process of survival itself becoming absolutely fatiguing. The curious make-up of the group. The nutsy Australian, who constantly jeopardized the group's security. The tough Irishman, who liked to take too many chances. The Brit, former publican, who got drunk daily from his secret cache of liquor. Then there was the mysterious Syrian, and the concern that he might betray them.

Dr. Morris recalled how their hopes for rescue ebbed, giving way to black despair as the Iraqis came closer and closer to their hideouts. The wondering who would flip out first. Kill himself. Go berserk. Give them away to become part of a human shield around some isolated Iraqi defense facility in the mountains or along the Tigris and Euphrates Rivers.

Worst of all had been the isolation, the paranoia, and claustrophobia, the terror of hiding and the fear of capture, which they wore like scratchy hair shirts every waking moment. The heights to which their anger and frustration soared. Waiting for the United Nations attack that never came. Praying for the Americans to bomb and storm the Iraqis even though they might have been among the victims.

So many times Dr. Morris had longed for the U.S. Marines to come charging ashore at Kuwait City. He knew them well. As a naval officer, he had served with the Corps in a series of embattled jungle hill stations in Vietnam. He was well acquainted with the sights and sounds and horrors of combat. Still, he wanted the Marines to drive out the Iraqi invaders.

Dr. Morris was shaken from his black thoughts by a smiling flight attendant, offering him champagne and a tray filled with McDonald's cheeseburgers. He and George Daher accepted the repast gratefully and were chatting amiably when his worst fear seemed to become reality.

Only moments before, the Pan Am captain, John Donahue, had announced over the intercom that the flight was ready to go. The jet would be taking off shortly. The Americans smiled in anticipation. Once aloft, they knew they would be safely out of Saddam's way.

But now Captain Donahue was back on the intercom, and his new announcement was draped in black. "I'm very sorry to have to announce something that's going to make you people scream. We're going to have a very, very long delay. I can't even tell you how long."

Dr. Morris was hit instantly with a cold wave of depression. He thought about slipping out of the plane and finding another one headed for the States. Right then, all he wanted to do was to go home to Boston and to Jill and his two daughters, Anna and Tricia.

Captain Donahue was on the intercom again. "I want you to know that we have American Embassy people here, and they are trying to pull every possible string to get us a fast clearance. So try to relax. Have some champagne. The bar is open to all."

Dr. Morris and Daher looked at each other, shrugged helplessly and grinned. Why not? They had already consumed free beer in the Pan Am lounge. Consumed champagne and McDonalds on the plane. Why not have a real drink? It was time to be patient, to try to relax, and to think positively. Yet, it was easier said than done.

Luck was with them finally. There wasn't to be an interminable delay. Captain Donahue's voice echoed jubilantly throughout the fuselage: "I've got good news. The German authorities have pushed us to the front of the line. We'll be backing out within ten minutes."

"Could it be," Dr. Morris wondered, "that we truly are going home? Whatever, let's just be out of here. Get us up into that big, blue, beckoning sky, and I'll believe it at last."

While he waited expectantly for the jumbo jet to become airborne, he considered his current situation anew. Here he was 47 years old; his only possessions a small cloth bag containing a few articles of clothing and his toilet kit. Everything else he and Jill owned had been lost, stolen, or left behind when he fled Kuwait City for Baghdad with false documents early in December. Everything including all his family's clothing, furnishings, jewelry, mementos, and the expensive German car he had to abandon in the desert during one of his escape attempts.

One thought took the greatest grasp on his mind. "I couldn't get it out of my mind. It gnawed at me. How in God's name did this ever happen to me? Selfishly or not, I kept thinking 'why me?'"

In his mind, he had always been a law-abiding citizen; one of eight children raised by strict Roman Catholic parents. They had instilled in him a keen awareness of the difference between right and wrong, imbued him with traditional values and the correct standards of conduct.

In turn, he had been a top student at the Boston Latin School. Suffered disappointment, but rose above it, when turned down for admission to Harvard College, the alma mater of his father and grandfather. He had gratefully accepted admission to the College of the Holy Cross. Gaining further scholastic honors, he had gone on to graduate from the University of Maryland Dental School. With the war in Vietnam entering its sixth year, he took a commission as a lieutenant senior grade in the Navy and was assigned to tender to the dental needs of Marine units at various hill stations in Vietnam. While no grunt rifleman, he had put his life on the line, voluntarily traveling with the Marines to outposts deep in the northern jungle to treat both military personnel and civilians

His love of travel and adventure brought him a ten-year contract with the United Nations Development Programme and World Health Organization, which sent him to train dentists and auxiliaries in Trinidad. It was there that he had met his wife-to-be, Jill Dopson, a graduate of the University of the West Indies, who specialized in educating autistic children. Two daughters were born to the family later—Anna, now eleven, and Patricia, now five. In time, WHO gave Dr. Morris a similar task in Guyana, South America.

After ten years with WHO, Dr. Morris returned to Boston to attend the Harvard School of Public Health as a Kellogg Fellow. It was then that he obtained the contract from the Kuwait government to upgrade its oral health care system.

Deep in thought within the Pan Am cabin, Dr. Morris was

riven with bittersweet memories of the good life his family had enjoyed in Kuwait City. Jill had been very happy living there. Earlier, on reaching Baghdad, he had telephoned her. By then she had been living for four months with his sister Joanne and her husband Jim McDevitt in South Boston.

In their conversation, she had revealed how much she missed life in Kuwait, how hard life was for her in Boston. Times were bad. The economy was deplorable. There was little work available. Everything was so expensive vis-a-vis Kuwait, where the government had subsidized so many facets of their lives, including a rent-free, three-bedroom apartment, free health care, and numerous perks and privileges.

He was a government consultant and was provided with an excellent compensation package comparable to U.S. standards for professionals. Indeed, the Kuwaitis, given all their oil wealth, could be arrogant in so many ways to peoples whom they considered their inferiors and whom they only allowed entry to perform the most menial tasks. In retrospect though, Dr. Morris didn't have a single regret about his life in Kuwait prior to the invasion. It had been A-okay.

So where had it all gone wrong? Why had he been in the wrong place at the wrong time? Thank God Jill and the girls had not been in Kuwait on August 2, 1990. Yet, ironically, he had been in frenzy in the days leading up to that date because Jill and his daughters had been visiting her family in Port of—Spain when the Black Muslims had staged their coup attempt.

There he was, believing he was safe and sound in Kuwait City, ready to flip out because his family was in the midst of a bloody uprising in the capital city of Trinidad some seven thousand miles away in the Caribbean. He had managed to telephone Jill to tell her to go to a safe house and insist that male members of her family remain with her and the girls. The international news was full of reports out of Port of Spain about the rebels looting, raping, and killing. Gory footage of the rebellion could be viewed almost hourly on CNN International in the hotels. He had never felt so helpless in his life.

He was snapped from these thoughts when several gongs sounded toward the front of the cabin. The 747 jet, the screaming whine of its four turbo-fan engines cut to a dull whine by thick insulation, quickly rolled down the runway and lifted into the evening sky. Within minutes, Dr. Morris and George Daher joined their fellow passengers in loosing a cacophony of happy cries, high fives, rebel yells, and waves of applause. The dentist was convinced at last that he was going home, home to America.

In his newly found bliss, Dr. Morris switched his thoughts to several songs that seemed to be appropriate for the occasion. One was "Welcome Home" as sung by Willie Nelson. It was from the Vietnam War era.

He hummed the words: "Welcome home, welcome home. There will be no parades, and there will be no flags . . . ." This time, though, he hoped it would be different. He, too, had come home from Vietnam to an ungrateful nation and had faced the scorn and indifference of the non-combatants.

This time there would be parades and flags. This time the survivors would not be mistreated. Deep in his gut, though, he realized that private citizens like himself, caught up as pawns in a foreign dispute, wouldn't rate such a formal welcome. Still, it would be great to experience such a reception.

As the Pan Am jet climbed to its cruising altitude, another song that went through his mind was "Somewhere Out There" from the animated film "An American Tail." He had adopted the song while in captivity, lulling himself to sleep with its message of hope.

> "Somewhere out there,
> Someone's saying a prayer,
> That we'll find one another,
> In that big somewhere out there.
> And when the night wind starts to sing,
> A lonesome lullaby,
> It helps to think we're sleeping,
> Underneath the same big sky.

> Somewhere out there,
> If love can see us through,
> Then we'll be together,
> Somewhere out there,
> Where dreams come true."

The words brought immediate thoughts of his family. They were out there somewhere. Under a blue sky or a soft dark night. Perhaps they were dreaming about him as he was thinking about them.

He and George chatted for a while about their escape from Kuwait and Saddam Hussein and everything that had befallen them in the past four months. George then dozed off. Still half-awake, Dr. Morris wondered anew how it had all come about. How some two-bit dictator—with a rag-tail army who couldn't defeat the Iranians in an eight-year war—could now place the peace of the world in such jeopardy?

Why didn't the U.S. government know more about the invasion? Why hadn't the Americans been warned to get out? He had been at an embassy reception the night before and there hadn't been a single word said about a possible invasion.

God how did it all happen? It seemed so long ago now. Way back in August. Last summer. 131 days ago. He had been so fearful for Jill and the girls in Trinidad. Then a single Iraqi shell had shattered his idyllic life in Kuwait and turned it into a shrapnel-studded nightmare.

Chapter 1

Kuwait Invaded

It was just a few moments after 5 a.m. It was a Thursday, a working day for us in Kuwait. August 2, 1990. I was in a deep sleep without dreaming after lying awake for hours, worrying about my wife and daughters in Trinidad. The latest news from there, however, had been cheering. Jill and the girls were okay, tucked safely away in a relative's house, and the Trinidad government was regaining control of the country. We would be reunited once again on August 10th in Kuwait City.

Suddenly, there was a tremendous explosion, a blast that brought me instantly awake in my eighth-floor master bedroom in the Al-Muthanna Mall apartment complex, facing on Al-Hilali Street and the Meridien Hotel. I sat up, shaking my head to clear it. What in God's name was that? What an incredibly ear-shattering noise!

I listened, but there was only silence. I swung my legs around and stood erect in the darkened room. At that hour, the city was still shrouded in the blackness of night although a slip of pink was beginning to spread slowly along the eastern horizon.

"Rob! Rob! Did you hear it? What the hell . . . ?"

It was Philip Balmforth, Jill's godson, a Canadian, who had arrived five days earlier from Jordan with the hope of finding work in the shipping business in Kuwait City. He was single and 25 years old. No sooner had he arrived for his visit than he discovered his passport had been stolen at the airport. Without it, he couldn't fly out of Kuwait City for Amman, Jordan, as scheduled the previous evening. Bad luck for him.

I went to the window, pushed aside the drapes, and looked out. Nothing. Only darkness and the lights of the city. I called to Philip. "It's okay. Not to worry." But I was worried. The noise had loosed a shock wave that shook the building. It was also very evocative, bringing to the fore bad memories of things I had been trying to erase for 20 years or more.

From my remembrances of things past, I recognized the sound of an exploding artillery shell. I hurried into the livingroom and peeked out. Everything appeared normal. Strange. After such an ungodly blast, I thought I would see police cars and ambulances rushing wildly about, sirens screaming and wailing.

"Rob, in here," Philip called. I went to his bedroom and saw him silhouetted like a dim cutout against the window.

"Can you see anything?" I asked.

"Not a thing. What the hell was it? Had to be something. I thought I was going to shoot through the ceiling," Philip said.

Side by side, we stared out the window. Daylight began to take hold and reveal more details of the city spread out before us. Then I saw it. "There, in the middle of the cemetery. A shell exploded. I knew it. See the crater? It's still smoldering. It was a big one. Heavy stuff."

Philip looked perplexed. "I don't understand. Who fired it? Where did it come from?"

I was grim-faced by then. "I'm sure we will find out shortly. Who knows? We might be in the middle of a coup against the Emir. It won't be the first try in Kuwait."

Within minutes, the sun rose and bathed the city in heightened light. The summer temperature would quickly soar to 120 degrees and even higher. In the burgeoning light, we could see other tenants at their windows in the apartment complex, the myriad night watchmen and old fareshis on the roofs of the lower buildings, and small groups of militiamen in the streets. All of them were now looking toward the spot where the shell had burst.

Apparently, the rising sun was the signal for whoever was trying to take over the city—or at least our central portion of it. "There," I pointed, "combat troops and armored personnel carriers."

Simultaneously, the sounds of small arms fire came to us as contingents of smartly-dressed soldiers and their vehicles flowed out from behind the National Bank of Kuwait building and along the length of Soor Street in the direction of the Kuwait National Television Center opposite our vantage point on the far side of the cemetery.

The attack was preceded by a series of rocket-propelled grenades, which erupted in small black bursts and in a rising crescendo of battle noises against the upper floors of the 16-story TV structure.

Despite the small arms fire that was directed at them from the smaller buildings clustered about the base of the tower, the unidentified troops continued their advance in a very professional manner. About then, I began to consider the fact that Kuwaiti forces were not up to such standards. I didn't want to even consider that they might be Iraqis.

Philip and I watched in awe as the phalanx of attackers ignored the bursts of gunshots sweeping their ranks and dashed forward. Gutsy guys, whoever they were. Pros. They quickly swarmed around the TV tower and shortly burst inside and overwhelmed the few defenders.

The two of us found it difficult to believe the military scenario that was being played out below us. It was as if we were leaning over a large sand table and a small-scale war was being staged for our entertainment.

Several minutes passed as the air echoed and shook with the roar of gunfire. Occasional tracers flickered like giant fireflies across the sky. We opened the windows to get a better view, and the level of the noise increased by several decibels.

"Wow, look at that," Philip cried, pointing to the right down Al-Hilali Street. I jerked my head about to see more troops deploying from Fahd Al-Salim Street in the vicinity of the Meridien

Hotel. I glanced at my wristwatch. It was almost 5:20 a.m. Where had the time gone?

Within moments, the troops rushed up Al-Hilali Street to halt almost directly below my windows. Without any wasted time, an officer approached three Kuwaiti militiamen, supposedly guarding the Saudi Airways office below, and ordered them to hand over their holstered guns. They did without any hesitation. I suspected then that the weapons had never been loaded. The officer then led the trio to the sidewalk where he motioned them to lie face down.

About this time of the morning, Kuwaitis usually began arriving in the city in their fleets expensive automobiles for the working day. Despite everything that was happening, they showed up as usual. One after another, their cars left the main highway to the left and turned down Al-Hilali Street to be stopped by the soldiers' roadblock.

It was not surprising that the occupants of the vehicles had no awareness about what was happening. Their rulers provided them with little news on the government-owned radio station. As for any noises of battle, the closed windows shut them out. They were sealed to hold the coolness of the air conditioning.

As they were ordered from their cars, the troops directed them to sit down on the sidewalk below us. They obeyed like sheep, few of them voicing any concern or anger. Mostly Muslims, they waited calmly to learn their fate.

At the time, some of the troops disappeared into our Al-Muthanna complex, a property of the Kuwait Investment Corporation. It was a huge building with three floors of mall shops and boutiques, and above were 13 floors of apartment units—actually some 450 apartments.

Philip and I wondered aloud whether they were going to loot the shops. Whether they would shortly be knocking on my door or bursting through it with weapons at the ready. Whatever, we decided to remain right where we were.

Meanwhile, the majority of the soldiers had advanced to our left up Al-Hilali Street and launched an attack on the City's main police headquarters. It was only some 150 yards distant, and we could see the fighting in detail. The strong point fell within minutes.

Now it was full daylight. Incredibly, despite all the sights and sounds of battle, the Kuwaitis continued like lemmings to swerve left off the highway and drive down onto Al-Hilali Street. Philip and I stared at each other in disbelief. Were the Kuwaitis blind? Deaf? Were they living in another world? How far out could you get? The whole scene had a surrealistic air about it.

By then I was sitting on a chair, crouched forward, to watch—in continued fascination—everything that was going on below us. Off and on, we had been trying to get some news of the ongoing events on the radio without luck. It was as though the world had no inkling at all about what was happening in Kuwait City.

Almost from the beginning, we were joined in my apartment by other residents of the building. Most of them were acquaintances unable to see what was going on from their own windows. By then, most of us were in agreement that the soldiers were Iraqis. Several of my visitors, lifelong residents of the Persian Gulf region, identified the initial wave of attackers as units of the Republican Guard, Saddam Hussein's elite troops. Whoever, there was no denying their elan.

If they were indeed Iraqis, what the hell were they doing? How had things come to such a pass? There had been periodic reports, gossip too, of trouble between Iraq and Kuwait, but we never figured it was serious enough to warrant an invasion.

Back in the spring, there had been a report that Saddam had demanded that Kuwait and Saudi Arabia forget about the 30 billion dollars they had lent him to fight the Iranians. In fact, he had told them to ante up another 30 billion big ones. They would suffer heavy reprisals if they didn't.

Such reports, however, were sketchy at best because again the government controlled what news, if any, the people would hear on its radio station and TV station. There was always the news on CNN in the various hotels, but we had no impression that CNN was paying very much attention to another squabble in the Gulf States.

In the month just passed, we had heard, informally, that Saddam was massing troops on Kuwait's border. By then, the United States, tired of Saddam's boorish behavior staged a naval exercise on the waters off the United Arab Emirates. Saddam protested but continued with his military buildup. In our own little world, we just thought of the situation as a lot of showy bluster and remained convinced that nothing would come of it. There was just no way Saddam was going to attack Kuwait. So we had blithely gone on with our lives. In any case, my mind was focused on the events in Trinidad and concern for Jill and my daughters. The hell with the crazy Iraqis!

It suddenly occurred to me that I should determine whether I could still call out. I picked up the telephone. It emitted the familiar, soothing dial-tone sound. I got through to Jill's number in Trinidad, but the line was busy. I quickly punched out the international area code for the States and within moments was talking to my sister Anne and her husband Ed Lynch in Hingham, a suburb of Boston. Here we were in the middle of a battle, and no one thought to shut down the telephone service. Bizarre.

I quickly informed them that I was convinced Iraq had invaded Kuwait. I could see Iraqi troops right out my window. There had been fighting. Lots of shooting. Bang! Bang! I told them about the heavy shell exploding that had awakened Philip and me.

I told them we were fine and that she should call CNN, CBS, *The Boston Globe*, AP, whoever—to tell them about my call and what was happening. We hadn't heard anything on the radio. BBC, no one. I said they could call me directly on my line for a first-hand report.

Ringing off, I called Jill again in Port of Spain and got right through to her, informing her of everything that had happened up to that point. I assured her that Philip and I were okay, but we were in one hell of a mess. I emphasized that it was no fun being trapped in the middle of a capital city being invaded by the Iraqis. Still shaking off the cobwebs of sleep, she replied that things sounded very bad for us, ominous even.

What with everything that had occurred since 5 a.m. that morning—and who knew what else was to be unleashed on us?—I snapped: "I don't need that kind of talk. I don't want to hear it. It's bad enough being here."

I instantly regretted my outburst. I apologized and inquired about her and our daughters. She said their situation was almost back to normal. I gave them my love, promised to call again shortly, and rang off.

As the early morning advanced—without any knocks on the door by the Iraqis—a steady stream of people came and went from my apartment. It was centrally located in the complex and provided an excellent view, a panorama actually, of the action being undertaken by the Iraqis.

Off to the far right beyond the Meridien Hotel, we could see along Fahd Al-Salim Street to the Sheraton Hotel, which someone said was being used as the Iraqi military headquarters. We could also look across the cemetery on the other side of Al-Hilali Street to the captured TV tower as well as the First, Second, and Third Ring Roads in the distance. As our eyes swept to the left, the main police station, various ministry buildings, and the expansive telecommunications complex came into view.

There was a lull in the action at the time. Little was happening in the far distance—neither right, left, nor to the front. Most of the activity was taking place below our windows as the Iraqis moved their militia and civilian captives about.

Checking around, I saw my neighbor, John Levins, an Australian; Dr. Robert Hansen, my colleague in teaching dentistry, who had come to Kuwait from Harvard University; his wife, Mona, and Mary McGee, a special needs teacher from New York.

There was also a Sudanese physician, whom I had seen on occasion in the elevator. He had brought along his short-wave radio, but there was still little news about the invasion. There was a fellow from Lebanon, whose wife, Rana, taught with Jill.

The cast of visitors kept changing in numbers, sex, and sizes throughout the early morning. It was like a small United Nations most of the time. Americans, Brits, Irish, Kuwaitis, and innumerable varieties of Arabs.

In all our many and excited conversations with each other, we came to a consensus that the Iraqis, having accomplished whatever their mission, would be withdrawing within a few days. We consoled ourselves that we only had to remain calm, out of sight, and out of their hands for several days or so, and then they would be gone. Talk about wishful thinking! Who was the poet who said something about " . . . hope springs eternal?"

Every now and then, we would be shaken from these peaceful thoughts and calming orations by outbursts of pistol, rifle, and automatic weapons fire—usually along Fahd Al-Salim Street between the Meridien and Sheraton Hotels, where there was a labyrinth of smaller streets, low-lying buildings, and criss-crossed walls. We could only wonder whether the Kuwaiti regular forces, or perhaps even armed Kuwaiti civilians, were putting up any opposition to the enemy soldiers. Within moments the firing would stop as abruptly as it began.

Off to the right, along the key Arabian Gulf Road, we spotted a heavy tank convoy headed south. We took it as an ominous sign. You didn't bother to bring up big tanks for a brief visit to your neighbor's country. Perhaps it was going to join in an attack on the royal palace some four miles distant in that direction. Spumes of black smoke rose into the sky on that horizon.

Philip made coffee, and some of the women went into the kitchen to prepare breakfast. The size of the crowd was constantly changing during this period. People just wandered in and out, many of them either hardly known to me or complete strangers. I suggested to Philip that he and I should keep an eye on some of them before everything in the apartment was missing. By and large though, most of the company was welcomed.

Quiet now descended over our section of the city. The sun mounted higher into the sky, the heat blistering the air. To our relief, the Iraqis moved their captives off the sidewalks and along the street to find shelter from the heat. Now and then, the soldiers would loot a Coca-Cola truck to give their captives a soothing drink.

One of our group suddenly pointed to the middle distance. "Helicopters! Look at them! They're shooting up something!"

As one, we peered across the sky to view the choppers as they began to launch an airborne assault on the police station in the Hawally district. There were perhaps five, maybe six, of the helicopters. There had been a series of muffled explosions in that area brought about no doubt by the helicopters. One explosion was more vicious than the next.

A ball of flame and a pall of black smoke rose from the earth. We figured one of the choppers had been shot down. Now there would be hell to pay!

Dr. Hansen had been photographing the helicopters and had a fine view of them through his zoom lens. "Damn," he yelled. "I think they're coming right for us!"

Instantly, I felt a cold ball of fear curdling in my gut. We glanced at each other, bewildered and white-faced, and again looked toward the helicopters.

He was right! The choppers, so reminiscent to me because of Vietnam, were headed directly toward the center of the city. It was as though they were approaching along an invisible line directly to my apartment on the eighth floor of the Al-Muthanna complex. I had this creepy sense that we had been selected earlier at some planning session as a designated target of opportunity. If nothing else, use up some ammo shooting up the Al-Muthanna, where all those foreigners lived.

Closer and closer they flew, their blades whirling in the clear humid air, engines emitting a terrible racket to all those hunkered down in terror within the city. Not Dr. Hansen, however. He was the picture of serenity and indifference as he kept his camera fixed on them through the open window.

Then it occurred to me. The open windows! Of course!

They were clearly visible to the Iraqi pilots. I realized they could see us crowded into the open windows as well as we could see them. We had made ourselves an inviting target for the trigger-happy Iraqis. My level of fear and apprehension jumped sharply. I looked around me. Didn't anyone else understand the danger we were inviting?

By then, the Iraqi choppers were only 200 yards or so away over the cemetery. They loomed larger in our vision and infinitely more ominous as they advanced in a rising crescendo of revolving blades and churning engines. Straight on. Straight for our complex. Straight for my apartment windows!

Memories of Vietnam flooded my mind on viewing the goggled-eyed helicopter crews through their Plexiglas windshields. At the open doors, gunners huddled behind their machine guns. They could fire at any moment!

"The windows! Damn it! The windows! They're targeting right on us!" I yelled. I pushed someone hurriedly aside and swung shut the darkly tinted glass.

As though snapped from a hypnotic state, the others rushed to follow my lead. Everyone was warning the others to get away from the windows. A final glimpse showed the helicopters skidding and yawing at slower speeds above the cemetery, approaching Al-Hilali Street and still fixed right on us.

I went back against the far wall, yelling for the others to get away from the windows. Take cover. Everyone moved like skittish rabbits flushed from their nests. The windows shook in their frames. The noise was deafening. I cringed involuntarily. Any second now, I thought, they will blast us with rockets and machine gun fire. We would be dog meat.

Somewhere in the apartment, a woman screamed. Someone else sobbed in my ear. I prayed like it was the old days, back taking a bloody pounding with the Marines on Hill 55 in the jungle of Vietnam.

Chapter 2

Battle for the Capital

The roar of the helicopter engines rose to a thunderous peak just outside my apartment windows. It was so overwhelming that I expected the helicopters to smash through the windows for a landing smack in the middle of the livingroom.

When would they open up with their 50-millimeter guns or whatever armaments choppers carried these days? I envisioned the bursts of deadly fire ripping away the entire front wall to leave us exposed in the bright sunlight to their rockets and missiles. It would be a turkey shoot for the Iraqis.

The walls now also reverberated from the massive airwaves unleashed by the churning blades. Incredibly, the reverberations stopped almost immediately, and the high-pitched wailing of the choppers receded simultaneously. I raised my head to stare at the windows. There was nothing to be seen through the tinted glass.

"What do you think, Rob?" Philip Balmforth asked at my elbow.

I looked at him, wondering whether I appeared as white-faced as he did. Shaking my head, I said I didn't know. "They're gone, that's for sure. And so damn quickly. How'd they do it?"

Philip considered my question a bit, then cocked his head. "I know what. Bet they went up over the roof. That would cut off the sound and shock waves quick enough."

Feeling more relaxed, I smiled slightly and said, "Not bad, young fella. Makes sense. In any case, they're gone for now."

Everyone who had been taking cover in the apartment began to emerge from their shelter. I think we all felt a little sheepish about then. Certainly none of us had acted heroically. It was almost a case of every man for himself. You know the old French bit about saving yourself if you can. (1)

Oh, well, I figured, nothing changes. I knew fear years before when shelled in Vietnam, and I had known the same fear only moments earlier. Twenty years really hadn't made any difference. The prospect of being torn about by flying lead and steel, in whatever form, would always be terrifying.

Dr. Hansen, clasping his camera, headed for the windows. While I could admire his *sang froid*, I didn't think he should be acting just then like Oliver Stone. I suggested that he wait a bit longer before cracking open one of the windows.

"An open window will stick out like a blackberry in a bowl of milk against all the glass. Bring those bastards right down on us again. Let's hold up for a few minutes."

Now everyone was about, coming and going from the apartment and out to the kitchen, preparing additional hot coffee and breakfast food. People were in and out of the bathroom, on and off the telephone, and trying to pick up any news about our situation on various radios.

Ever the frugal Irishman, I urged my guests to keep a record of their long-distance phone calls and be prepared to ante up any charges to my service. Hell, they were direct-dialing all over the globe. My friend, John Levins, the Australian, had already made a series of calls to Australia, mostly to media outlets, to begin creating his own living legend.

Over a period of time, all of us had taken to peeking through the windows to see what was going on in our vicinity of the city. Cars were still being stopped along Al-Hilali Street, and their occupants hustled away at gunpoint. There never was any resistance. Smoke rose from several widely separated spots. Occasionally, we could hear gunfire in the distance.

Because of the curved facade of the complex, I could see other residents at their windows. A few even waved on sighting me. I smiled and waved back, wondering who the hell they were. People definitely were friendlier at such times. Showed that old spirit of "we're all in this together, and let's make the best of it."

At the time, however, I was still confused. What was "this" we were all in together? Were the Iraqis in town just for a short visit to spank the Emir and his government for daring to ask for payment on their bills, or were they in Kuwait for the long haul? Where would we foreigners, particularly we Americans, fit? Saddam Hussein had been our boy for years. We loved him when he was kicking Iran's backside—our surrogate for getting even with the Iranians for seizing our embassy in Tehran and holding Americans hostage for more than a year.

I had to wonder, though, whether Saddam Hussein ever really loved us in return. He was a well-known taker, not a giver. I had heard that he had never made promised reparations to the families of the men killed aboard the U.S.S. Stark, when one of his fighters loosed an Exocet missile into her hull three or four years before. No, it never seemed to bother him that he hadn't made good to the survivors.

There he was—always at the front of the line—taking everything he could get his hands on from the United States, Germany, Russia, England, France, Brazil, Argentina. You name it. He was a dictator and tyrant who never met a weapon system he didn't like.

Philip once again calling to me shook me from this reverie. "Planes, Rob. Bunch of them. Over to the right. Look like jet fighters, and they're headed right for us!" I was at his side in a shot.

Philip pointed in the direction of the Gulf of Kuwait. "Down low. 'Bout two o'clock." I felt my heart beginning to pick up the beat. "You're beginning to sound like a fighter pilot yourself," I chided him. "I have them. One, two—I count six."

As we studied the planes headed in our direction, we agreed that they were F-I Mirages. The French had made a gift of about

30 of these sophisticated single-seat fighters to Saddam Hussein. Now he was showing off these jets to the enlightenment of Kuwait City residents. "Mirabile dictu." Then we picked up the increasing whine of their engines.

"You don't think they're going to attack the complex, do you Rob?" Philip asked. "Sort of pick up where the copters left off?"

I studied the rapidly approaching Iraqi jets. They had zoomed in over the Gulf and were flying on a course fixed directly on the Al-Muthanna business complex, where we were located.

"Well, if they are going to hit us, we're all dead men. With their weaponry, they'll blow this place into little pieces. Why would they bother anyway?"

We remained at the windows with some of the others, including Dr. Hansen and his ubiquitous camera. I had to admit he was getting some great shots. First, the Republican Guard troops, then the helicopters, and now the Mirages. He would get a hell of a price for the photos if he could get them quickly to one of the networks or wire services.

Neither Philip nor I ducked away from the window as the Mirages roared in concert overhead. We had been so quick to scurry for safety when the helicopters came at us, but with the jets, there hadn't been any time. One moment, the jets were flashing across the Gulf, and the next they flew right over the complex.

The noise of their passage was deafening, and the air shook as they sliced across it only a few hundred feet above the Al-Salhiya Cemetery across the way. They disappeared in the direction of the central commercial area, northward, and to the rear of the Muthanna complex.

A moment later they reappeared to our right over Arabian Gulf Street, which ran along the Gulf of Kuwait. For the next few minutes, we were treated to a spectacular air show as the Mirages circled repeatedly over the cemetery and our apartment building. It was as though they were gearing up to launch an attack on some special target. But which one?

At the time, I don't think any of us thought it was going to be us. We each had concluded that we were of little importance to the Mirages. They had much bigger fish to catch than despised infidels. As a result, we felt little fear and showed less worry about their aerial demonstration than our earlier experience with the helicopters

The jets soon lowered their speed and dropped their landing gear, signaling to us that they had fixed on their target and were about to loose an onslaught. They circled above us once more and then headed straight as an arrow northward behind us.

Philip and I and some of the others dashed for the bedroom for a better view of the jets' target. "It's the Sief Palace, I bet you," Philip cried. He undoubtedly was right.

We could view the Iraqi planes again headed for the central commercial area in the direction of the palace, which was located on the waterside of Arabian Gulf Street. Being the seat of government, the Sief Palace would have to be considered a prime target.

Then, too, the area around it held other key buildings serving important functions. They included the Council of Ministers, Ministry of Foreign Affairs, Environmental Protection Agency, the Ministries of Public Health and of Planning, the Grand State Mosque, and the Kuwait Stock Exchange. They presented a veritable shooting gallery to the Mirages.

The bedroom had quickly become overcrowded as my guests squirmed and wriggled for a viewing site. We could clearly see the preparations for an aerial assault on the Sief Palace. The jets, flying at a very slow pace, lined up one after the other, readying to fire their rockets and heavy guns in the direction of the palace.

This scenario was played out almost directly in our view. Others came in from rear apartments and reported that they saw the missiles crashing into the palace, scattering debris at every point of the compass. During a segment of the attack, I was on the phone to *The Boston Globe*, giving them a running account of what I could see.

Afterwards, I just watched the proceedings quietly, unbelieving. It all seemed so unreal. Here was a city of much beauty and discipline, where my family and I had known many happy times. Now it was being blown apart. Why? Nothing was making any sense. Periodically, I was filled with rage and cursed the Iraqis for their destruction and bloodletting. Mostly though I just watched their activities in silence.

As the air attack on the palace began to wane, we saw thick smoke erupting from several sites in the far distance to the south and slightly west. I went back to the telephone to tell other reporters about the bombing of the Sief Palace. I could now report to the media that the Emir's palace was under attack from the sky, an attack that intensified throughout the early afternoon.

As the hours passed on that hot August day, we mostly continued to watch the war unfolding before us, conversed quietly, ate and drank, talked around the world on the phone, watched a flow of people come and go in the apartment. Many of these people were unknown to me but appeared halfway respectable. Others were residents of the complex, whom I had seen about or with whom I had a nodding acquaintance. They seemed to think that my apartment was the best situated to view all the activity.

By mid-afternoon or thereabouts, it became obvious that Kuwait City was by and large in the control of Iraqis. They had moved quickly and neatly to capture the city with a minimum of damage. Now there was only an occasional burst of small fire heard along Fahd Al-Salim Street. We speculated that it came from members of the Kuwaiti army, retreating after their failure to hold the Emir's Palace.

As the afternoon deepened, the noise of battle intensified in the direction of the Emir's palace. A die-hard band of Kuwaitis undoubtedly was putting up a final fight. Geysers of debris and flames shooting into the darkening sky told us that the palace was being bombed. The big size of the explosions and the volume of their detonations convinced me that the Iraqis were pulverizing the palace with bombs from artillery pieces, tanks, and aircraft.

At that point, someone, probably the Sudanese doctor with the short-wave radio told me there had been a report from some English-speaking station that the Emir and his personal staff had fled the country before sunrise and were safe and sound in Riyadh, Saudi Arabia.

The report sort of surprised me because it implied that somehow or other the Emir had been forewarned in time to elude the Iraqis. Not by very much time, but enough to get away. How exactly wasn't known then although we figured among ourselves that he probably hopped aboard one of his speedy helicopters for the short trip to Saudi Arabia or might even have gotten away in one of his highly tooled limousines down the Al-Safr Motorway or the Fahaheel Expressway.

A few negative voices argued that the Emir should have stayed in Kuwait City and rallied his army to fight the Iraqis. Most of us though were in agreement he could do far more for Kuwait alive in Saudi Arabia than dead, no matter how heroically, in Kuwait. *Real politiks* once again overwhelmed romanticism.

My feeling was that the Emir could do more for his country as a free man in Arabia. I argued he would in effect be another DeGaulle, who rallied the Free French to his cause in World War II and joined them to the Allied forces in breaking the Nazis' hold on his homeland. Similarly, the free world would join forces with the Emir.

After a while, the discussion fizzled out because people wanted to prepare their evening meal and get themselves locked behind their own apartment doors before nightfall. Shortly, most of the crowd had left.

Looking around, the only ones remaining were Philip, my wife's godson, Bob and Mona Hansen, and Mary McGee, the teacher from New York. We agreed among ourselves to stick together for a while longer. Mrs. Hansen was particularly anxious about returning to her apartment, fearing capture by Iraqi soldiers

Together we prepared a light dinner and passed the evening away trying to put the day's events into perspective. It was probably still wishful thinking, but we were of a mind that the Iraqis would pull back to their border after beating up on the weaker Kuwaitis.

As night fell, there was little to be seen or heard throughout the city except for a periodic outbreak of small arms fire that died away almost as soon as it began and the tracer bullets that passed by the windows—left to right, right to left. From my experience in Vietnam, I attributed the firing to trigger-happy soldiers whose levels of nervousness were increasing sharply in the gathering blackness.

Philip had been playing with the television set to get any program possible, but the only viewing available was from the Kuwaiti government's own station—the one that had been seized earlier in the day by the Republican Guard.

Incredibly, despite being in Iraqi hands, the screen was filled with Kuwaiti propaganda films about the Emir and his government, their generous contributions to their people's welfare, and the strong, aggressive army they had built to defend Kuwait's borders to the death. There was not a word nor picture about the day's devastating events. Rather, like every day except the Sabbath, the station showed government-made films with martial music in the background. One of the military films was especially ironic, depicting as it did all the modern weapons, personnel carriers, aircraft, and so on that the Kuwaitis possessed. We couldn't help chuckling over these films. They were just too Kafkaesque in our circumstances.

Someone remarked about "all those billions spent by the Kuwaitis for a modern army. I ain't seen it today." I had to agree. About the only real fight, to my knowledge, that the Kuwaitis had put up that day had been at the Emir's palace. Realistically, though, there was no way the Kuwaitis or most other Arab armies in the Middle East could stand up to Saddam Hussein's powerful military force.

We flicked off the television set and turned on the shortwave radio left behind by the Sudanese doctor. We listened to the British Broadcasting Company's World News, hoping for any tidbits of information that would enlighten us about our situation. The BBC had little news of any value to us. Actually, we knew far more about what was going on than the news people.

I couldn't help wondering what was happening to all the information I had been giving over the phone during the day to

The Boston Globe back in the States. If they were broadcasting it, why was the BBC not picking up on it and using it in the broadcasts? Surely, CNN had to be disseminating our information. While we didn't want our names to be used, it was eyewitness stuff right from the midst of the fighting.

"Damn! I wish there was someone who could tell us what's going on," Philip said disgustedly. "Even the damn embassy is useless. Tried calling them again and again and couldn't get an open line. We could be dead for all they care."

I nodded my agreement. "The whole country could have fallen for all we know, but don't count on the embassy to let us know. They aren't worth the powder to blow them to hell."

Mary McGee inserted at that point that maybe the embassy had been blown up or taken, and we should not look for help from there.

I nodded again. She had a point. My experience with the embassy was to stay about as far away as possible. The less you had to do with them, like lawyers and doctors, the better off you were.

Generally, the embassy people had an attitude that tended to put off American citizens. Like, "Why are you bothering us or me with this foolishness? Don't you know I'm important? I'm busy. I don't really have time for such matters. And besides, I must get ready for the 'pahty' at the Emir's palace. Only the best people are invited."

When it came to bedtime, I suggested that we all remain together. There were three bedrooms. Philip and I could double up. The Hansens could have a room to themselves, and Mary McGee could have the third.

The Hansens thought it was a splendid idea. Mona Hansen obviously was upset—what with all she had been through and witnessed during the day. She expressed the need for extra protection.

Mary, however, passed on the idea. She said she would return to her own apartment even though she had had several close encounters during the day with Iraqi soldiers. While going back and forth during the day between my place and hers, Iraqis, passing her in the hallways, had brushed against her and offered remarks she assumed were of a lewd nature. After noting the number of her apartment, they had returned on several occasions while she was there to knock and seek admission.

She refused the suggestion, however, that Philip or I accompany her down to her apartment. She was a tough lady, whom I was sure could use her voice loud enough to raise the dead in the cemetery across the street. She slipped through the doorway with a wave goodnight, promising to call us as soon as she arrived safely. Within a minute or so, she reported she was safe behind her doors.

Surprisingly, I was to sleep fairly well that night, little realizing then it was just the first of more than 120 days I would pass in Kuwait City in deep hiding from the Iraqis. I was comforted in my sleep by the knowledge that Jill and the girls were out of danger back in Port of Spain.

Tomorrow? I would worry about tomorrow when tomorrow came.

Chapter 3

Pillage and Rape

When I awoke the next morning, the apartment was still cloaked in darkness, and I listened in vain for any sounds of battle. I was alone in the master bedroom. Philip was in Anna's bedroom after Mary McGee had decided to sleep in her own apartment downstairs. The Hansens were in Patricia's bedroom.

For a few moments, I lay without moving, blinking my eyes to adjust them to the dim light just beginning to filter through the shaded windows. There was not even a sound to indicate that anyone else was up and about on that Friday, August 3rd.

Momentarily, I wondered whether the events of the past day had only been a dream. My Celtic nature was constantly conjuring up fantasies, mostly concerning things that go bump in the night. Did you ever imagine your arm hanging over the edge of the bed and a hand coming out from under it and grabbing your wrist in a shockingly cold manner? Those were the kinds of fantasies I'm talking about.

I began to scold myself, wanting to believe that there hadn't been an invasion by the Iraqis, while simultaneously knowing it was true. Such a horrific thing couldn't have occurred! Don't be a fool. It did. If you don't believe it, go and look out the windows.

As always when I faced danger, I immediately acted to confront it—to prove that it was unreal or to confirm its reality and then act to contend with it. I slipped out of the bed and went into the livingroom for the best view of what might have transpired the day before in Kuwait City.

Gingerly pulling apart the shuttered drapes, I peeked first into the Al-Salhiya Cemetery. Foolish me. Always the dreamer. There was the crater created by the exploding Iraqi shell in the early dawn of yesterday.

My eyes focused on the expanse of Al-Hilali Street below to view the uneven ranks of civilian cars and trucks abandoned at gunpoint by the Kuwaitis. In the dim light I could make out Iraqi soldiers, wrapped in military blankets and ponchos, sleeping in small groups against the cemetery wall, the back of trucks, and even alone in some of the vehicles.

Here and there other Iraqis were standing, smoking, and talking among themselves while heating water on tiny oil stoves for their morning coffee and tea. Only a few seemed to be on guard duty or intent on carrying out some official responsibility up and down the length of the street. Bastards!! They really were here in the city. Would that it had been a nightmare. My inspection showed the damaged police station and the radio and television complex. In the distance, I could just make out whorls of white and gray smoke rising from the vicinity of the Emir's palace.

I prayed again that the Emir had gotten safely away and that he already was rallying the free world to come to the rescue of his country. How great it would be to see the U.S. Marines storming into the city at the forefront of our rescuers.

There were footsteps behind me. I whirled about expecting to confront some ugly looking Iraqi intent on ripping me open with his bayonet. How's that for imagination?

It was Philip, another early riser, who, like a doubting Thomas, had to see for himself to believe that we were truly holed up in an occupied city.

"Sorry, Rob, I didn't want to wake the others," he offered.

I felt a bit foolish and apologized. "Guess we all have the jitters. Had to come look and see whether I had dreamed it all. Same for you?"

He admitted to the same and made his own aperture to gaze out on the city. Then he came up with the $64,000 question.

"So what's to become of us? What's the plan?"

I assured him they were good questions but had to 'fess up that I had no instant answers. "We'll have to talk about it. Get together with some of the others for a council of war. For now, I don't think we're a top priority for the Iraqis. But if they're not leaving, then you can bet they'll come looking for us."

Philip nodded; his young face a grave image. "You can count on it. Nothing like grabbing a bunch of infidels as hostages. Gives you lots of leverage in dealing with the big boys."

I agreed about the hostage bit, but the world had changed, and I wasn't convinced that the powers-that-be in Washington, London, Paris, wherever were swayed much anymore by any dictator holding their nationals as hostages.

When you play for big stakes—fortunes in oil, entire countries—it's no big deal to sacrifice hundreds, even thousands of hostages on the altar of pragmatism. After all, everyone, including innocent civilians, should have the opportunity to find out how sweet and fitting it is to die for one's country. The rules had changed.

I doubted whether any consideration would be given to our safety vis-a-vis bombing the hell out of the Iraqis. What the hell? Who could be opposed to the liberation of Kuwait?

Immersed in these black thoughts, I went into the kitchen to put water on for coffee and to see what was available in the way of food for breakfast. Quickly washing and dressing, quietly though so as not to disturb the Hansens, I turned on the short-wave radio to listen to the news reports.

The BBC was reporting that Iraq had implemented a full-scale invasion of Kuwait and its forces had suffered little losses in overwhelming the Kuwaiti army. There had been reports of summary executions, out-of-hand murder of civilians, and a plethora of rapes and looting. There was no indication whether the Iraqis intended to remain or get out of the tiny country.

The Americans were outraged and dispatching naval forces to the Persian Gulf. The United Nations Security Council had already condemned the invasion and was to meet again during the day to decide on what other actions to take.

The Hansens soon joined us, and we all sat around the table discussing the latest developments. We expressed the hope that the speedy condemnation by the UN and the threat of action by the US would send the Iraqis packing in a hurry.

Dr. Hansen wasn't convinced. He was of a mind that Saddam Hussein's egotism and bully boy pride would not permit him to be ordered out of Kuwait until he was good and ready to leave if ever. Mona agreed with her husband.

I suggested that we wait and see while maintaining a low profile in the Al-Muthanna complex. Just sit tight. Keep the drapes drawn so as not to draw the attention of the Iraqis and our doors locked at all times from now on. Yesterday's open door policy was history. Here on out, we would keep the door locked at all times and ask who was there before opening it.

When the Hansens went back to their apartment to freshen up and check on its status, we locked the door behind them. While Philip took up his post at the window to keep us apprised of what the Iraqis were up to, I fiddled with the TV set. Damned if the screen wasn't continuing to show the same Kuwaiti propaganda tapes.

I laughed aloud. It was all so bizarre. Here were the Kuwaitis touting all their wonderful military capabilities without their new masters apparently making any effort to stop the programming. Maybe the Iraqis figured it served as therapy to mesmerize the Kuwaitis into deep-sixing what had happened to their country.

I couldn't think of any other reason why the Iraqis would allow the programs to be seen over and over again. Surely, they had someone with them who knew how to turn off the tapes or could force one of the surviving employees of the station to do it for them.

Of course, there were so many weird things that had occurred since the initial shell burst in the cemetery 24 hours or so earlier. Take the telephones. Nothing had been done to keep us from calling out or receiving calls from around the world. The Iraqis must have known the complex was filled with non-Kuwaitis, many of them detested infidels, but to my knowledge, they had yet to come looking for us.

Then there was the unremitting stream of motor vehicles coming down off the expressways to end up at the Iraqi roadblocks. That had gone on for hours without one car taking note of it and attempting to turn around and get away.

It was just one surrealistic incident after another. Write it as fiction, and Hollywood would dismiss it out of hand as unbelievable.

I left the TV on with its blaring martial music and went into the livingroom to join Philip at the windows. He was bemoaning his bad luck in losing his Canadian passport and not being able to leave as scheduled.

"Just think, Rob, I could be in Amman now if I had my passport. I still think one of the Arabs stole it at the airport."

Playing my man of wisdom role, I noted: "Wouldn't doubt it for a minute. Canadian passports bring a good price, but then think about all the fun you would have missed. Think of the heroic stories you'll have to regale all the girls back home with. And besides, what would I have done without you? At least Jill knows you're in good hands."

At the mention of Jill's name, we both became more serious, expressing gratitude again that she and the girls had come safely through their ordeal in Trinidad.

"Would you believe it? Jill and the girls getting caught up in that rebellion, and now we're smack in the middle of this invasion. No one could've planned for any one family getting involved in so much international fighting. It's like some big shot somewhere has got it in for us. How else can you account for such bad luck?"

Philip pointed out with sagacity that things were not as bad as they appeared. Jill and the girls were out of harm's way in Port of Spain where the rebels had surrendered. As for ourselves, we were alive and kicking. The worst that could happen to us was to wind up captives of the Iraqis. We would survive and go home eventually, and we would all live happily ever after.

"I'll buy the bit about Jill and the girls, but if you believe that scenario about us, you're blowing smoke. We're in big trouble, young man, believe me. Saddam's henchmen wouldn't hesitate a minute to dispose of us and any other foreigners if it suited their purposes. Look how they gassed thousands of their own people and the Kurds, and never once uttered any remorse. Hell, the world hardly noticed. Our own country never condemned them for it. We were too busy helping arm them to kick the crap out of the Iranians."

"It's called *realpolitik*, Rob. You know. Whose ox is being gored, by whom and why, and all that. Meantime, why don't we just try to lighten up and figure out what the hell we're going to do?"

I nodded and looked down on Al-Hilali Street, which by then was showing much more activity. There were few civilians to be seen, but soldiers were everywhere along the length of the street.

"Look at the bastards," I cried. "They're looting the shops down below."

There were more than 130 shops and boutiques of all kinds in the complex, and the Iraqis finally had gotten the message that they didn't need credit cards to help themselves to the merchandise. It was strictly carte blanche for them. Their gold cards were AK-47s.

Increasingly, as we watched, the hordes of looters became larger, staggering and stumbling out from the Al-Muthanna Mall with bags and boxes of every possible type of products. Whatever you can buy in a mall, they were taking for free.

It was comical to watch the Iraqis load their loot into the abandoned cars and attempt to drive them away. Arabs traditionally are terrible drivers because most of them never had the opportunity to learn to operate motor vehicles. Again and again, they would manage to get cars of every make and description started only to crash into another car or a pole or a wall within 30 to 50 feet.

Streams of soldiers continued to enter and exit the mall, and many of them attempted to drive away in one of the hundreds of cars and trucks left empty the day before. Some of the smarter ones stashed their loot into cars at the head of the line or off to the side. They could then drive them away more easily from the solid mass of vehicles, which had turned the street into a huge parking lot.

Additional soldiers, obviously of a more intelligent bent, simply hailed one of the taxis, which had already appeared on the city streets. They shoved in their bags, boxes, armfuls of clothing, and electronic equipment and drove away. The taxis showing up early that way didn't surprise us at all. Business was business, and the Arab drivers had mouths to feed and bills to pay.

I quickly realized that the soldiers involved in the looting were not members of the Republican Guard. Those elite troops must have pushed on farther south toward the Saudi border and into the oil fields. Those who had taken their place were inferior-type Iraqis. They were nowhere near as sharp in their bearing, discipline, and uniforms. Second-raters obviously—perhaps even militia.

My belief that they weren't the Republican Guard was reinforced when I noticed their officers were shabbily dressed and made no effort to stop the looting. In fact, the officers shortly joined them in order not to be left out of the frenzied thievery going on in the shops and boutiques.

As I said, there were a few civilians about, discreetly clad in Arab wear, dishdashas and sandals, and all. Apparently, they believed their Semite features and clothing would spare them from the attention of the soldiers.

Later in the morning, I noticed that more civilians were taking to the streets, apparently believing that their Arab brothers would not bother them since they were of no importance. It worked well for the truly Arab types, but a trio of Indian males, who came strolling down the street, was not so lucky.

While they didn't look like looters to me because they were only carrying small bags rather than large overstuffed ones like the genuine looters, they were ordered to halt and explain themselves. Despite their noisy protestations, I had the distinct impression they were about to be arrested, possibly even shot on the spot for looting, if you can believe it.

One Indian wasn't buying the Iraqi charge and bolted, dashing across the street through the maze of cars to hurdle over the cemetery wall. The Iraqi interrogators were slow to react. When they got to the wall, the Indian was zig-zagging in a whirlwind manner toward the opposite side. By the time the soldiers loosed a few rounds of revolver and rifle fire, the Indian had leaped over the far wall and made good his escape.

The sounds of the gunfire brought Philip running into the livingroom from the kitchen. "What's up? Are we under attack?"

I quickly explained to him what had happened, and we both watched open-eyed as the Iraqis turned their wrath on the other two Indians. I don't know what they were yelling in the way of protest with their arms covering their heads, but it did them little good. The Iraqis set upon them with their fists and hurried them away down the street and out of sight.

Later in the day, when the Iraqis had their fill of looting, growing numbers of civilians began to participate in the wide-scale thievery.

On my first venture out of the apartment since the invasion, I moved quickly along the hallway to the elevator, prayed no Iraqis were aboard, and went down to the underground parking garage to check on my car. I was a bit nervous when I exited the elevator, wondering whether Iraqi guards would confront me.

There were no guards, but there was pandemonium. Arabs, loaded down with computers, vacuum cleaners, stereos, every imaginable type of home appliance, VCRs, and TVs were scurrying in and out of the mall doors to load their cars with the stolen goods. Nothing bashful about this gang. They had driven their cars right into the mall parking lots so they had only a short distance to cover with their bounty.

A quick look showed my car was okay, and I went back upstairs in a hurry, once again missing any Iraqis, who might have been prowling the hallways in the apartment complex above the Al-Muthanna Mall. I used my key to get back inside and made a mental note that Philip and I should come up with some sort of secret knock to identify ourselves before entering.

Secret knocks, I thought to myself. What's next?

By this time, Mary McGee had returned to pass the second day in the apartment. Mary said she had had an uneventful night except for some occasional noise in the hallways. She was still of a mind to return each evening to her own apartment, although she expected to be continually harassed by Iraqi soldiers, who obviously would rape her in a moment if they had the opportunity and could overcome her intimidating manner.

Throughout the day people came and went but only by knocking first and being asked to identify themselves. John Levins was in and out. I saw the Sudanese physician and the Lebanese man briefly on several occasions. A few of them were thoughtful enough to bring food, mostly in the way of condiments and other non-perishable items.

At one point there was a heavy knock at the door, and I decided immediately that the Iraqis had come for us at last. With all the different types of nationalities living in the complex, including so many types of Arabs, someone by now must have informed them of our presence. You name them, we had them: Egyptians, Palestinians, Syrians, Iraqis even, Saudis, Lebanese, Yemenis, and on and on. You had to bet that among them, there had to be a few who would be more than delighted to see us westerners apprehended and taken away.

But to our relief, the newcomer was another Australian. His name was Max. Counting John Levins, we now had two Australians in our midst. He was about 50 or a bit more, short and stocky, and in a business that sold various green plants to the Kuwaiti government. As he was a friend of Mary McGee, we tried to convince him to hang around for a while. Max, though, was one of those restless souls who couldn't remain long in one spot without getting uptight. All too soon, he was out the door and down the hallway to the elevator. That was the last we saw of Max that day.

I'm not sure who first told us, but sometime that day we had the first inkling of myriad rapes occurring in the Al-Muthanna complex itself. Filipino women, living on the lower floors, became the special targets of the Iraqis. Maybe it's stereotyping, I don't know for sure, but there were stories going around that Iraqis had a lascivious fascination for Filipino women.

I don't know whether it was because they were brown-skinned, gentle, smaller and slimmer than Arab women, and carried themselves with dignity and grace. Whatever, the stories bruited about were that the Iraqis were obsessed with them and would make every effort to have them, forcibly or however, to fulfill their fantasies.

Most of these Filipino women were married and worked in the hotels in the vicinity of the complex. During many of the rapes, the husbands were knocked about and constrained by the Iraqis while the soldiers took turns with the women.

If the husbands protested too much, they were badly beaten. Many had been arrested and taken away. In efforts to escape the Iraqis, many of the Filipino women had dashed down the street and across it to the Meridien Hotel, where they had sought entrance. By that time, however, the hotel was filled with refugees and the hotel doors were locked to these women. There just wasn't room for them. With so many people filling every available space, the hotel's management had decreed that only the relatives of people who worked there would be permitted entrance.

We heard that the Filipino women beat on the big glass doors, crying and begging to be let inside. It was apparently a heart-rending scene because the lobby was jammed with people who could clearly witness the women's pleading but could make no move to help them. Some of the hotel occupants were pushed right up against the glass doors and were only a few feet away from the anguished faces of the Filipino women.

Philip and I agreed it must have been a terrible scene. You would think a few more bodies could have easily been absorbed, but where do you draw the line? One or two more people in the lifeboat might be just enough to swamp it. Then they would all drown instead of one or two poor souls.

We then got into a discussion about the question of "am I my brother's keeper." Most agreed that we were but only to a point. It was very difficult to choose to be a completely moral person, unselfish to the point of death—when one's family and dearest friends might also suffer because of one's desire to achieve a true state of nobleness.

It was about this time that my neighbor, John Levins, who had been in and out of the apartment most of the day, returned once more to tell us that there was an Irishman on the ninth floor in need of assistance.

Earlier in the day, John had brought us several pieces of interesting information. In one of his trips about the neighborhood to try and identify other westerners, he had gone into the Plaza Hotel and found it was nearly empty of Americans and other foreigners. He was unable to learn whether they had been rounded up by the Iraqis and taken away or whether they had managed to flee on their own for the border.

The Plaza Hotel was part of the Al-Muthanna complex, almost like a segment added onto the far right wing of the structure. If you looked out the livingroom window, it was located around the curve of the building to the right—almost diagonally across from the Meridien Hotel.

If the news about the vanished guests was not enough, John also reported that the Plaza was being occupied by the Iraqis, not just military types, but by members of their dreaded secret police, the *Mukhabarat*. There were not many in the hotel as yet, but an Arab employee had informed John that many more were expected and that the Plaza was the designated headquarters for the secret police.

Talk about shocking news. Not only was the Iraqi secret police moving into Kuwait City in force, but they were locating their headquarters right in our complex. I think I blanched at the news. My heart, I know, picked up the beat again. At that moment, I realized irrevocably that we had to take action. Make a plan. We just couldn't act as though nothing had truly happened, that we were not participants but just onlookers. Such an attitude could only lead to disaster—with us at the head of the parade.

Chapter 4

Iraqi Confrontations

John took me off into a corner to tell me that the Irishman on the ninth floor, whose name was Paul Kennedy, had endured a frightening confrontation with some Iraqi soldiers and wanted to know whether we could help him.

The name didn't ring a bell with me, and John explained he lived one floor above but in the adjacent apartment block. Since the mall complex was so expansive, it was divided into connecting segments. Each segment had its own entrance and banks of elevators. With so many residents of the complex coming and going from a variety of entranceways, it was not surprising that I didn't know Kennedy.

According to John, Kennedy was married to a Thai woman, who fortunately was home in Thailand. The Kennedys, though, had been renting their other two bedrooms to a pair of Thai women, friends of the wife.

Earlier that day, there had been a heavy banging at the door, and the Irishman had opened it to be confronted by two Iraqi soldiers, who pushed him aside and strode into the apartment. When Kennedy started to protest, one of the soldiers stuck a big revolver in his stomach and prodded him back into the apartment.

While Kennedy was held at bay, the second soldier went looking for the two Thai women. John said it was obvious the

Iraqis had spotted them earlier and had made a point of finding out where they lived in the complex.

One of the women, who had quickly hidden behind a curtain in her bedroom, dashed shrieking for the bathroom where she locked herself in. The second one was not as quick and was grabbed by the Iraqi.

Kennedy protested vehemently, much to his credit, only to be warned in Arabic to shut up or he would get a bullet in the belly. At least that's the gist of what he thought the Iraqi snarled at him.

John said the soldier ordered the Thai woman to strip and fast. She apparently understood enough Arabic to understand what he said and removed her clothing. Without any wasted motion, the Iraqi doffed his uniform and, naked as a baby, lunged for the woman.

But try as he might, he could not get her into a position where he could force himself on her. All this time, Kennedy was listening to her screams from the livingroom where he was under the gun of the other Iraqi.

The soldier, intent on raping the woman, was now enraged and struggling to unsnarl the convoluted entanglement she had made of her arms and legs to prevent his attack. Her friend in the bathroom, hearing her piteous cries, joined in with her own.

It was then, according to John's account, that a third Iraqi soldier came into the apartment to assist his buddies in their efforts to carry out the rape. Kennedy told John that he looked like a direct descendant of Ghengis Khan with his big ugly face and that he wouldn't have hesitated a moment to cut your throat with the 12-inch knife he was wielding.

Kennedy was convinced of this because the Iraqi came right up to him and stuck the point of the knife into the soft skin under his chin. In effect, he was warned to stay put or be prepared to gain a second mouth.

He left Kennedy and his guard and went over to the naked soldier. It wasn't clear to Kennedy whether he planned to bugger the soldier or help him rape the woman. Whatever, when they got into a discussion, the woman ran out of the bedroom and yelled to her friend to let her into the bathroom.

Disconcerted by this unexpected escape, the trio of Iraqis made no motion to break down the door. They would get into that type of activity later. Instead, the soldier got dressed when the knife-wielder said something about getting out of the apartment.

He went to Kennedy and waved the knife once more under his chin. "Give me your watch, or I'll cut your throat." The Irishman handed it over, but after close scrutiny the Iraqi returned it with a look of distaste. It wasn't up to his standards.

Kennedy told John he wondered at that point whether they intended to kill him anyway. A bit of blood sport. As his last request, he mentioned he would like a cigarette.

One of the soldiers pulled out a pack and offered him a smoke. Together they lit up and took several puffs. The Iraqi with the knife shook his head and put the knife back into its sheath. Then in broken English, smiling, he said, "Smoking can be dangerous to your health."

On that humorous note, the trio went out and slammed the door. When Kennedy heard their footsteps fade along the hallway, he dashed to bolt the door.

"And that's his story as he related it to me," John said. "I think we've got to help him. What do you think?"

I thought we didn't have any choice. Kennedy was one of us—a westerner, that is—and I felt we also had a responsibility for the Thai women. There could be little doubt that the Iraqis would return to get what had been denied them. Their passionate lust for Asian women was a force that constantly drove them to commit any number of unspeakable crimes.

"Okay, bring them down. Be careful though. You don't want to run into that bunch of bastards again. They'll make quick work of you and Kennedy to get at those women."

John looked at me as though I was losing it. In his mind, I'm sure, he was convinced that he and the Irishman would make mincemeat out of the Iraqis if both sides just went at it with their fists. Spare me the Rambos of the world—no matter how good intentioned. They only leave a trail of broken bodies in their wake.

Happily for us, John and Kennedy and the Thai women made their way to my apartment without encountering any Iraqis. Their arrival added even more of an international cast to the people already in the various rooms.

Let's see. There was Philip and I. The Hansens. John Levins, now this Paul Kennedy and the Thai women, whose names I don't recall because they didn't hang around for long. Mary McGee and Max. Several Arabs, including the Lebanese businessman, the Egyptian computer expert, and the Sudanese physician. They would be seen one minute and gone the next almost on a half-hour to hourly basis.

Then there was an Englishwoman, Jane Anderson, who kept drifting in and out as though trying to make up her mind whether we were made of the "right stuff" or not. Jane lived above on the ninth floor and was also experiencing some harassment from lowly Iraqi soldiers. When they met her on the elevator, she said, they evinced this sudden urge to touch her, mostly on the breasts and thighs.

Because there were so many people in my apartment on any one occasion I actually never had a real opportunity to talk with her. I doubt she knew that it was even my apartment she was visiting. Probably thought I was just another hanger-on.

It was late afternoon when Kennedy and the two Thai women had entered the apartment. I recognized immediately that the women were in a state of shock. It was so traumatic for them— after their near rape by the Iraqis—that they could hardly speak. It was obvious that they couldn't deal with us at all. It appeared as though they were as afraid of us as of the Iraqis.

Kennedy explained that they not only felt terrorized but helpless because their husbands, who were employed on the other side of Kuwait City, couldn't get through the Iraqi roadblocks and checkpoints to join them. In their culture, women were terribly dependent on their menfolk and became almost basket cases when separated from them for any length of time.

The big question was what could we do to ease their fears and make them feel more secure among us? We finally decided that Kennedy and the women should stay in the master bedroom until their husbands showed up.

This was explained to them, and they nodded their understanding quickly. There was no doubt they felt very safe in Kennedy's company. We showed them the bedroom and the connecting bathroom and how to lock the various doors. Their faces lit up with gratitude.

Kennedy said they would need some extra mattresses. John and I went off through the complex to Kennedy's apartment to obtain them. It was only my second time out of the apartment since the invasion. After seeing and hearing what the Iraqis had been up to, I was apprehensive about the venture. As far as I was concerned, the women could have the bed, and Kennedy could sleep on the floor sans mattress.

John, for his part, didn't seem to have the slightest hesitation about barging through the hallway and up the elevator to Kennedy's place. I thought the slightest footstep would bring the Republican Guard hot on our heels. Here we were, strolling about like Tom Sawyer and Huck Finn.

We retrieved the mattresses without difficulty and slipped back downstairs in stealthy fashion like the last of the Mohicans. That is, I did. John made no effort at all to hold down the noise level, banging away against the walls and cursing anytime the mattresses caught him. If I had had a gun, I would have shot him no matter how much noise resulted.

Once they felt they were truly out of harm's way among us, the Thai women proved to be good companions, offering repeatedly to do little chores. Their cooking was especially welcomed because there were no great chefs among the men, and the western women never had to do much of it with such plentiful cheap labor available in Kuwait during normal times.

It wasn't long after this episode that Bob Hansen had a frightening experience. It all started with Mona Hansen, his wife, who like others, had begun to pretend that nothing truly unnatural was happening to us. The old ostrich head in the sand bit. "If I don't see it, it doesn't exist. At least for me. The world is falling down around me, but if I refuse to acknowledge it, then it isn't happening to me anyway."

Of course it isn't happening to you unless you happen to be standing on ground zero.

She had bundles she wanted to mail back to the States. In Kuwait, at least in peacetime, all such bundles had to be wrapped in muslin, which was then stitched to hold the loose ends properly together. She planned to send these bundles to Dr. Hansen and herself as though there was no reason they wouldn't be home to accept delivery. They had been scheduled to return to the States on August 15th.

It wasn't just two or three bundles or bags. It was a series of them. She apparently thought she could mail them home cheaply through the Kuwaiti postal service. Bob Hansen, going along with her, kept making trips back and forth to their apartment to obtain more things for her to wrap in muslin, stitch gracefully, and prepare for the big posting.

It was on one of these trips, obviously the last one, that he was no sooner in their apartment when there was a heavy banging on the door. Without thinking who it might be, Bob went to the door and opened it to be confronted by Iraqi soldiers.

They were insistent about coming into his apartment to sniff about. Bob Hansen was never one to flinch before anyone, and he wasn't about to be put down by these intruders. He admitted to us that he was scared but managed to remain in control and literally chased them away. He could be very authoritative, indeed, when he felt put upon. The Iraqis had felt the full brunt of his scathing denunciation—although they probably didn't understand a word he was saying to them.

We realized he must have been very frightened by their appearance because he was still rattled when he arrived with his latest supply of items for wrapping and stitching.

Obviously, it was the last such trip he made that day. He said the thing that bothered him the most about the appearance of the

Iraqis was the fact they were not top-of-the-line troops. They were more like militia, who had only recently been called up and thought they were in Kuwait for a holiday of rape, pillage, and murder to their hearts' content. A little gift of R&R from their leader, Saddam Hussein, the butcher of Baghdad.

Bob also had the impression that the complex was rapidly filling up with this type of Iraqi soldier. They were no longer just looting the mall shops below but now were smashing the glass windows and doors and breaking anything else that served as any kind of an impediment to their activities. If it moved, carry it away. If it doesn't, smash it!

"Second-raters. Bush league. That's what they are," he exclaimed. "We'd be much better off if Republican Guard were still in the city. At least they know the meaning of the word discipline."

From what he told us, we concluded that time was growing short before we all could expect a visit from the Iraqis. They had to know we were in the building. The city was crawling with Palestinians and others friendly to their cause, who must have snitched on us by now.

Bob's experience cast a pall of gloom over us. It wasn't like him to admit to fear, but he acknowledged the encounter with the Iraqis had scared him badly. What had upset him the most was the caliber of the soldiers occupying the city. They were hardly disciplined, in his mind, and seemed capable of any outrage.

During the day, I had made numerous attempts to reach Jill by telephone in Port of Spain. Her number was programmed in my machine, and I had only to touch a few numbers to complete the call. The problem was that the lines were busy all day long.

This was very exasperating for me, but there was really no one to blame as a way of letting off steam. Obviously, many other people around the world were also trying to reach loved ones on the island, people just as concerned as I was about my family.

I finally got through and had a warm conversation with Jill and my daughters. They were all in good health and out of danger. Jill was already trying to make reservations to fly to Boston.

There was little I could tell her about our situation except to say that the Iraqis still hadn't made any concerted effort to round up the foreigners. I told her a little bit about what had been going on in the city but not enough to alarm her. It would serve no purpose except to make her feel as helpless as I had about her and the girls when the rebellion was going on in Trinidad.

I didn't know it then, but it was the last time I was to talk to her from Kuwait City. Efforts to use the phone the next day were to prove fruitless. Somehow or other the Iraqis had stumbled on to the fact the phones were still in use. They then shut off the international service although we could still call in-country.

Before signing off, I told Jill I was disappointed we wouldn't be together on August 10th to belatedly celebrate our wedding anniversary. It would be a disappointment, but we would celebrate at another time. I'm not sure how convincing I sounded, but I did feel at the time that somehow we would be together again. Where and when, I wasn't sure.

That was also the last day I was able to use the phone to talk to my sister Joanne McDevitt and her family in South Boston, several other relatives, and various media people. Joanne reassured me she was passing along my information to the media and that she was hearing it piecemeal in local news reports. In my calls to the media, I brought them up-to-date on what we had witnessed and heard on that second day. Again, I asked that I not be quoted as a source because we had no way of knowing what retribution, if any, the Iraqis would take against captured Westerners for disseminating such reports.

Getting off the phone, it seemed to me that the apartment was full of smoke. A non-smoker, I was especially sensitive to cigarette smoke and felt my eyes beginning to water. The problem was the place was full of people. About three-quarters of them, particularly the Arabs, were puffing away, some of them chain-smoking one butt after the other.

Without thinking, I made a foolish mistake. I pushed my way through the mob and opened several windows. Nobody seemed to notice or think anything of it. For myself, I stood and breathed the fresh, but humid, air from the outside.

I was thinking how hot it was at that time of the year, how humid it got, and how fortunate we were to still have electricity to drive the air conditioning—we wouldn't melt away like so many sticks of butter—when suddenly there was a sharp rapping at the door.

I knew immediately. Iraqis! From down on the street or some lookout, they had seen the windows opened and concluded we were spying on them. Even worse, taking photographs and film footage. "Idiot," I called myself. I didn't have a moment to warn the others because one of the so-called guests had already gone to the door and pulled it open.

I knew from the awesome expression on his face that they were Iraqis even in the split moment before I actually saw them. He was pushed aside, and they surged into the apartment. The non-com in charge already had his revolver in hand and was waving it about while jabbering excitedly in Arabic.

Philip and I just stared at one another momentarily as all conversation broke off instantly at the sight of the uniformed men. It was as though everyone was struck dumb on cue.

"He says no one is to move," the Sudanese doctor translated. "No one is to leave the apartment by any other exit."

The non-com gestured to two of his men, who went to check and guard any other exits to the outside that they could find. John Levins moved slightly as though to block their way, but he was roughly brushed aside and cursed.

The physician said aloud, "I would suggest that we remain calm and just do what we are asked. I wouldn't do anything foolish. You're dealing with some rough men here."

I have to admit I was scared. I kept seeing myself hustled away to be tortured and then shot or bound and sent to be a hostage somewhere in the backwater of the desert. My imagination was having a field day, but I wasn't enjoying it.

Chapter 5

Forays and Forages

The non-com snapped off several orders in Arabic, which were relayed to us in English by the Sudanese doctor. We were to produce our identity cards or whatever we had in the way of identification for scrutiny by the Iraqis.

Fortunately, all of us had some form of ID on our person, mostly in the form of a Kuwaiti government-issued ID card. While his compatriots watched us closely, the non-com took each of the IDs and studied them without comment.

I thought it was remarkable he didn't ask a single question of any of us. To me, he looked like he was a middle-aged reservist, undoubtedly called up for the Kuwait attack. I wondered whether he knew how to read.

When it was my turn, he just stared at my head photo on the card and then at me. Talk about cold brown eyes that didn't betray the slightest emotion. It was like looking into twin graves.

He handed the card back and turned abruptly about to return to the doorway. Now what? He must know that many of us were westerners with Americans among us. I bit my lips to keep them from quivering ever so slightly from a mixture of fear and apprehension.

Then he spoke rapidly and sharply to the Sudanese physician, who just listened without replying. Finally, the non-com looked angrily at him and surprised us all by shepherding his men out of the apartment. Before slamming the door, he walked straight up to John Levins and requested to bugger him! John turned grim-faced and pale. The non-com smiled and went off.

Everyone just stared at each other with raised eyebrows. Is that all there was to it? They were truly gone? Why hadn't they grabbed any of us? The non-com would have liked to have taken John with him.

I asked the physician, "What did he say to you at the end? Something about Americans? I caught that."

The Sudanese replied, "He wanted to know what I, as a Muslim, was doing with you infidels."

"What did you tell him?"

"I just told him you were my friends. What else?"

I smiled and hit his shoulder lightly to show my appreciation. Funny guy. Didn't know him before yesterday, and now he seemed like part of the family.

As evening encroached on the city, the Thai women prepared a light meal for the group, which by then had thinned out with many people returning to their own apartments.

At the end of that second day in occupied Kuwait City, there was Philip and myself, Bob and Mona Hansen, Mary McGee, John Levins—when he wasn't slipping in and out of God knows where—the two Thais, and Paul Kennedy, who was as elusive as John in his nightly peregrinations. The Englishwoman, Jane Anderson, was sighted periodically, and Max, the other Australian, was still to be seen again.

Quite frankly, I believed by that time of the day we were all bored a bit. We had been more or less on a high all day, watching the Iraqis below and wondering each time there was a knock on the door whether they had come to do all kinds of horrible things to us. Now there was a bit of a letdown. They had breathed in our faces and gone away without inflicting any physical abuse or threats of any kind.

The crazy TV set was continuing to show only the Kuwaiti government film with the martial music thumping relentlessly in the background. I came to the conclusion that the Kuwaiti

Resistance, if there was such a thing so early on, had set up a secret transmitter, which the Iraqis had yet to uncover.

"There has to be a secret transmitter," I insisted. "How the devil could they keep showing those pictures otherwise?"

Mary McGee suggested in a sarcastic tone that perhaps the Iraqis were well aware of the programming and could not care less. "Keeps the populace doped up. Like what Lenin said about religion 'being the opiate of the masses.'"

Philip chimed in that he was inclined to agree with Mary. The TV films offered no threats to the Iraqis. With their army, they could take on just about all the Arab states at once and win.

Right about then, I realized that I could use some exercise. I really wished I could have teamed up with my good friend, George Daher, the landscape architect from Pennsylvania, for about three hours of tennis at the SAS athletic club. We used to play two or three times weekly. Worked up a good sweat and got rid of a lot of the tensions we had picked up in our daily lives.

But tennis, of course, was out as were any other activities offered at the club, including squash, boating, swimming and myriad exercise opportunities. Besides, George was nowhere to be found in these early days of the occupation.

I called over to Dr. Hansen to learn about any new developments. He was leaning over with one ear cocked to a small short-wave radio.

"For what it's worth, the BBC says they hear that the Iraqis might announce they'll begin pulling out of Kuwait on Sunday or thereabouts."

I brightened perceptibly, and Philip and I grinned at each other. "That sounds like good news to me."

"They say it's only hearsay at the moment. Any definite announcement will come out of Baghdad tomorrow. Think we better hold off any celebrating until then," Bob said solemnly

I had to agree even though I made a mental note to pay close attention to the radio during the next day. It would be Saturday, August 4th. I suggested aloud that we should take turns listening to the radio.

Later in the evening, when we seemed to have run out of conversation, Mary asked who played bridge. It ended up that Dr. Hansen and I were card players, and Philip volunteered to sit in and be the fourth hand while learning the game.

The Thai women had retired by then. Mona Hansen was stitching her muslin covers for the packages to be mailed back to the States. I can't recall whether John Levins and Kennedy were about, as they constantly announced they were off "to get some fresh air." Jane Anderson had disappeared again after probably deciding we were not the "right stuff" on a 24-hour basis.

About mid-evening, John did return from one of his foraging expeditions. I don't know why, but there wasn't any liquor in my apartment. We all had looked forward to a good stiff drink, but John had been unable to find any.

He reported that the mall shops had been completely looted and smashed. The only shop left intact was an English-language bookstore. The Iraqis and their Arab supporters hadn't bothered to clean it out because they didn't read English.

So what did John bring back to us? Two books. One on tank warfare and the other about combat aircraft. I think they were both Jane's publications, the London military book house.

I pressed him to explain why he had taken only those two books. Did he have pretensions to succeed von Clausewitz as an expert on war? He refused to enlighten us in the matter.

"You just wait and see, mates. These books will come in mighty handy before we're out of here. You can believe it." Other than that, he had nothing more to say about the results of his nocturnal wanderings.

Philip tried to get a rise out of him but to no avail. "John, those books look very interesting, but right now, we could all go for a stiff shot of Scotch, gin, even a beer. That's the big priority right now."

John only grinned in response and kept his head buried in his tank warfare book. I prayed that he wasn't planning on seizing a Russian-built T-72 tank to go joyriding about the capital. Even worse, he could be trying to determine how best to take one out with a homemade Molotov cocktail.

I had to shake my head physically to free it of the images of us all standing blindfolded before a firing squad with our backs to a clay brick wall.

"Rob, a penny for your thoughts," Philip inquired. "You're out in the cosmos again. Bridge, remember? Cards? It's your bid."

I made my bid and went back to my thoughts. It was true we were out of liquor, but that shouldn't be too difficult to rectify. It was our food supply that was my big concern. Even with the small group we had now, there was food for only about five days. We would definitely have to start planning how to survive—especially if the Iraqis announced during the next day that they were in Kuwait for the long haul.

When the Hansens decided to call it a night, Mary McGee also bid us farewell and returned to her apartment. Once again, she declined the offer of a companion to her doorway. I'm sure she was apprehensive about encountering Iraqis in the darkened hallways, yet determined that she was not going to be intimidated by them. John had gone to his place for the evening, and Kennedy had come in from his nightly wanderings to sleep in the bedroom with the Thais. At that point, only Philip and I remained in the livingroom.

"So, Rob, with a little bit of luck the Iraqis will announce they're pulling out tomorrow, and soon they'll be gone. I'll be off to Amman, and you'll have this place all to yourself again."

"Sounds good, Philip, and I hope it works out that way, but I'll believe it when I see it. I wouldn't trust Saddam Hussein any farther than I could toss him. I don't think I could even raise him off his feet. The man's lied all his life, and I don't expect anything different now."

After a bit, Philip yawned discreetly and went off to the bedroom we were sharing. How ironic, I thought, that he could have flown out of Kuwait City for Amman on Wednesday night if he had not lost his passport. Instead, Philip had ended up being caught in the vise of the Iraqi invasion.

Yet, overall, we couldn't complain. We were alive and healthy and had hardly felt the impact of the invasion. In my case, I knew my family was safe and sound in Trinidad and not caught up with me in Kuwait. It terrified me to think how different things would have been if they had been with me. It's one thing to be able to take care of yourself or at least to think you always can. However, with a wife and two young girls, I would have been a wreck, worrying every moment that something terrible was going to happen to them, and I wouldn't be able to help them.

Our food situation was still on my mind when I went to bed that night. In the dark, I listened to the sounds of war. There were sporadic bursts of gunfire and the roar of engines from motor vehicles below or the flights of aircraft above.

We would definitely have to replenish our food supply. I would have to talk seriously to John about it. If he was determined to go roaming about, he might as well be a "midnight-robber" and help stock the larder.

I got out of bed and took a last look at the city. Just then several machine guns opened fire. I watched in awe as lines of tracers lazily arched through the night sky and hammered the Saudi Airlines building. The tracers were so close I swore they were going to hit our complex.

The next morning Philip and I discussed the food situation with John. Fortunately, I had risen early and caught him before he was off again. I had the impression that John saw himself getting his orders for the day and was preparing himself mentally to carry them out.

I figured if he saw himself as Chuck Norris or Clint Eastwood, I wasn't about to shake up his sandbox. Just bring some food, John. That was all I requested. The question as to whether he was to buy it, borrow it, or steal it never came up. I would just as soon not know.

Outside the complex there was an eerie quiet, almost a deathly stillness as though the city had been abandoned. I could hear only the faintest of noises. A scrutiny of the city showed very few troops and civilians about. On Al-Hilali Street, many of the motor vehicles had been driven or hauled away. There was a driveway through the remainder.

Urging Philip to keep a close ear to the BBC news reports, I slipped out of the apartment and went down on the elevator to my level of the parking garage. The scene was different from the one viewed from our windows.

My car was still there and didn't appear to have been touched in any way. No signs of forcible entry, broken or cracked windows. I checked the fuel level. It was still the same so no one had siphoned off the gasoline.

The thing, which was different though, was that the garage was filled with Arabs, still coming out of the mall with loot. They were jamming their stolen items into rows of cars. All the time there was a constant jabber of Arabic—curses and impatient cries—and seas of tense faces.

It seemed that everybody wanted to grab what was left and get out of the garage as quickly as possible. There was a very desperate air of urgency permeating the huge concrete expanse as though the thieves expected the Iraqis to show up at any moment and execute them.

I gave them all a wide berth, but they had no interest in me although I was an obvious Westerner, at least in my dress. Maybe they thought I was Russian if they thought about me at all.

Philip couldn't believe it either when I told him what I had seen. John Levins had given us the idea that the entire mall had been cleaned out except for the bookstore. Obviously, John could not have personally checked every shop and boutique and especially their stockrooms.

"That's it," Philip said. "The stockrooms, of course. They were overlooked to some degree by the first few waves of looters. Why go in the back rooms when everything you wanted was laid out in front like a big buffet table?"

He inquired whether there were any soldiers among them, and I shook my head. "No Asians either. Strictly Arabs. The street-type. Probably Palestinians. The only soldiers I've seen were out on the street."

I asked whether he had heard anything on the BBC broadcasts about the Iraqis withdrawing. Not a word. Bob and Mona were up and about and also had promised to keep an ear tuned to the BBC.

"As we discussed, Philip, if the Iraqis aren't getting out, then we've got to decide on a plan of action. We just can't wait to react. We have to act. So start giving some thought as to what we do if Saddam Hussein says he's here for the long haul. Do we stay? Do we go? If we stay, how do we get by? If we go, how do we go? Don't just focus on the fact that we have wheels and can drive blithely out of here. Give it some real thought."

Once more on the third morning, my apartment began to overflow with visitors. Again, many of them were known to me like Mary McGee; Jane Anderson, who had deigned to test us for another day; the Sudanese physician; the Lebanese businessman; the two Iraqis; the regulars like John Levins, the Hansens, Paul Kennedy, and the Thai women; and others with whom I now had a nodding acquaintance—Westerners and Arabs alike.

Intermixed with these people at various times were a goodly number of strangers to whom the word had gotten out that my pad was a good place to meet kindred spirits of all colors and flavors. Sort of a safe port in a bad storm. To my relief, most of them were smart enough and aware enough to bring food for the group, including fresh eggs, crisp vegetables, fancy canned goods, and odd cuts of meat.

John and Kennedy had gone off early—John for foraging and Kennedy for God knows what. I had to remind myself that Kennedy could move about far more easily than we Americans and John, the Australian. While he might portray an air of derring-do, Kennedy was never in much danger because as an Irishman, he was a national of a neutral country and Iraq was friendly to certain groups in Ireland. Iraq had no quarrel with Ireland. He had to be careful though not to be caught assisting other Westerners.

If I remember correctly, Kennedy was given very specific requests to dig up some good booze on his trips about the city. It was even suggested that he go to Aer Lingus and obtain a few bottles of liquor. He had been hinting that he was well connected there.

Returning from one of his mysterious missions, Kennedy was trailed into the apartment by a British couple. The man's name was Mike, but I don't remember his wife's name because I took an instant dislike to her. In my mind, I quickly baptized her Frau Dracula. Here's how it came about.

Upon entering, Kennedy reported he was hot on the trail of the booze and hoped to be successful obtaining a supply by the end of the day. Mike and Frau Dracula had followed along, as though waiting to be introduced, but Kennedy had no awareness of their presence and left abruptly.

At the time, we had been talking among ourselves about the continued rape of the Filipino women living on the lower floors of our complex and our frustration because there was nothing we could do about the situation.

John Levins, who had just returned from outside, said he had heard the Iraqis were carrying out an unending orgy of rape against the Filipino women housed in an apartment building adjacent to the Meridien Hotel. The place was filled with Filipino workers, and the Iraqis had made the women the target of their lust and villainy.

"It goes on without let-up from what I've been told," John said. "Any of the men who interfere are badly beaten or just hauled away to be shot for all we know. I went by the hotel, and there was a line of soldiers going in and out with guards at the door. It's like one of those unpaid brothels the Nazis set up in occupied countries."

I was dismayed at hearing this report, and my feelings were shared by Philip and Bob Hansen, who were huddled with me at the time. "I feel so damn helpless. To know this cruelty is going on, and we can't do anything. Who do we tell? We've already told the media about all the raping and looting, but they're there and we're here, and they can't do anything either."

"This mass rape, though, is something new," Philip said. "Why don't I try calling CNN or whoever and tell them about it? Might set a fire under the world if they report it."

I was just about to tell him to go for it when this woman I had dubbed Frau Dracula retorted, "Oh, that's ridiculous. Surely you must know," she added in a very imperious voice, edged with a hard Germanic accent, "Oriental women are the targets for this type of treatment because of their nature. They deserve just what they get."

Before I could speak up, John Levins was all over her. "Are you daft, madam? We're talking about rape—not a little petting in the back seat of the automobile. Rape!

R A P E! You know—when a man rips the clothes off a woman's back and rams himself into her."

He was really lighting into Frau Dracula, who gazed at him with narrowed eyes that registered total disbelief. Could this white man be taking the side of some Filipino menials? Raising his voice to her in that way?

"Your graphic language is uncalled for, sir," she hissed. "Michael, are you going to let him talk to me like that?"

Before Michael, who was heavy-set and looked like he was no pushover, could say a word, John went on. "You ought to be ashamed of yourself. I'll say it again. Filipino women are the salt of the earth in my estimation, and you do them a terrible disservice in speaking about them in such a manner."

Without another word but with a look that could kill, Frau Dracula turned about, took Mike—who I think was a diplomat-type—by the arm and sideslipped through the crowded room to settle in a quiet spot off in a corner.

"Bitch!" John sputtered. "Did you hear her? And she's not alone, you know, Rob. The world's full of bitches like her. What did the Filipinos ever do to her? Can you believe it?"

"Not a Westerner we'd want to brag about, John, believe me," I responded. "Who the hell are they anyway?"

"I thought they were friends of Kennedy's," Philip interjected. "They came in with him and followed him right over to us. Did anyone catch their names?"

I was still feeling a sense of embarrassment over the woman's outburst. "All I know is that his name is Michael. Hers I didn't catch, but then it wasn't offered. I can only think of her as Frau Dracula. She had such a mean look about her. Ugly, too. Look at her. That mouth, so full of hate and bigotry. I hope they know enough to leave soon."

As though sensing my outrage, Mike and Frau Dracula worked their way over to the door to make their exit. Philip took off like a shot across the room to be sure that the door was locked behind them. They went out without a word of thanks, and the bolt was shot home quickly to bar any more unexpected arrivals.

"We've got to watch that door," I said when Philip returned. "Got to man it. Even locked, we have no control over who's coming in. There's a knock and whoever's by the door just opens it. Let's make up a big sign and tape it to the door. Something like 'ask for names before opening!'"

Philip thought that was a good idea. He went off to look for paper or cardboard we could use to make the sign. I yelled after him to check on the BBC and see whether anything was being said about the Iraqis getting out of Kuwait.

The Iraqis must have heard us and decided to show us they were still around. Twice in the next half-hour, different units of Iraqis knocked and demanded entrance. Both times we had to produce our ID papers, while fearing they were going to haul us away. But again, they just looked at us disdainfully and left.

"Let's give the bastards a few minutes and then get out of here ourselves," John suggested. "You must be getting cabin fever by now. It'll be good for you. We'll go along to the Evangelical church and check on Pastor Maurice. Great mate. Make sure he's okay."

I was taken aback by his suggestion. Just like that. Go out walking about among the Iraqis. Hell, what if they were still in the hallways? Had just received orders to apprehend all Westerners? We would make it easy for them.

But then again, why not? It would be good to get out for a bit, stretch the legs, and breathe fresh air—even if it was hot and humid.

To help me make up my mind one way or the other, I went to the window and cracked it just a bit to study the street below. It was getting onto near noon. While there were a lot of people in the street, things seemed fairly quiet. There were few uniforms to be seen.

Most of the motor vehicles had been driven or towed away except those that had been wrecked by the Iraqis. There were more civilians than soldiers. Many Arabs, some Far Easterners, and even a few Westerners, whom I didn't recognize. The few Iraqis about didn't appear to be paying any attention to the civilians. I could not see any checkpoints or any efforts being made to impede the foot traffic.

"So, are you on, Rob?" John pressed. There was a bit of a twinkle in his brown eyes as though he knew I was being my usual cautious self before making any decision.

I decided to surprise him. "You're on, John. Should go about a bit and test the waters. Let me tell Philip what we are up to."

Philip was working on the sign and reported that there was no news on the radio about the Iraqis pulling out or about any round-ups of westerners. On hearing that, I felt more comfortable with my decision. In truth, though, I still considered John a bit of a loose cannon and had to wonder whether I was making the right choice.

Still, the Evangelical church wasn't more than a 100 yards or so down Al-Hilali Street past the Meridien Hotel and across Fahd Al-Salim Street. What could happen to us in such a short stretch? We were about to find out.

Chapter 6

Captured

Philip reassured me he would keep an ear cocked to the radio reports and a sharp eye on the door. By then, he had posted his sign, warning everyone to check on any arrivals before opening the door. I said we wouldn't be long, and off John and I went.

We encountered no Iraqis in the hallway, elevator, or in the lobby below as we pushed our way gingerly out onto the covered sidewalk. We could really feel the heat and humidity, and I regretted ever leaving my air-conditioned apartment at the steamiest part of the day in Kuwait.

John gave no signal that he had noticed any change in the climate and walked off to the right toward the corner of Fahd Al-Salim Street. I hurried to catch up.

"John, slow it down. We'll draw attention to ourselves if we look like we're in a hurry."

"Not to worry, Rob. Ain't many of the buggers about right now. See for yourself."

He was right because I had seen few Iraqi soldiers since exiting the Al-Muthanna complex. The walkway and street were thronged with Arabs, in both western and native dress. I didn't spot any Westerners. The mall areas were an unforgettable scene of destruction with broken glass strewn everywhere. The gutters were filled with discarded boxes, paper wrapping, and smashed electronic products like big television sets, VCRs, computers,

Walkman headsets, and telephones. Apparently, the looters had fought each other over many of the items and destroyed them rather than let one or the other have it in quality condition. The ransacked Pizza Hut was already being used as a public toilet.

Serves them right, I thought. What a mess! Especially when compared to how clean the Kuwaitis had always kept the streets and walks before the invasion. They had plenty of Asians to keep them spit and polish clean then.

"What say we give the Meridien a look?" John said, quickly crossing Al-Hilali Street with me once again trailing in his wake. I was beginning to get more tense because I was conscious of far more uniformed personnel around us as we approached Fahd Al-Salim Street. I remembered, too, that the Iraqi secret police had taken over the Plaza Hotel, which was right on that corner.

I was about to suggest to John that we forget our trip to the Evangelical church when he bounded up the stairs to the entrance of the Meridien and pushed against the large glass door. Instead of the door opening, John bounced off it slightly.

"The goddamn thing is locked," John muttered. "What the hell? Why is it locked?"

I was at his side, peering through the glass into the expansive lobby. It was filled with all sorts of people, but no one was coming forward to open the door. We banged on the thick glass.

"They're not going to let us in, John. Remember how they wouldn't let the Filipino women inside? The bastards. Only registered guests, employees, and their families. C'mon, let's get out of here before we attract attention to ourselves."

John scowled and hesitated momentarily but then went off with me. "Bloody bastards. Nothing wrong with our money before the invasion. All too glad to see us then. What?"

"These are bad times, John," I said in an effort to reassure him. "Everybody's trying to do what's right for their people. Forget it."

We went around the corner on Fahd Al-Salim Street, crossed the street, and ducked down an alley between several buildings, heading in the direction of Gulf Street. A quick look behind showed no one following us, a bit of a disappointment to me. Right along, I had this idea that we were high up on any list of foreigners to be picked up when the time was right for the Iraqis. It wasn't that I thought we were so important. It was just we were so obviously Westerners and detested infidels.

As we went along the alley, the sky was a bright blue with only a few puffy white clouds scudding across it. The narrowness of the walk had shut off most of the city noises although we heard a dog bark occasionally and a female voice calling to someone.

At the end of the alley, we came into a wide-open area fronting the church. Scattered about were several stands of palm and date trees and rows of greenery—giving the site the semblance of an oasis.

I don't know why, but I just didn't like the appearance of the grounds. There wasn't a soul about. So quiet. Almost a deathly stillness. I envisioned the church door bursting open, and a throng of soldiers rushing out to seize us.

John was oblivious to my imaginings and strode across the grounds without speaking. He was like a character out of a Rudyard Kipling novel, who shows utter disdain for any danger as he marches into the mouths of the cannon armed with only his walking stick. I couldn't help thinking that like the Marines of old, we should have first reconnoitered the area. But then, it was too late.

Without the slightest warning, an Iraqi soldier fell out of the sky to confront us with his AK automatic weapon. I was not so much taken aback by the danger he posed but in wonderment as to where he had come from.

"Can you believe it?" John said. "The bloody Iraqi was in the tree. Thinks he's Rambo jumping out of it like that. Scared the bloody piss out of me, he did!"

I was still speechless from the shock caused by the sudden appearance of the Iraqi, but I could still appreciate John's honesty. Nice to know he could admit to fear like the rest of us.

The soldier muttered some words in Arabic and gestured with his free hand as though we were to give him something. What? A bribe? What?

"Wants to see our ID cards," John guessed. "Hand it over and we'll soon be on our way."

This was quickly done, and the Iraqi studied them without any comment. I was beginning to relax. Just a check. That's all. Nothing to get in a funk about. We would be on our way shortly.

Once again, I had figured incorrectly. The Iraqi said a few more words and gestured with his weapon for us to move along. While he did not appear openly hostile, there was a look of determination about him.

"We're to go along with him. God knows where," John explained. "Not to worry, mate. It'll be all right. You'll see."

With an expression on my face of hopelessness, I followed John in the direction pointed out by the soldier with the barrel of his weapon.

I knew it. I knew it, I thought. I should have never listened to John. I should have laid low. Stayed right there in the apartment with Philip, and this wouldn't be happening. Damn John!

In my innermost mind, though, I recognized I could not blame John for my predicament. He hadn't forced me to accompany him. It was my decision to do so. Now I would have to live with that decision. Take responsibility for my actions.

We didn't have much of a walk at the point of the Iraqi's gun before we came to a guardpost. Within moments the commander, a friendly lieutenant, came out and scrutinized our identity cards.

"Dr. Morris?" he asked, looking up at both of us. I nodded and gave him my most benign smile. I hoped that we could end this relationship with the Iraqi army right then and there. "An American?" He spoke in fairly good English. "And, Mr. John Levins, Australian. Two birds of a feather, yes?"

Since we were not sure of his meaning, neither of us responded while continuing to give him our best "hands-across-the-border" grins. Just give us back our ID cards, and we would be out of there in a flash. I yearned to be one of those characters on Star Trek where bodies vaporize, disappear and reappear within seconds in human form at a safe distance millions of miles away.

"Fact is, you aren't my responsibility, gentlemen. Going to have to send you along to the police station on Al-Salim Street."

John jumped in at that point. "Sir, I don't understand the problem. We were just going by the Evangelical church over there for a visit with Pastor Maurice. Nothing more. I can assure you we have no quarrel with you or your people. Why don't you just give us our ID cards, and we'll be on our way?"

The Iraqi officer smiled. As an Arab, he was used to people trying to constantly bargain with him. It was his way of life.

"I'm sure you don't, Mr. Levins, and I have none with you or Australia. I will return your cards, but you must go with this soldier to the police station. Strictly a formality. I'm sure you'll be out of there in a few minutes. You must be off now."

I only had to look into his dark brown eyes to glimpse the steely will power that laid just behind the facade of civility and good humor to know there was nothing more to say.

I tugged at John's sleeve and beckoned to him that we had to be off. He shrugged and turned away. Nothing ventured, nothing gained was his attitude. We didn't end up walking to the police station. The officer directed us to be driven in an army vehicle. We clambered aboard, and off we went up our very own Al-Hilali Street, around the corner onto Fahd Al-Salim Street, and along it for one block to the Safat police station.

Piling out, John and I went inside under the watchful eye of our guard. Just preceding us were six members of the Kuwaiti militia with their hands held up. Collectively, they were a mournful looking lot, who were then contemplating all the terrible things that could be done to them.

They were ushered into a large office while we were kept under guard in the hallway. We didn't have to wait long before they filed out and passed us by without a word. I wondered momentarily about their fate before we were ordered into the office.

Awaiting us was another Iraqi officer. A major, I believe, who was even more polite than the officer on Gulf Street. Once again, we produced our identity cards, which he quickly studied before addressing us.

To myself, he said in a pleasant English voice, "You're an American? A dentist?"

I answered yes to both questions. He already knew I was both from the information on my ID card.

"And you, Mr. Levins, you're an Australian? You're in import-export?" John responded in the affirmative to those queries.

Then without any further conversation, he ordered us to be taken to the Sheraton Hotel. My heart jumped instantly. Damn! The Sheraton Hotel, as we already had learned, was being used as the Iraqi army's headquarters in Kuwait City. Now we were in for it. I was convinced that our transfer there portended no good for us.

As we went out of the police station, I became very apprehensive, very angry. The Sheraton Hotel was at the intersection of Al-Soor Street and Abu Bakr Al-Siddi Street near the Al-Jahra Gate, an area now known as the Sheraton Round About. The location was on the northern side of the city and one of the main entrances to the capital. As a result, it had great strategic importance to the Iraqis and determined their decision to make it their headquarters for the invasion force.

"This is a bad move, John, going to the Sheraton. I can feel it in my bones," I muttered.

"I couldn't agree more, Rob. It's a bad idea, but what's to be done about it?"

Suddenly, I let loose. "How the hell did we get into this fix? We were crazy to leave our building. I never should've let you talk me into leaving the apartment."

"Hey, Rob, leave off. No one twisted your arm to come along. I could've just as easily gone out by myself. Knock it off!"

When we exited back onto Fahd Al-Salim Street, there was general confusion generated by the scores of military vehicles parked along both sides of it. There was every type of military vehicle—troop carriers, big and small, staff cars, commandeered autos and trucks, and many smaller vehicles, mostly Toyotas.

Incredibly, our guard just went off and left us alone while he tried to requisition one of the Toyotas. We stood on the steps of the station and watched him disappear into a swirling mob of soldiers, who apparently were waiting to be transferred to God knows where.

I wasn't sure why the guard had gone off to get one of the Toyotas. The Sheraton Hotel wasn't much more than a hundred yards away, and we could have walked there in a few minutes.

Without looking at John, I said in a low voice, "I don't really want to go to the Sheraton. I think we should just sort of split. No one's paying the least bit of attention to us. Let's just walk away."

John readily agreed and asked how best to get out of the area. I said we could go along the front of the station for about 60 feet and duck around the corner. The only problem was when we turned that corner, we would be in a very open area which stretched for some distance. If they came after us and caught us in the open, we would be an easy target for their guns. I felt decidedly squeamish about that.

"Do you think they'd really shoot us?" John asked.

"Those bastards wouldn't hesitate for a moment."

"So, what do we do—go or not? No one's paying the slightest attention to us. Look at them. Hundreds of Iraqis and not one who gives a damn about us."

I desperately wanted to escape. All I had to do was walk down the steps, turn to the right, walk along for 60 feet, and go around the corner. Once there, we would be out of sight of most of the Iraqis. We would have to force ourselves not to break into a run at that point. I could see the Iraqis blazing away at us with their automatic weapons.

John and I looked at each other, and we saw the fear of being shot down in each other's eyes.

Our contemplated escape became moot because the guard yelled to us from a Toyota he had managed to squirm through the maelstrom of traffic and pull up before the station.

We grumbled to ourselves and went down to the walk and got into the vehicle. "Indecision will do it every time," John muttered aloud.

I noticed then that the guard had turned about and was just staring at us. I bet myself that the cretin didn't know where he was to take us. My belief became an act of faith. In a very authoritative voice, I ordered him to take us to the Meridien Hotel. Once there, we could probably slip away from him and get back to the Muthanna complex.

As I sat back, congratulating myself on my cleverness, the guard began to turn about to drive off. John spoke up, almost indignantly, "No, no. It's the Sheraton, not the Meridien. Take us to the Sheraton."

I bent forward and looked at him. "Are you insane? For God's sake, shut up." I turned to the guard. "The Meridien. The Meridien Hotel." I added a few Arabic expressions, denoting "please" and "thank you."

John incredibly regarded me as though I was the one who was crazy and repeated, "The Sheraton. It's the Sheraton Hotel we're supposed to go to."

He no sooner finished when I rammed my elbow into his ribs, hoping he would get the message as I glared at him. If my eyes had been laser beams, he would be only a memory.

As calmly as I could, I told the guard again, "Take us to the Meridien."

But John, in his own incredibly insipid manner, leaned forward to put his mouth only inches from the guard's face and said, "Take us to the Sheraton. Now!"

The guard stepped on the gas pedal, and we pulled away into the dense traffic in the direction of the Sheraton. I had nothing left to say at that point. John obviously had convinced himself that the right thing to do was to go to the Sheraton. Once he had achieved such a mindset, there was no way to argue with him.

I was absolutely livid, seething with rage. To think that we could have conned the guard into taking us to the Meridien, where I was sure we could have made our escape but John could only focus on going to the Sheraton as ordered by the Iraqi major.

How could any one person be so stupid? So obstinate? So unenlightened? What hell did we face now, I wondered, because of his quixotic, naive nature? I could have strangled him right there in the back seat of the Toyota and happily faced any punishment, knowing I was free of such a foolish man.

I growled at John, "You son-of-a-bitch, getting us into this jam. You're crazy, and I'm just as bad for listening to you. I'll get you some day for getting us into this!"

It was only a short drive to the Sheraton. Again, there was another traffic jam in front of the Iraqi headquarters, and we had to get out and walk the last 50 yards. I looked about, searching the alleys of the souk in a vain effort to see a way out of our dilemma, but the guard was most attentive and kept close to us.

I looked up at the main entrance and remembered the times I had entered through it to meet with family and friends on happy occasions. Now there were red-bereted Iraqi soldiers, members of a crack Republican Guard Unit, armed with submachine guns at the doors. They had only expressions of disdain for us. I cursed John once again and followed him into the hotel, the guard at our heels.

Chapter 7

Escape from Headquarters

Once inside, our guard turned us over to other Iraqis, who indicated we should hold up for a moment in the lobby. While waiting, I noticed the manager, whom I had also known when he was the manager of the Meridien. He was walking toward me, and I prepared to say hello when I caught a slight headshake, which I took as a signal not to acknowledge our acquaintanceship.

Whatever his reason for not wanting to talk to me, I respected his wishes, and he passed by without a word. I believe he was an Iraqi, who had trained at the Cornell University Hotel Management School. My impression was he tended to be pro-western but not at that moment when he might be observed by so many of his countrymen.

I looked about the lobby and saw the six Kuwaiti militiamen formed up two by two. We were told to be seated and then ordered to get into the double files with the Kuwaitis and several other civilians who had been brought into the hotel.

A soldier beckoned us to "fall in" and follow him off to the right of the lobby. We all trailed behind him up a winding staircase and into the main ballroom. About 45 people, seated in a large semi-circle in the middle of the room, greeted us.

I recognized quite a few of them, including a German dentist, two British friends, and another man, who worked for the Kuwait Danish Dairy. Others were familiar to me in varying degrees—

people whom I had seen about the city, in the health field, or perhaps at various social functions which were always being held in normal times.

We were told to take chairs beside the wall and move into the circle. Seating myself, I was chatting with some of these people when a Englishman I knew from the beach—his name was Paul—came by to say he had been picked up just after filling his car's gas tank at the Sheraton Round About.

A Polish physician said that was exactly what had happened to him as well. He had no sooner driven into the round about when he was waved over to the side of the road and taken into custody.

Several others said they had been picked up while walking just like John and me. Hadn't done a thing. Just walking. An Air India crew said they were guests in the hotel when ordered into the ballroom.

A Richard Simontelli told us he was from Boston, but I didn't mention my roots there. He was a guest in the hotel. I had decided by then that the best thing for me to do was just to be friendly and cooperative but close-mouthed. I was going to be a good listener and leave the talking to others.

Meanwhile, John reverted to his gadfly nature and was circling about the room, collecting everyone's name on paper napkins. If we were to be detained, he said it was important we figure a way to get the list of names to people on the outside who could help us. He soon slipped the napkins to a Spanish diplomat.

Several hours passed, and the group now numbered more than 60 people of many nationalities. There were some diplomats among us, who requested diplomatic immunity, but the Iraqis refused to release them. Another diplomat came into the room, thinking he was going to win their release when he, too, was arrested and ordered to remain with us.

The diplomat complained to the commander of our guards, a middle-aged soldier, who was very dignified looking and wore the red beret of the Republican Guards. The Iraqi officer listened politely but said there was nothing to be done for any of us immediately. Meanwhile, he would look into the status of the detained diplomats. His remarks had to be translated into English.

About five o'clock, we were treated to a typical Arabic buffet, but we were getting tired, impatient, and wondering loudly what was to become of us. By then, the diplomats, up on their high horses, were visibly upset about their situation.

Within an hour, the commander returned to tell us through the translator that we had been detained for our own protection. There were many bad elements loose in the city, and the Iraqi army still had to deal with them. The streets could be very dangerous for us. It would not be for long—although we had no idea how he measured time.

Several of us said we didn't appreciate being taken into custody and wanted to be permitted to leave immediately. In reply, he said this would not be possible but added that the diplomats were free to go. With that, the diplomats, their superior airs most apparent, stood up and went to retrieve their passports and documents before leaving the Sheraton. The Spanish official was among them. (1)

Watching the diplomats file out of the ballroom, I felt even more frustrated and very angry. How come they were able to leave, and we couldn't? Of course, I knew the answer. Just because they were diplomats. Somehow it still didn't seem fair. Some crummy clerk in a two-bit consulate or embassy received precedence over citizens of great and powerful countries.

Next thing I knew, John was on his feet, demanding to know what they intended to do about us other diplomats, who had not been carrying papers with them at the time of detention. He went on in English, and the translator seemed confused. John was not only speaking quickly and in an irate voice, but he was also stuttering, a disorder he had.

The translator whispered to the commander, and the commander said something back. The translator then asked how many in the group were diplomats without papers.

I raised my hand immediately, and John was right behind me. The German dentist looked at me, and I nodded for him to follow suit. An American Air Force man I knew slightly also raised his.

The commander gazed about the room, saw no other hands, and with several guards accompanied us into the hallway. With the commander at his side, the translator asked us each individually "to explain our case." Instinctively, I knew from the tone of his voice and the looks he had been giving us that the translator was on our side. All we had to do was make our stories realistic.

We were told to produce whatever documentation we had available. I showed the commander my Kuwaiti government-issued ID card, which stated my name and the fact that I was a dentist. The commander asked in Arabic: "And who are you?" I stated that I was an employee of the United Nations Development Programme.(2)

The translator took my cue and pounced on the saying: "Very good, very good. United Nations. United Nations." The commander took his fellow Arab at his word and ordered me to stand off to the side.

Next up was John, who showed one of his calling cards, which simply noted that he worked for an Australian trading company. He used it to claim that he worked for the Australian Embassy. He was also motioned over to the side with me.

The American officer was next. I almost vomited when he launched into an obsequious, demeaning speech about being a representative of the United States, who was there to offer any assistance required by the Iraqi government. When his bum-kissing statement was half-translated for the commander, he was ordered to stand off to the other side of the hallway by himself.

The German dentist stepped forward after he had quickly asked me what he should say. "Just tell them you also work for the United Nations Development Programme," I whispered. It worked for me, why not for him? He was placed with John and me.

This process was no sooner completed when a door to the ballroom swung open and an Englishman I knew by the name of

Nigel hurried out. Obviously upset, visibly pale, and shaking, he went right up to the commander and said he wanted to be released at once. The commander asked Nigel why he should be allowed to leave.

Nigel spluttered, "I just don't want to stay here. I want to leave. I don't want to be here. I have my rights."

The translator repeated this claim, and the commander said, "You must understand that we're protecting you. We're keeping you here for your own safety. Now return to the ballroom at once."

We stared as one at Nigel, wondering whether his outburst was going to foul up our little plan to get away. I was waiting for him to complain about us, but he kept quiet and went back to the ballroom.

The commander spoke to the translator, who said softly, "Go. Go right now."

Thinking he meant, "Go. Go get your documents," we headed down the hallway for the winding staircase to the lobby. We figured Iraqi guards were right at our back, but a look behind showed that we weren't being followed. "Stay cool," I urged. "Let's not blow it. Just keep walking. Down the stairs and then out of the lobby."

Crossing the lobby, I saw the manager again and gave him a wink, saying facetiously, "I'm sorry, I'll have to pay my bill later. Goodbye". He appeared incredulous and gave no reply.

As we approached the main door, I said, "Straight through, gentlemen. Like we are on official business. Going to get documents requested by the authorities."

Once back into the beautiful fresh air, the German dentist went off to the right to return to his villa in the Behbehani complex behind the Catholic cathedral, and we started up toward Fahd Al-Salim Street. As earlier the street was jammed with hundreds of Iraqi soldiers with their myriad vehicles.

Would they stop us? Not one soldier blocked our way or bothered us in any way. Most said nothing. A few, relaxing on the grass and eating their evening rations, nodded and said hello to us.

"I can't believe this, John," I said. "We're walking through the whole damn Iraqi army and not one of them cares diddly about us. Can you believe they just accepted that baloney about being diplomats and sent us out without any escort to get our documents?"

Because of the adventure we had just shared, mostly due to his initiative, John was temporarily back in my good graces. It would take some time however to get over his insistence about going with the Iraqi guard to the Sheraton Hotel.

Rounding the corner onto Fahd Al-Salim Street, we threaded our way as discreetly as possible through throngs of soldiers and civilians. Again, not a soul stopped us nor sought to question us. I was looking straight ahead, avoiding any possible eye contact. I figured John was doing the same.

As we passed the police station, where we had been briefly detained before being transferred to the Sheraton, John suggested, "What say we take a left here and go down and visit our friends? We never did get to see Pastor Maurice."

I gave him a look that clearly indicated I thought he was insane and kept right on walking to the corner of Al-Hilali Street where I turned right up past the Meridien Hotel and headed straight for the Al Muthanna complex.

"John, you're impossible. After what we've just been through. Wanting to go cavorting through the streets to make house calls on people. Where do you get your brains? I'm going straight home, John, and I'm going right up to the apartment and staying there."

We got into the building without incident and moments later entered the apartment, acting like a couple of escaped mental patients. Half-laughing, we jokingly told the group we were never going out again. We had been picked up, and it hadn't been much fun.

Philip was very relieved to see me, imagining all sorts of terrible things had happened to me. What would he have said to Jill and my daughters? I had just vanished into thin air?

"They're doing it, Philip," I said. "They're picking up all the Westerners. They're after us. No bones about it. They're transporting people to Baghdad or wherever in Iraq. We heard the first load of hostages are being sent out. Probably this evening."

I had picked up this information from Paul, an Englishman at the Sheraton, but had kept it to myself. I had no way of knowing how John would have reacted to the news while we were still in captivity. Probably would have gone off half-cocked and got us shipped out, too. (3)

We were telling about our run-in with the Iraqis and our imaginative escape when Dr. Hansen came into the apartment, obviously very shaken. He explained that the Iraqis had come to his apartment again and rummaged through it quite extensively.

"They didn't actually trash the place, but I can tell you that they put a scare into me. Malicious bastards. Seem to delight in frightening people."

Looking around, I noticed that Max, the Australian, was aboard. He was not a resident of the complex, but given the round-up of Westerners, we had convinced him to stay overnight in our complex. Up to that point, he had been thinking about driving back to his own place. Can you just see him tooling his car through one Iraqi roadblock after the other and getting away with it? No way!

Once our story had been told by John—with a few embellishments—and we had answered a series of questions, I called the United States Embassy to give them a report.

I talked with an employee by the name of Gail Rogers. I don't remember her title. Whatever, she apparently considered our capture and escape very unimportant because she was terribly patronizing. I no sooner began to tell her what had happened to John and me when she told me to calm down. Flabbergasted, I asked her what she was going to do with the information. She replied, "I'll think about it."

"That's not good enough!" I replied. "I want to know what you're going to do about it. You, the United States Embassy. I insist that you do something about it. Americans in Kuwait have a right to know what's going on."

Very matter-of-factly, she said, "I'll give the information to my supervisor."

"And what's he going to do about it?"

"We'll all talk about it."

"What the hell does that mean? 'Talk about it.' What good is that going to do?"

At that point, I couldn't stand her condescending, bureaucratic manner any longer and slammed down the phone.

"Bastards!!" I yelled aloud. "I don't think they give a good goddamn about us at all." (4)

A short time later, I received a call from a military attaché at the embassy, inquiring about the Air Force officer, who had been detained by the Iraqis. I described him, deciding not to say anything about his unctuous statement. My caller explained the description fitted that of a United States military advisor to the Kuwaiti government, and he hung up.

We passed the remainder of the evening discussing the day's events, particularly the round-up of Westerners, played several rubbers of bridge, and called it a night.

Chapter 8

Foiled Flight

Philip was up and about early on Sunday morning, August 5th, and said there had been a BBC report about the Iraqis announcing their departure from Kuwait. I brightened immediately, but Philip added that the report was being denied by both the Saudi Arabians and the Americans. Some Iraqi vehicles had been seen traveling north to the border, and the erroneous conclusion was that the Iraqi army was headed home.

"It wasn't so," Philip said. "The equipment only went a short distance before the Iraqis either stopped it in place or turned around and came back to the capital."

"Probably just a feint to try to fool the Saudis," I said. "Iraqi bastards might still invade Saudi Arabia, too."

"They better hurry if they intend to," Philip said. "Washington's bullshit, and President Bush is pressuring the United Nations to take action against Iraq. Calling for world-wide sanctions against Iraq and planning to send troops and aircraft to the Saudis."

"Good," I replied harshly. "Kick the shit out of the bastards. The Marines will kick Saddam Hussein's butt in short order."

"Yeah, yeah, the Marines," Philip teased. "Remember Lebanon. You got your butts kicked there."

"Hey, it was a sneak attack," I could only respond weakly, recalling with sadness the terrorist attack on the barracks which left some 240 sleeping Marines dead.

Philip quickly changed the subject to our own situation. "So, where are we, Rob? I think the Iraqis are here to stay. What are we going to do?"

"Good question, Philip. Maybe it's time we just got the hell out of here. Get in the BMW and just take off down the highway for the Saudi border. Who knows? We might just get through."

The apartment gradually filled during the morning with the regulars. The Hansens; John; Kennedy and the Thai women; Mary McGee, who had lived through another uneventful night; Jane Anderson, still trying to make up her mind about us; and the other Australian, Max. The Sudanese doctor came in, followed by a friend of Kennedy's—a Lebanese fellow named Tony, a very mysterious type, but very quiet and always the perfect gentleman.

Tony, unlike some of the others, brought some food that he was willing to share with us. He lived up above on the ninth floor. He was a gem, who shortly would leave for Lebanon. Before going, though, he would provide us with the key to his apartment, giving us more space, extra beds, and telephones among other things.

New arrivals would bring stories about further looting, rapes, and round-ups of Westerners. There were more and more reports about Iraqi soldiers prowling the hallways of our complex even breaking down doors to get into apartments whether occupied or not. We couldn't help wondering when the Iraqis would come back for us, especially since they knew Americans were in the building.

Among the newcomers were two Iraqi businessmen, one of whom was married to a Kuwaiti. In all fairness, they were both pleasant and sympathetic to our position, but they were still Iraqis—the people who had invaded little Kuwait and inflicted so much death and destruction. I hadn't forgotten how the Iraqis had picked me up. As a result, I didn't want anything to do with them.

To my surprise and disapproval, Bob and Mona Hansen accepted an invitation from one of the Iraqis to be his guests in his apartment in the Jabriya section of the city. In my mind, Mona had gone around the bend because of the events of the past four days. That's why she was all for the idea. She convinced Dr. Hansen that they should go, and I refused to argue with them. If they wanted to go off with the enemy, let them!

To keep our minds off our situation as much as possible, we passed many hours playing bridge. Occasionally, one of us would check out the window to see what was happening in the street. Nothing had changed. It was filled with Iraqis and military vehicles.

Once again, I went downstairs myself to the garage to check on my BMW and was appalled to see Arabs, mostly Palestinians, still stuffing hundreds of cars with loot from the mall. I couldn't believe that there was anything left to steal. But as Philip had said earlier, they had probably discovered many of the stockrooms and storage spaces brimming over with attractive merchandise.

Later in the day, civilians became more daring and began pulling up before the mall directly below us on Al-Hilali Street. While the men sat at the wheel, ferocious-looking obese women would waddle into the shops and boutiques and return minutes later with armfuls of loot. Once their individual vehicle was stuffed, off they would go without a word of protest from the Iraqi soldiers.

When we became weary of playing bridge, Mary McGee showed us her new board game she had jokingly created called "Expatriate's Guide to Kuwait." It mostly dealt with all the screwy bureaucratic crap we had had to put up with in peacetime Kuwait.

Her game took into account the constant fingerprinting of foreigners, the need to carry one's ID card at all times, the inability to drink alcohol, how to deal with the Kuwaitis in the way they expected, how to enter and exit the country, and stuff like that. To add to the fun, Philip and I came up with a few more rules that she had overlooked. We also thought we should add a section on the "Expatriate's Guide to Wartime Kuwait" and what to do if you became trapped in the middle of it.

We all died a little bit when the Iraqis came to the door and again checked our ID cards. We were sure they were going to take us into custody "en masse," but they just scowled and left.

"This is getting to be a little too much for me," Jane Anderson said and went off to her own place.

"I couldn't agree with her more," Philip said. "This building is filled with tension. With waiting. With anticipation that those bastards will come back at any moment and take us away. We've got to think about getting out of here."

We were all of the same mind when Monday morning rolled around, and the Iraqi presence seemed even more threatening and overwhelming. Each new arrival brought additional stories about rape and looting, more round-ups and executions of Kuwaitis.

"Why do the Iraqis hate the Kuwaitis so much, Rob?" Philip asked.

"Plain old envy, Philip. Another case of the 'haves' versus the 'have-nots.'"

"I understand with all their oil, the Iraqis are fairly well off compared to a lot of other Arabs."

"Yeh, they've plenty of oil, but they don't know how to market it like the Kuwaitis. Besides, old Saddam Hussein spends 40 to 50 percent of his budget on military stuff rather than on his people. He sees himself as a modern-day Suleiman the Magnificent."

"Who was he?" Philip asked with a wrinkled brow.

"Read, read, read, young man. Something your generation doesn't do, but that's how you learn."

Just then, the married Iraqi from the day before entered. He informed us he had gotten his wife out of the country into Jordan. From there she was on her way to Lebanon.

We all felt happy for him, instinctively reacting to his sense of joy in this accomplishment. His news started a general discussion about how it was time for us to give serious thought to leaving, if not the country, at least the Al-Muthanna complex, where the danger to us seemed to increase by the minute.

For the past few days, I had been in touch on the telephone with Bill Colwell and his wife, Luz Marina. Bill was the senior attaché at the U. S. Embassy and suggested that some of us move into his house, which was empty because he and Luz had been staying nights at the embassy.

On the spur of the moment, I called Bill at the embassy, and he assured me the invitation stood and that other Westerners would also be welcome. I thanked him profusely and rang off.

Bob and Mona Hansen then came into the apartment and claimed they had passed a very peaceful night in the Iraqi businessman's home. I expressed my relief but couldn't help adding that I had to wonder why they would want to sleep in the enemy's house.

Neither of them said a word in response. Probably knew they had been out of line.

In any case, they were lucky they returned when they did. Hearing about the Colwell's invitation, they expressed an immediate wish to join the group making the move. The other members of the group would be Philip, Mary McGee, Max, and myself.

We passed the remainder of that Monday listening to the BBC, playing, checking on the activity in the street, and trying to make telephone calls to our various friends and official contacts. For me, it was a big disappointment not to be able to call my family and friends at home and the various media to keep them informed about what was happening in the capital.

I did, however, maintain contact with Jill's brother-in-law, John Evelyn of St. Kitts in the Caribbean, who was employed at a Getty Oil Company facility close to the Saudi border on the sea to the south. On my last call that day to John, he informed me he was going to attempt crossing the border in a caravan of buses. That failing, he said he would go with a few friends in a small boat out to sea a bit and then head south until they hopefully were in Saudi territorial waters. (1)

I wished him luck but envied his location only a few miles from the Kuwait-Saudi border. Just a hop-skip-and-a-jump, and he was free from the danger of being rounded up by the Iraqis, who were already in his vicinity.

After a restless night's sleep, I packed a small bag for my stay at the Colwells' place in the Abdulla Al-Salim section of the city. It was an embassy property located in one of the top Kuwaiti residential areas across from the government-owned ice rink. Yes, an ice rink, right in the middle of an Arabian city. Great spot to cool off on hot evenings. (2)

None of us packed very much for the trip. A change of clothing, toiletries, stuff like that. We didn't figure on a long stay. The Marines would be storming ashore within a few days, and our nightmare would be over.

Surprisingly we drove away from the complex in two cars without incident although the garage levels were rapidly filling up with die-hard looters. In all the turmoil and tangled mass of ruined cars and moving vehicles, the Iraqis paid us little heed.

We were proceeding down one street when Philip spotted a roadblock in the distance with a line of cars backed way up. With little lost motion, we turned about and went around the long way, taking a right at the Al-Murgab Health Clinic to drive to Al-Soor Street. There we hooked a left and went along to Abdulla Al-Mubarak Street, turning right, and proceeding to Al-Maghreb Street and the Abdulla Al-Salim section.

No sooner had we parked the cars outside and gone into the spacious two-story house when sporadic gunfire erupted from the direction of the Emir's and the Crown Prince's palaces.

As though it were a signal, the gunfire was rapidly followed by outbursts of weaponry throughout the city. At our new location, we had an excellent vantage point from which to view the city. We remained transfixed at the curtained windows, watching the activity. The tracers marked the line of bullets across the sky like strings of Christmas lights.

"What's up, Rob?" Philip asked.

I really didn't know but guessed that small units of the Kuwaiti army or hastily formed Kuwaiti underground forces were still putting up a fight. The Colwells' house offered us an excellent view in the direction of the Al-Muthanna complex. About halfway across that space was the radio and television center captured by the Iraqis on the morning of the invasion.

There wasn't a soul about, but suddenly there was an intense fusillade of small arms fire. All eyes fastened on the communication structure, but there was little to see—just billows of smoke to mark the firing of weapons and spurts of debris and dust to show where the slugs were hitting.

"What the hell is that all about?" Max queried. Again, no one could truthfully say because there were no troops to be seen on either side. I figured once more that some Kuwaitis were letting their oppressors know they hadn't given up the ghost.

One thing we had to chuckle about when we entered the house was the state of disarray. Luz Marina had been packing to move with Bill for new duties in Baghdad when the Iraqi invasion occurred. In fact, the very day of the onslaught, the Kuwaiti movers showed up as though everything was normal in the country and continued to pack the household items. How's that for a conditioned mindset?

Most of the smaller items were still in various size boxes and cartons, but the key items like the furniture, including the beds, tables and chairs, TV sets, VCRs, and telephones were in place. The Colwells had left plenty of food in the refrigerator and pantry along with all the necessary pots and pans and silverware. There was even linen for the beds.

If the invasion had come a few days later than August 2nd, we would have been hunkered down in an empty house without any food or communication. Then again, we probably would have never moved there.

To sort of pay our way, we had agreed to answer the telephones for the Colwells. The embassy phones had been shut off by the Iraqis, but all the key callers had been informed earlier to contact the Colwells numbers as a back-up system.

We worked out a schedule so the several phones were manned within reason around the clock. Almost immediately we began receiving messages, many of a cryptic or arcane nature, making no sense to us. Dutifully, we wrote them down and logged them into the duty book.

The plan called for Luz Marina to come back to her home about noontime every day to collect the messages. Almost from the first day, though, she came accompanied by an embassy employee named Paul, a commercial officer of some type whom I knew slightly.

One or the other was constantly on the phone, talking about the Filipinos whose lives had been disrupted by the Iraqis. Apparently, thousands of them had rushed to their own embassy seeking protection. Their embassy, in turn, had requested aid from the United States ambassador.

To my surprise and dismay, the plight of the Filipinos seemed of far more importance to our embassy than the fate of American citizens. The Filipinos figured in most of the phone conversations involving Luz Marina and Paul when they were present.

I couldn't help wondering why U.S. Embassy employees weren't concerning themselves about their fellow citizens. Where were they? Were they in need of help? I had to believe the Americans in Kuwait City had to be number one on the Iraqis' hit list—if not now, sometime soon.

Within a few days of our going to the Colwells, it became evident to me that our embassy had no system to keep track of Americans living permanently or temporarily in the capital.

They obviously had no list at all of Americans anywhere in Kuwait. Without such a list of names, addresses, and telephone numbers, there was no way the embassy could possibly be supportive in an emergency like the one we were experiencing.

Sure, if you made a point of going to the embassy and saying, "I'm John Jones, an American, and I'll be in Kuwait City at such-and-such an address for the next two weeks or month or year. Here's my phone number, and I would appreciate your making a record of this information so I can count on you to alert me to any potential danger or threat and support me in the event of dire straits." Maybe then, just maybe, they would have a record of your presence in Kuwait. But even that wasn't so.

As always, the onus was on you as an individual. Don't be so callow to think that the embassy was going to inconvenience itself to determine whether you were living for a time in the country.

Paul Kennedy came by during the first 24 hours or so to check on our situation. He always seemed nonplussed by the presence of the Iraqis in the city. In fact, he was never in danger because Ireland was neutral in the brouhaha. Accordingly, it was no big deal for him to appear like Mr. Cool.

As for myself, I wasn't too keen on his coming to and going from the Colwells. He could unintentionally bring the Iraqis down on us. All they had to do was to follow him to see what he was about, and there they would be at the door. Until he identified himself as an Irish citizen, he was just another Westerner running loose.

On his initial visit, he said he and the Thai women were in need of food. He wanted us to take him to the local cooperative supermarket to see what was available. Off we went to the cooperative, one of which was located in each district of the city. It was a self-contained organization with a food cooperative, health center, schools, TV and shoe repair shops, service stations, a shop for cooking gas. Just about anything you would need in a small community.

Unfortunately for us, the Kuwaitis in this particular cooperative had panicked and cleaned out most of the food from the store in a few days after the invasion. There were only condiments to be picked over. A true forager, especially for food, Kennedy was disappointed about the remaining items and shortly returned to the Al-Muthanna complex.

In addition to my BMW, the Hansens also had a car at the Colwells. A third one belonged to Pastor Maurice of the Evangelical church, whom John and I were on our way to visit the day the Rambo-acting Iraqi soldier dropped out of the tree and took us into custody.

Because the pastor's wife had been molested and assaulted by some soldiers, he had decided it was time for them to flee to the United States Embassy. On the way, their car was stopped at a roadblock. One way or another, the pastor's car wound up in the Colwells driveway, riddled with bullet holes.

When told about the pastor, I couldn't help but think that he was already safe in the embassy when John and I had gone off to visit him on the third day after the invasion and we had been apprehended.

Several days passed while we continued to take messages for the embassy. Luz Marina and Paul came by to collect them and use the phones to talk to their contacts, informers, or whatever. Their central concern continued to be the Filipinos. I heard very little conversation about any Americans. You had to wonder who the hell the embassy was working for.

Through this whole period, right from the first day, I was treating myself for colitis. Within a few days, I ran out of the medication and couldn't obtain any more because of the confusion in the city and the inadvisability of traveling about. As a result, my stomach and bowels became tangled into painful knots at odd times. The only thing left for me to take were pain pills, whatever kind were available. Because of the colitis, I lost my appetite and began losing weight to the point where people noticed.

Obviously, what with everything else happening to us, I became more anxious about finding some way of getting out of Kuwait. It was past time to attempt an escape from the city and run for the border. "It's no big deal," I told the assembled group of Philip, the Hansens, Max, and Mary McGee. "We go out on the Second Ring Road for just a short distance, turn left, and we're on the Fahaheel Highway. Just stay on it, and it becomes the Al-Safr Motorway, which will take us right to the Saudi border."

"Just like that?" Max said questioningly.

"No. Not just like that, but it's simple and direct. We could be at the border within an hour or so. It's worth a shot."

"Yeh, it's worth being shot," Max contended. "Nothing is ever simple. The Iraqis must have set up roadblocks along it—especially at the border. I'll sit this one out. There's no great urgency for me to leave."

In the end, the Hansens also decided to stay in the Colwells' home with Max while Philip and Mary would take their chances with me in a dash for the border. We made our preparations in the way of water and gasoline and prepared to be off. Good-byes were said and good luck expressed.

I didn't have any worry about the car being in good condition for the trip. It was a big BMW 635 coupe, vintage 1985, with the engine recently tuned. As far as I was concerned, the BMW was in the best possible shape for the 140-kilometer dash to the border.

Off we went, nervous but confident that we could somehow circumvent the Iraqi net and cross the border. We hadn't driven more than 30 kilometers when the Iraqis netted us at a roadblock by Green Beach, an old swimming haunt in better days.

We acted as though we hardly knew there had been an invasion. Why in the world would anyone want to bother us? We had a very amiable conversation with the soldiers, several of whom spoke some English, but they were adamant about our returning to Kuwait City.

I thought fleetingly of gunning the BMW and driving off in a beeline of burning rubber and shrieking engine. It was only fleetingly because the Iraqis always held their weapons at the ready. Anyway, they would just call ahead, and the guards at the next roadblock could start shooting before we even stopped.

We were a dejected, sheepish trio when we circled about and drove back to the Colwells. Our welcoming committee of Max and the Hansens was most generous and warm in its greeting and listened attentively while we provided the details of our escapade.

Chapter 9

A Dash for Saudi

The day after our abortive escape attempt, Mona Hansen began to act rather queerly. Once again it was over those packages she had been wrapping in muslin to post back to the States. No matter who was about to go out for whatever reason, she would ask them to swing by the post office to see whether or not it was open. She was quite anxious to get all her sealed packages, boxes, cartons—filled with God knows what—mailed home.

For the three days or more we had been in the Colwells' home, she had continued to wrap and stitch the muslin covers. I was never sure what the hell she was putting into the packages or where she had gotten the contents. I can't recall that Bob or she had returned to the Al-Muthanna complex for anything.

It was a bit irritating to be constantly pestered by her about when the post office was going to open or to drive by and see whether it was. For the most part, I intended to roll with her barrage of requests, but Max was another story.

He was definitely of a mind that she was acting irrationally. Here we were in the midst of a war, concerned for our very lives, and she was only worried about sending her things back to the United States.

I remembered very well Max telling me back at my apartment that her unceasing harping on this issue was driving him crazy. "I swear I'll throw her out the window, Rob," he said in exasperation. "So shut her up. Just shut her up, or I will. All eight floors. I swear it!"

As the days passed, and Mona kept up her requests about checking the post office, Max began to get annoyed beyond measure with her. Fortunately, the Colwells' house consisted of only two floors. Mona would probably come to little harm were he to launch her from the roof.

Desperate to lower the tension, I suggested we should try escaping by taking another route. The five members of the group asked which one I was considering.

"We slip out of here, pick up the Sixth Ring Road, go left along it to Jahra, then around the Al-Atraf Road interchange, and head southwest for Al-Salmy. It's close to the border of Saudi, and we can look for a way to slip across."

"That's fine, Rob," Max spoke up, "but Al-Salmy, as you know, is also about the same distance from the Iraqi border. The place could be crawling with Iraqis set to invade Saudi Arabia."

Max had a good point. Al-Salmy probably was about nine miles from the Saudi border and eleven or so from the Iraqi border. It's located where the borders of the three countries converge.

"You're right on that point, Max," I said, "but let's just think of this as a scouting expedition. A chance to check out the route. We can turn around as soon as we spot an Iraqi checkpoint. At the same time, if we get lucky and the opportunity presents itself, we'll go across the border."

Max, Mary, and Philip had no problem with that idea and agreed to accompany me. The Hansens passed, wishing us a safe return.

I had assumed Max and Mary would ride with Philip and me in the big BMW, but they were adamant about taking the pastor's car, a small Mitsubishi sedan. Even when I pointed out that my BMW could do twice its speed, Max insisted on driving the second car.

I shrugged. To each his own. Max was just one of those independent cusses who always had to believe they were in control. With me at the wheel and his life in my hands, maybe he figured he didn't have a chance. A sense of humor does help.

After checking the gas tank levels and stowing away extra water supplies, we drove quickly away and soon were at the roundabout at Al-Jahra and driving southwest down the highway to Al-Salmy.

There was Iraqi military traffic everywhere, but no one paid any heed to us although my mouth dried out rapidly whenever an Iraqi auto or military vehicle passed us. Since they had been picking up Westerners, I expected to be stopped and arrested at any moment.

In way of a disguise, we all wore dark glasses and hats to somewhat hide our light skin and features. I also had the sun visors down and the tinted windows up to retain the coolness from the air conditioner. Both vehicles still carried Kuwaiti registration plates.

We weren't more than a mile down the highway from the interchange when we spotted an amazingly surrealistic scene comprised of hundreds of brand new cars with their hoods up, abandoned at a Kuwaiti warehouse. In peacetime, the site had been a Chevrolet car lot, storing mostly Chevrolet Caprices.

"How do you figure that, Philip?"

"Dumb Iraqis. They don't want the new cars. They don't know how to drive them. It's the batteries they took. Slow down. You can see they've stolen the goddamn batteries. Can you imagine? What a waste."

"Imagine an American breaking into a $30,000 car and only stealing a $50 battery," I laughed.

I was so intent on taking long sideways glances at the disorderly mass of disabled cars that I almost ran head-on into an Iraqi roadblock no more than 1500 feet farther along the highway.

"Rob!" Philip shrieked. "Rob, for Christ's sake, hold it up. A roadblock!"

I slammed on the brakes and slowed to a crawl. Actually, I hadn't been going that fast because we were scrutinizing the car lot and the BMW's powerful brakes could stop on a greased dime.

As I slowly drove up to the waiting Iraqis, who already had their weapons aimed at us, I glanced in the rear view mirror. Max had apparently spotted the roadblock before we had and had halted way back near the lot. No flies on Max. And those that were had to be paying rent.

My heart was beating faster, but overall I wasn't too scared. Philip assured me that he was all right. "Just be cool, friendly. Do what they say," he said.

"Not to worry," I said. "I'm a man of peace."

Whatever, it didn't make any difference. The Iraqis were very insistent that we had to turn around and go back to Kuwait City. They kept waving their weapons at us and gesturing with their hands for us to turn around and go back the way we had come.

I wasted no time doing exactly that, and Max swung out in front of me as we went back up the highway.

I was unkindly shaken from these thoughts when a group of Iraqi soldiers suddenly appeared from the side of the road and waved for us to halt. One minute there was nothing but the sand piles along the highway without a soul in sight, and the next second we were being confronted by what seemed to be a full squad of hostile Iraqis.

They had waited for Max, who was some 200 feet ahead, to go by before they leapt out in front of us. I thanked the powers-that-be again for the BMW's brakes. Without their quick grab, I would have smeared half the soldiers over the surface of the road and then died with Philip in a hail of bullets.

"Dumb bastards!" I yelled as the car came to an abrupt stop. As the soldiers approached, I noticed that Max had stopped some 200 yards down the road to await the outcome.

Once again, the Iraqis made no big deal over the fact that we were Westerners. We soon established the fact that all they wanted was some gasoline for their armored personnel carrier, which was stuck off in the desert.

I indicated that their need was understood and to help themselves. One of them whipped out a section of hose and within minutes had siphoned off about three gallons of my gasoline. I wondered how far that much would get them but kept the thought to myself.

All the time they were jabbering away and laughing among themselves. Philip and I just kept smiling and acting like we were their brothers-in-arms.

Spotting one of the Iraqis wearing a winter woolen cap in the day's 120-degree temperature, I couldn't stop myself from laughing. I pointed out the cap to Philip and got him laughing. The Iraqis sort of stopped moving about and looked at us with blank faces. What did the westerners think was so funny?

The one with the cap walked over to me. My heart sank, and my mouth felt like it was lined with dry tree leaves. He had taken his rifle off his shoulder, and I wondered whether I was going to die. To die for laughing at his foolish winter cap out there in the desert.

He started talking in Arabic and his buddies crowded around. Obviously, he was asking me what was so funny. With quaking heart, I used hand gestures and a few Arabic phrases to tell him.

As one, the Iraqis stared at me with expressionless faces, and then they looked at one another. "We're in for it now, Rob," Philip croaked.

But it was our lucky day. First one Iraqi and then another grinned foolishly and broke out into laughter, each in turn pointing to the soldier's cap. When he finally joined in the merriment, I knew we were out of potential harm.

They gestured that we must be off, but first the Iraqi soldier took off his cap and insisted that I take it as a souvenir. I really didn't want the filthy headgear and especially from any Iraqi who had helped to shatter my life.

"Take it, Rob. For the love of God, take it, and let's get out of here before they change their minds," Philip begged.

I smiled and reached for the cap. Taking it, I held it aloft. The Iraqis smiled back and turned away to head for their APC. Philip and I walked quickly to the BMW to drive off in a burst of speed that generated the beaming admiration of the Iraqis.

Speeding to catch up to Max, who had taken off down the highway as soon as he saw us returning to the BMW, I could only express gratitude that the Iraqis hadn't insisted I put on the woebegone cap. I envisioned it crawling with lice. Ugh!

I was about to throw it out the window when Philip stilled my arm. "No. Hold on to it. It's a great souvenir. Make for a great story when all this crap is over."

"Yes. I'll give it to John. He's a great souvenir collector. Can put it with his collection at the complex."

In hardly any time at all, we were back at the roundabout and on the Sixth Ring Road headed for the Colwell's house.

The four of us piled into the house and admitted right up front to the Hansens that we had had no luck getting out of Kuwait or finding a way to get out. I added that it had been "a complete waste of time."

That was a mistake because Mary hopped right on it and said, "I could've told you that, but you wouldn't listen. How many times have you been out looking for a route to get away? Two, three? You people just don't know your way around out there. Especially in the desert."

Philip bit. "What's the desert got to do with it? We were in our cars, not trekking across the desert like Beau Geste."

"Why don't you just leave it, Mary?" I said calmly. "You thought enough of the plan to go along with us. We took our best shot, and it didn't work out. It's not the end of the world."

With that remark, I got broadsided. "Best shot! A drive down the highway to the first Iraqi roadblock, and we all come running back with our tails between our legs. I suggest you stop trying these little boy tricks and figure out something that's going to get us out of this place."

My ire was rising, and I could feel my cheeks flushing. "You want to sit here and do nothing? Wait for the Iraqis to come for you and go off with them like a lamb? Go ahead! What makes you an authority on escapes?"

She glared at me. "I'll remind you, Doctor—and as one, you're supposed to show some smarts, some intelligence—that I lived in Egypt for a long time. I learned there to know the desert, to live in the desert, and to survive in the desert. Until you do, your escape attempts will only prove fruitless."

I looked at her in disgust. "What the hell does the desert have to do with anything? We didn't try to cross the goddamn desert or even talk about it. All we tried to do was to drive down one of the freeways to the border."

Before she could jump in, I added, "Why don't we just drop it, Mary? We're talking on different wave lengths."

I recalled then that she had been married at one time to an American employed in Egypt. Because of her knowledge of Egypt, she apparently had convinced herself she was an intimate of the desert. God only knows how living all the time in Cairo allowed her to become an expert on the shifting sands.

With that, I walked away and went into the bedroom to freshen up and take another pain pill for my colitis, which had been further irritated by my verbal exchange with her.

By that point, I was depressed about everything that was going. Realistically, too, I had to admit the air of tension was tightening throughout the household. Everyone was getting on each other's nerves and lashing out verbally at one another.

Dinnertime that same day brought another verbal onslaught—with me against the whole pack except for Philip, who didn't join in on either side. It was my turn to make dinner, and I whipped up six eggs for omelets, figuring there were six of us, and six eggs should do it. I planned to serve each person a one-egg omelet with one piece of toast. Rations were tight, and it was the best I could do for the evening meal.

I no sooner had the eggs whipped and was working on the toast when Max came into the kitchen, quickly diced an onion, and flicked it into the bowl.

I didn't say a word. I figured, screw it! I've got colitis, and the onions will do a job on my guts. In a dash, I whipped up an additional egg in a separate bowl for myself.

You can imagine what hit the fan when I brought out the omelets and placed them on the table. Almost in tandem, Mary and Max, the two M and Ms, fired off at me.

"Six eggs—and what—more for yourself?" Mary sputtered. "We're running out of food, and you used up the eggs. There're just six of us."

"For Christ's sake, Rob, are you losing it? Seven eggs. We'll all starve to death at this rate!" That was Max's contribution by way of thanks for my preparing the dinner.

"Why don't you just sit down and eat the omelets?" I replied. "I cooked six eggs for the six of us, but old Max here came out to the kitchen and cut an onion for that batch

Max opened his mouth to protest, but I cut him short.

"You know I have colitis. Onions are one of the worst things in the world for it. I whipped up another egg. Without onions. So I took an extra egg. Big deal. I'll be happy to share it with anyone of you."

Max blurted out, "You really ought to get your ass kicked, Rob. Bloody doctors. You all think you're so smart."

I jerked about to confront him. I caught the look of alarm and apprehension in the faces of Mary, Mona and Bob Hansen, and Philip.

"Let's make one thing clear, Max. I acted with the best of intentions for everyone. You're the horse's ass who put the onions in the eggs, not me. I was the cook for the evening meal, but you had to butt in.

Max rose from his chair and was braced as though to make a physical rush. "What am I, a mind reader? How am I supposed to know onions aren't good for your queasy stomach?"

"Just ask," I told him. "Just ask before going off half-cocked like some idiot from the nuthouse."

"Are you saying I'm crazy?" he demanded, his voice limned with anger.

"Just don't tell me that I need my ass kicked," I replied, trying to keep my voice on an even keel but sensing the ship was flipping over. "No one kicks ass here. No one! And that includes you. Now, let's all cool off and eat up. Goddamn eggs are getting colder by the moment."

Max glared at me for a few moments but then sat down without further comment. Mary was already seated with the face of a frustrated dowager. Philip was picking at his omelet.

Bob Hansen braced me immediately. "I don't understand why you are making such a deal about the eggs, Rob. I'm very disappointed in you."

Because his wife was present, I didn't tell Dr. Hansen what I thought he could do to himself.

I held my hand up like a traffic cop. "Stop, Bob! Stop right there! I don't want to listen to any more of that talk. I don't need you all to carry on about the eggs."

I went into the kitchen and noticed the small bowl in which I had whipped the egg sans onions. Where the hell was the omelet? I went back to the dining area. It was nowhere in sight.

I returned to the kitchen. The egg could not have just disappeared even though the others had quickly eaten the original six eggs. In the sink! There in the sink I saw the plate which had held the egg. It was empty!

I went back into the dining room and faced the silent quintet. "Excuse my language, but who ate my omelet? Who's the bastard who ate it. C'mon, confess!"

Dr. Hansen flushed. "There's no need for that language, Rob. There are women present."

"That's beside the point," I riposted. "I want my omelet. I cooked it and I want it!"

"Don't look at me!" Max warned. "I never touched it. Who took it in the kitchen when you and I were arguing?"

Ask the right question and you might get the right answer. I looked at Dr. Hansen.

"You, Bob. You were out in the kitchen with Mona when I was getting into it with Max. You took your omelet out into the kitchen and ate both of them."

Sonofabitch! He did! I couldn't believe it. A Harvard man, and he wouldn't admit he had eaten the eggs.

I paused while he sat there silently and Mona fluttered about him with her head and hands. "And you had the gall to question why I was making such a big deal out of the eggs. You're a hypocrite, and you know what kind."

In a most calm voice, he said—as if some innocent Captain Dreyfus—that I was obviously distraught and should consider going to my room to rest.

Can you beat that? He refused to respond to the charge but tried to turn the facts around to make out that I was off my rocker.

"If that's your position, so be it. You and I both know what you are. It's the 'L' word. Don't ever do it again."

I walked into the livingroom, munching on my lousy piece of toast. Philip came by to check on me. Are you all right?"

"Yeh, I'm fine. I'm not the one threatening anyone. I'm not the one who's a liar. I'm okay. How about a cup of tea and a chat?"

The house was puffing up with tension like a giant balloon. It was filling every nook and cranny. Hardly anyone was talking to anyone else. Mona Hansen was wordless, probably realizing the truth of what I had said about her husband.

Eggs! Eggs! Forget the goddamn eggs! I chastised myself. You're beginning to sound like that paranoid captain in "The Caine Mutiny." Humphrey Bogart. He went around the bend when he thought a crewmember had stolen some of his strawberries. Knock it off! You'll be goofy, too.

It was true. The tension was just waiting to explode like a German zeppelin under aerial attack. Except for Philip, there was no one I particularly wanted to be with then in such close quarters. Maybe we should consider going back to the Al-Muthanna complex. I decided to talk with Philip about it.

Incredibly, the ordeal was not over. Early in the evening, the Hansens had gone out for a walk in the darkened neighborhood—believing there were few, if any, Iraqis about in such an out-of-the-way section of the city. Bob returned after a few minutes, saying something about Mona wanting to get some extra fresh air.

I was glancing disinterestedly at the lit-up TV set, bored out of my gourd with the same Kuwaiti government films with the music of John Philip Souza echoing relentlessly in the background as all the Emir's wonderful military equipment passed in review. Peace and quiet. That's all I wanted. Peace and quiet and the opportunity to go home to my family. To get away from the turmoil, bickering, and all the bloody realities of the invasion. Goddamn Saddam! Bastard! Should be taken out and shot wherever he was.

It was not to be. Mona Hansen rushed into the house and circled about to inform everyone that there was a rumor we were about to be gassed. Talk about a rise in the tension level.

"Wait, Mona! Where did you hear that? Who told you that?" I was irate when she refused to answer. She only glared at me. Bob hurried to her defense. He started on me again with the psychobabble bull shit about why was I so upset?

I stood to face him and told him to buzz off. "Don't give me that crap again, Bob. It was your wife who charged in here with the rumor about being gassed. Not me! I don't believe it for a minute. How could the Iraqis gas the city without either killing many of their own people or ordering a massive evacuation of their troops and friends?"

"All she did was to report the rumor. You're making a big deal out of it," he countered.

"None of us should be dealing with rumors or spreading rumors if we can't substantiate them or at least provide a source for them," I shot back.

Anyway—Max, Mary, and I gave enough credence to Mona's story to pass several hours turning the entire second floor into a so-called "safe room"—mostly with rolls of tape. Naturally, there wasn't a gas attack that night.

Chapter 10

Mired in the Desert

For the most part, the next day passed uneventfully. While we had discussed the possibility of returning to the Al-Muthanna complex, the final decision to make the move was put off for another 24 hours. For my part, I tried to regain my composure after the battering I had taken the evening before from the group.

I wasn't totally lucky in this matter because Mary braced me during the morning to help her straighten out the budget we had set up to handle the food. I didn't know what the problem was. The budget had been working out to about five dollars apiece daily—an amount each of us could easily handle.

I decided to use the meeting to gain an edge over her and let her know I didn't appreciate her attitude.

"You manage the budget, Mary. Whatever you think is fair. Just let me know what my share is, and I'll give it to you. It's no big deal, and I know you can handle it."

She appeared to be taken aback by my position as if she were looking for the straight ball and I had tossed her a curve. Only she wasn't sure whether it was a curve or not. Perhaps it was a spitball. While she was still off balance, teetering in effect at the plate, I whipped a fast ball by her.

"I want you to know, Mary, that I am very disappointed by your attitude toward me—especially since I think I've been very supportive of you and tried to let you know I was there for you."

She started to speak, and I gestured with my hand that I wasn't through. "No, I don't want to turn this into a discussion or into another argument. Your attack on me over those lousy eggs last night was completely uncalled for. Seven crappy eggs. For Christ's sake! It was ridiculous."

By then, Mary was almost beside herself and bursting to speak, but I was not going to have any of it. "You just weren't there for me when I expected it. It was a big disappointment and so has your constant criticism of my efforts to find some way for us to get out of here. Here on out, just bite your tongue and shut up if you can't do anything more than criticize."

With that, I turned and walked away, a big smile creasing my lips. She remained speechless, but then I heard her calling for Max. Later that day, they announced they were leaving to go to his hotel room in the Al-Salmiya section. Obviously, I was not heartbroken to see them depart.

The Hansens remained decidedly cool toward me during the day, but I paid them little heed. My conscience was clear. I had tried to help them both from the beginning, offering them my apartment and the safety of numbers from the very first day of the invasion.

I believe it was Luz Marina, who tipped us that a group of Americans and Brits were to meet that night at the SAS Hotel on Arabian Gulf Road in the Salwa district to discuss a mass escape.

Philip and I drove a slow circuitous route to the meeting to avoid any Iraqi roadblocks. The Hansens had declined to go along with us.

At the meeting, one character after another rose to speak about the best way to get to the Arabian border. Each one sounded more deranged than the last. One guy was totally out of control as if he were scared to death. He rambled on and on and finally said he would do whatever was agreed to by the group.

A Brit I recognized, whose wife was a dentist, was very keen on getting away from the Iraqis. He was obsessed with the idea that the invaders wanted to rape his wife.

"They're all crazy, you know, Morris," he whispered. "Lost it already. Just listen to their ideas about how best to escape. They've lost touch."

I mostly listened and finally inquired whether anyone present had a four-wheel drive to make it across the sand. No one had a four-wheel drive, but it was agreed an effort would be made to get one. Anyone who wanted to make the attempt to flee was to be at the basement of the Latiffa Apartments in Farwaniya, a town about 30 kilometers south of Kuwait City, by 6:30 in the morning.

Philip admitted he thought the attendees were mostly gonzo. "I never heard so much crap in my life, Rob. Couldn't agree more with that Brit friend of yours."

Driving furtively through the back streets of Kuwait City in the dim light, I told him about the rumor I had picked up from another acquaintance on the way out of the hotel. The talk around was that the Kuwait-Saudi border on the Gulf would be open in the morning to anyone wanting to leave the country.

Philip became visibly excited. "Do you believe it, Rob? What do you think?"

"I'm thinking it through, Philip. Do we go south to check out the rumor? It sounds almost too incredible. Or do we meet with the others in the morning at the Latiffa apartments and try the road again to Al-Salmy off to the southwest?"

Philip came up with an excellent compromise. "Why not get up very early and dash down the highway in the BMW to the border at Al-Nuwaisib? If the rumor proves false, we can turn around and probably still get back in time to join the others for the trip to Al-Salmy."

Damned! If he hadn't hit the solution smack dab on the head. "Beautiful, Philip. Jill would be very proud of you. Yeh, I like it. Get away around 4, 4:30, and we could pull it off. If we get lucky, we won't even have to go back to the back to the Latiffa apartments. We'll already be gone bye-bye."

Even the Hansens saw the beauty of the endeavor and said they would follow us in their auto, an arrangement I would eventually regret.

We packed as many of our personal belongings as we could that night and stored them in the trunks and back seats of the two vehicles. I was full of anticipation, convinced that one route or the other would lead us to freedom and back home.

Just before we left shortly after 4 a.m., I asked Philip to call Max and inquire whether he had heard the border to the south was open. If he and Mary didn't want to make that gambit, then they might consider linking up with the small group convening that morning at the Latiffa apartments. Mona, hearing the discussion, said that we were not to call Max and Mary. They had stated specifically on leaving the day before that they didn't want to be contacted. The hell with them, I thought, and went out to the car in the darkness of the pre-dawn.

With my BMW capable of hitting 140 miles per hour, Philip and I could drive down the Al-Fahaheel Expressway to the border in less than an hour. Unfortunately, Dr. Hansen's car was not capable of such speed. Usually he puttered along at 45 miles per hour. Can you believe it?

On that drive, his speed was not to be a factor although it would prove otherwise later. The fact was we hadn't gone more than 30 miles south on the expressway when we found ourselves mired in an endless stream of cars, vans, and trucks loaded with refugees who had heard the rumor.

Three, four abreast, we waved and chatted back and forth to each other, expressing our hopes for freedom. The throng counted thousands of Filipinos, Egyptians, Saudis, and Thais. Everyone was in a gala holiday mood even though we had slowed to a snail's pace.

All too soon, our mood changed when we came to the Green Beach turnoff and learned there was a very tight Iraqi roadblock ahead. It was almost the same spot we had gained a few days earlier on our dash to the south.

When it was finally our turn to approach the Iraqi guards, we argued in vain for five minutes to be allowed to continue, but it was to no avail. They were adamant that we turn around and return to the city. Westerners were not to be allowed to proceed. There was nothing for us to do but turn around and drive back.

"All's not lost, Philip. We can easily get back to the Latiffa apartments and hook up with those guys going to Al-Salmy."

Philip pointed out we hadn't brought too much water along—so confident were we that we would get across to the south. I said we had the speed to cover the distance in quick time, and the lack of a big water supply wouldn't be a factor.

So off we went northward to Fahaheel and the Latiffa apartments, cursing all the while because Dr. Hansen wouldn't pick up the speed. In my anxiety to return quickly, I took the wrong road, and we lost even more time.

It then became too late to make the 6:30 meeting. I decided to try and catch up with the Latiffa group farther to the north along the Sixth Ring Road in the area of Al-Jahra, where we could take the road southwest to Al-Salmy. We soon were on a two-lane paved road—resembling some back woods road in New England—covered with drifting sand instead of snow. Within moments, the wind picked up and blew the sand in greater depths across the road to the point where I had to ram my BMW through it to keep moving.

I was so busy concentrating on watching the road and hitting the sand piles correctly that it was some time before I noticed Bob Hansen's car was no longer behind us. I cursed and came to a quick halt to turn about and head back up the highway to find him. It was in vain. I went all the way back to the Sixth Ring Road at the interchange without seeing a sign of him.

"We'll head toward Al-Salmy again, Philip," I said. "Keep an eye out for any sign of his car. Perhaps he had an accident or pulled off the road for whatever reason."

Very slowly, I drove back down the narrow road we had just come up, scanning both sides of the road for any sign of the Hansens. Nothing. There wasn't even a turnoff he could have taken.

"He's gone back to the Colwells, I bet," said Philip.

I had to reluctantly come to the same conclusion although it bothered me he could disappear so quickly since he drove like a turtle.

Without the Hansens to slow us down, I drove faster along the road, using the speed and bulk of the BMW to toss the sand drifts aside in beige sprays. Philip and I were looking for the turnoff into the desert, which would allow us to skirt Al-Salmy and the Iraqi roadblocks in the vicinity.

"There!" I said excitedly "See the opening in that big sand dune? Look at those cars going in and out."

As I approached, I had to wonder why cars were coming out. If it were an escape route, why would anyone want to come back in our direction?

The dune towered about eight feet in height on both sides of the cut. I was moving very slowly through it when a car with a Brit at the wheel came out. I asked whether the cutoff led to Saudi Arabia.

"Right on," he called back, "but you'll never make it. It's all sand. Follow along behind me. I know a better way."

He drove away through the cut, but I had my mind set on that route and instead went some 20 yards into the desert. Stopping, Philip and I just looked around and couldn't believe what we saw in front of us. Surely, it was the world's biggest and ugliest mirage.

The desert was a panoramic stretch of vehicles and humanity struggling in a snarling, confused mass to make headway toward the horizon shimmering in the distance. It was like watching a battle scene from the movie, "Lawrence of Arabia," without the rapid arms fire and bursting shells, but the frustrated yells and curses equaled the sounds of war.

"I thought it was a mirage at first," Philip exclaimed. "God, it's incredible! All those people walking about, kicking their cars, the rows and ranks of the cars and trucks and vans and everything else."

I asked an Egyptian, stopped momentarily beside me, for the direction to Saudi Arabia. He pointed straight ahead. "*Rohr sitta!*" he replied in Arabic. "Straight ahead."

That's exactly what I did. I floored the gas pedal, and the BMW surged ahead. In beautiful fashion. However, like a fool who should have known better I took my foot off the pedal. A no-no when driving in sand. The wheels dug instantly into the sand, and we came to an abrupt halt.

Only a few minutes passed before a friendly Kuwaiti pulled the BMW onto a flat dry spot even though I had asked him to tow us back to the road. Since I still faced toward Saudi Arabia, I decided to "rohr sitta" again. I jammed my foot down on the gas pedal, and we shot across the desert I really thought we were going to roll all the way to the border.

Some 300 hundred yards along the desert floor, the BMW's front wheels crunched deep into the sand to bring us to a roaring stop. I knew better than to try to rock it out; the spinning wheels would only bury us deeper.

Other cars were stuck all around us. Fine. We would help them get out, and they would help us. Like two good Samaritans, we managed to push clear the cars blocking our immediate way.

During this clearing operation, Philip thought he had spotted the Latiffa people and went to investigate. It was indeed the few Americans and Brits from the night before who had agreed to give the desert escape passage a shot.

Unfortunately the four-wheel-drive vehicle they had obtained was stuck like most of the other vehicles. With it, they were perched at a standstill on a flat dry spot, wondering what their next move should be—onward into another sand trap or backward to the road.

Philip left them and returned to give me his report. My Arab friends and I had pushed the BMW free. With Philip and I ensconced once more in its roomy interior, we shot another couple of hundred yards deeper into the desert where we became stuck for the third time in the treacherous sand.

Spotting some Egyptians in a mired Toyota pickup behind us, I went back and offered them two bottles of booze if they would help extricate the BMW. Only I didn't say the bottles contained liquor. I let them think they held water. However, one of the Egyptians took a quick swig and instantly spit it out in a fine spray along with a string of obscenities.

He bore such a surprised comical expression that his fellow Egyptians burst into belly roars of laughter. Actually, they had no aversion to liquor and asked him to share his find with them. Instead, he ran off as they chased laughingly to catch him and help themselves to the booze. Crazy bastards, I thought. Took my booze and didn't give us a push.

By then it was past 8 o'clock in the morning, and the sun was high over the horizon. The temperature was going up toward 110 degrees. I was beginning to feel light-headed and sick to my stomach because of the combination of colitis, heat, and anxiety about our situation.

We could not just walk away from the BMW. It was loaded with most of our personal belongings and valuables because we had believed we would get away to Saudi Arabia that day. It was impossible to run the engine to have the benefit of the air conditioning because it would overheat quickly in the hot, dry air.

We asked many people to help push the BMW free, but they were wrapped up in their own efforts to break loose from the sand. Desperate, I headed for the road, hoping to find a truck to tow the car out.

Philip and I set off across the desert to gain the road about a third of a mile away. I used a cement storage tank that rose above the dune as a landmark to guide on. It shimmered crazily in the heat like a sinuous cobra.

Christ, it was hot! I knew then how the French foreign legionnaires must have felt when they went trudging off to fight the Tauregs or whomever in the Atlas Mountains. I realized, too, that even if we got the BMW freed, we couldn't go any farther into the desert. Our puny water supply would be the death of us.

I began to worry about Philip and what I had gotten him into. In my mind, he was a boy, Jill's godson. I was responsible for him and would have to answer to the family if anything happened to him. On his part, I don't think he felt that way at all. He always pulled his own weight, seldom complained, and generally was the best of companions in our many ticklish situations.

Still, he was dependent on me for getting him out of the desert. At least I had a passport and could prove who I was. He had lost his and could not prove his citizenship.

I chastised myself for getting him into our current mess. All we had to date for our escape attempts were failures. One after another. Now we were in the desert, the BMW jammed up to its hub caps in the sand, and the two of us were ready to be done in by sunstroke if we didn't get to the road and shelter in a hurry.

Gaining the road, we tried to thumb a ride. More than half an hour passed under the sweltering sun before a Toyota Land Rover with eight smiling Pakistanis aboard stopped for us. They were very cordial and told us that they had been reconnoitering the length of the road to determine a good escape route.

All the way back to Kuwait City I kept thinking about our bags and valuables left in the BMW. I had locked them in the trunk in the belief that no one would break into it. The doors had been left opened. I didn't want anyone to smash the windows to get into the BMW.

We thanked the Pakistanis profusely for the ride back to the Colwells and wished them good luck on their escape attempt. It was past noon when we arrived. The house was strangely quiet, bereft of any human occupants.

I had hoped we would find the Hansens in residence on our return, but neither they nor their car had turned up. Then I really began to worry about them—whether they had been rounded up in a sudden Iraqi onslaught against the Westerners.

I hoped one of the Colwells or someone from the embassy would come by as usual so I could report the Hansens disappearance, but no one did. I called a Kuwaiti friend, Adnan Muqaddam, and he agreed to go out to the desert and help us retrieve the BMW.

We waited until late afternoon for the sun to get lower in the sky before we left in Muqaddam's small Suzuki four-wheel-drive jeep. It was in vain. Iraqi soldiers turned us back at a roadblock just below the Al-Atraf Road interchange.

Disheartened, we drove back to the Colwells and passed the remainder of the day taking calls for the embassy and hosting various visitors to tea and biscuits, whatever we had. Throughout the day, there were many visitors—Americans, Brits, Kuwaitis, whatever.

Many of these people we had known in a slight way in the pre-invasion days. Some were well known to us like an American woman and her husband, who was a Kuwaiti pilot; the principal of my daughter's primary school; professional colleagues; and businessmen. They shared their fears and worries with us, warned us against trying to escape across the desert, and gratefully accepted our hospitality.

Funny thing about them though, they would be talking to you one day, and then you would never see them again. One way or another, they would escape across the border to Saudi Arabia in four-wheel-drive vehicles, many of them jeeps, but without ever once offering to take Philip and me along. How weird can people be?

In my mind, this selfish spirit and conduct was compounded by the loss of the Hansens. Had they been apprehended? Crashed in the desert? Murdered in the sands? Or had they just taken off without a thought for us? (1)

We called all over town trying to find some trace of them. No one had seen them or had any idea of their whereabouts. My frustration built when I called Max's hotel and was informed that both Max and Mary McGee had driven off in Pastor Maurice's car and had not been seen for a day or two.

Philip was convinced we had been betrayed by the former members of the initial group we had formed after the invasion. "Jesus, couldn't they even tell us they were leaving so we wouldn't have to worry about them? Now I know how Christ felt except that we're surrounded by Judases."

Chapter 11

Swindled in the Sands

First thing in the morning, I called a dear friend, Mohammed Attai, an Iranian, with whom I had stayed in contact since the invasion. He was a very wealthy man and had assured me he would provide me with as much money as I needed. As always, he said not to worry because the Americans would soon be on the scene.

By then, I was not easily convinced of that possibility but thanked him for his generosity. My pressing need, I said, was for a four-wheel-drive vehicle and the equipment necessary to get the BMW out of the sand. Items like shovels, rope, and lumber to shove under the wheels.

Mohammed said he did not have a four-wheel-drive vehicle, but the rest of our needs could be found at the lot behind his house in the Jabriya district.

Well, it would have to be Adnan Muqaddam's little Suzuki jeep once more to the rescue. He quickly agreed to be of further assistance, and we arranged to return to the desert late in the day.

Meanwhile, Philip and I were manning the phones to handle the calls for the embassy. About mid-morning, John Levins, Paul Kennedy, and Jane Anderson came by. Great, I thought. Reinforcements for our desert trek.

Once again, however, I was reminded that there are few people you can truly count on in this world. "The mass of men lead lives of quiet desperation," probably because they deserve to.

When I requested their help to free the BMW, I received a collective look as if I had gone soft. All three, like a singing trio in perfect harmony, said no way. They were too busy. Kennedy was more specific. There was no possibility of his taking his bloody car into any desert. The plight of my BMW spoke for itself.

Okay, fine. How about joining us in Adnan Muqaddam's Suzuki jeep for a ride to the desert in the coolness of the late afternoon? They should think of it as a free sightseeing trip into the mysterious sand wastes of Arabia. Their girth and brawn would be of immense help in freeing the BMW.

Once again, I was made to feel as if I had gone daft. In unison, they gave reasons why there was no way they could lay their bodies on the line to free my BMW. They were scurrying from the house for fresh air within minutes.

After Philip, Adnan, and I picked up the supplies from Mohammed Attai's lot, we went along the Sixth Ring Road to the interchange and swung onto the narrow road into the desert. I had geared myself up to believe that we were going to have clear sailing but then we spotted an Iraqi army patrol on the road.

We let Adnan talk in Arabic with the Iraqis and explain we were going to retrieve our bogged-down car lost the day before. The Iraqi in charge glared at us but declined to ask for our IDs and waved us on. Adnan said that since we had no baggage, the Iraqis must have concluded we weren't trying to escape.

We turned into the opening and soon spotted the BMW out in the desert. It was no longer mired in sand but standing on a dry, flat area. How the hell did that happen, I wondered?

The answer was soon forthcoming. Nearby the BMW, a large Ford pickup truck with a 4.2—or a 5.0-litre engine was parked. Two berobed desert Arabs, Bedouins, came out from behind the truck.

Philip drew a quick picture for me. "They've hauled the BMW out, Rob, and now they're going to steal it."

The hell they are, I thought. My mind was a whirlwind of conflicting thoughts. Still, we were not back in the city. There weren't any Iraqis about. This was the desert. These were desert types, and most times they carried weapons.

The gist of it was they claimed the BMW was theirs even when I produced my owner's documentation. It probably meant nothing to them since they couldn't read. Adnan tried to reason with them in Arabic but had no luck.

One of them slipped into the BMW and sat behind the wheel. We held the door so he couldn't close it. With a screwdriver, he got the engine started, but we still prevented him from closing the door.

All this time, I was watching for one or the other to whip out a revolver or an ugly looking dagger and wave it at us. I prayed they weren't the assassin type.

To my relief, we finally convinced the Arab to get out from behind the wheel and to let me get in, which he did after more minutes of arguing. I wasn't certain how he had turned on the engine, but the wheel lock was still firmly in place, and I couldn't drive off.

The Bedouin urged me to let him demonstrate how to free the wheel. I was looking for more magic, but he just stepped on the gas. The BMW shot straight ahead like an arrow in flight and rammed into a big dune. With a smile creasing his lips from one end to the other, he got out of the car and gestured.

"The son-of-a-bitch. He did that deliberately," I screamed to Adnan and Philip.

"You've got it, Rob," Philip said calmly. "He figured he'd pulled it out in the first place, and since he couldn't have it, he'd give it back to you like he'd found it. Are there any nice people left in the world?"

The Arab's pal mocked us with a duplicate grin on his scarred face. I don't think they would have hesitated a moment to have fought the three of us if we had decided on that course of action.

I wasn't about to since I had no idea what weapons, if any, they carried under their dishdashas.

When they drove off, our main antagonist in the Ford pickup and his pal in a Chevrolet sedan, I noted the latter's registration numbers—1161. I swore then that I would get back at him when the war was over. (My list of malefactors on whom I was to exact revenge one day in the hazy future was growing daily.)

When they were out of sight, we began immediately to tackle the problem of freeing the BMW from its sandy roost. We quickly learned that the Suzuki jeep was not up to the job. It had a big heart, but unlike the little train that could, the jeep couldn't. It strained the ropes to the limit, and the engine whined for mercy, but the BMW still squatted indifferently.

All this time, of course, we had the hottest sun in the world beating down on us. It was so hot, we soon were feeling ill. The sun was dropping lower in the late afternoon and would soon go down. If it had been truly high above and we had continued to labor, I'm certain the heat would have killed us.

"All right," I conceded, "let's leave it off for today. Maybe we can get out here again tomorrow."

I doubted that we would. I thought of fashioning a cross from the wooden boards and jamming it into the sand beside the car. That's how I truly felt about the BMW. It was a traitor, deserter, and should be left to die in the goddamn desert with the rest of the faint-hearted. (1)

I dropped that thought instantly when Adnan announced the jeep was stuck.

Under the searing sun with Adnan at the wheel, we rocked and rocked the jeep until I thought I was about to become a blob of melted flesh and bones on the desert floor. Finally though, the jeep launched itself free like a rousted rabbit and rolled to a stop where the BMW had been held fast earlier.

"Hey, Rob," Philip called, "here's some of your stuff in the sand. It's all over the place."

I felt a little burst of joy. I had been convinced that I had lost everything when I saw the BMW's trunk had been forced open and the contents removed. Maybe the two Bedouins hadn't gotten away with everything after all.

In the end, I recovered a David Roberts' print—he was a 19th century English illustrator, who had traveled throughout the Middle East—my tennis racket, tennis shoes, a jar of peanut butter, and my personal telephone book.

That was all I had left of Jill's and my personal possessions after three and a half years in Kuwait. Everything else of a personal nature that I had packed and stored in the car—several suitcases stuffed with our favorite clothing, some jewelry, and more personal items—was gone. Stolen!

I caught myself up. It was not the time to be either angry or self-pitying. Most of the stuff could be replaced later. I reminded myself, too, that our really personal family things like photo albums and the kids' mementos were hidden away in the apartment. Besides, I was alive and together Philip and I would get out. I thanked God again that Jill and the children had not been in Kuwait when the Iraqis had invaded.

On the drive back to the Colwells, I convinced myself that the recovery of the BMW was a lost cause. The Bedouins would reappear as soon as we were out of sight and haul it off to some desert chop shop.

Deep in my innermost being, I was feeling like a terrible failure. Why could others get away? Escape across the desert? Why couldn't I pull it off with Philip? I had let him down badly.

It was about 8 p.m. when we got back to the Colwells. Adnan dropped us off and returned to his empty house. His wife, an American from Ohio, was away in the States on vacation. Their daughter was one of my daughter's best friends. That's how I knew Adnan.

Adnan was very supportive of Philip and me, providing us with the necessities and at least trying to help us with other requests when possible. He was especially helpful in supplying us with food.

Strangely, however, like so many others, when he had worked out his escape plan, he never called to see whether we might have fitted into it or even to say goodbye. He just left without a word. Another friend who slipped away without a goodbye for us.

Luz Marina came by later in the evening and listened with a look of disgust on her face when we told her about our latest desert venture. She grimaced, laughed aloud, and gave us condescending looks.

"When will you learn, Rob? I told you what would happen. Told you that you'd lose your BMW in the desert. Why do you do it? Please. Just sit tight. Hang on. Everything will be okay because the U.S. government will make it okay."

I listened to her latest lecture about our embassy in disbelief. She was so goddam condescending, had such a superior attitude like we civilians just didn't know what was going on.

Well, in my mind, there was nothing to know because the embassy wasn't doing anything for us.

" . . . and I'll say it again, Rob. You're a fool to keep on trying to escape. It's foolish and dangerous. Leave it off. The embassy will look after you."

I would remember her words in the weeks to come when the majority of the embassy personnel and their families had gone home, leaving the ambassador and a few staffers behind and the U.S. flag flying overhead. Also left behind were Philip and myself and other Americans, who refused to give themselves up to the Iraqi occupiers and take their chances as human shields before some military facility.

Luz Marina must have sensed my rising anger because she changed the subject, demanding to know the whereabouts of Pastor Maurice's car. She reminded us that the car had been left in the driveway when the pastor and his wife had taken refuge in the embassy. I then reminded her she had given Max permission to use it to go shopping.

"But that was two days ago at least," she retorted. "He should've returned it. You're responsible, you know, for the car."

I just looked at her in disbelief and shook my head. "No way, Luz Marina. I never touched the pastor's car. Max took it to go shopping—and with your permission. It's ridiculous for you to say now that the car is my responsibility."

Ever the lady, she attempted to remain cool, but it was obvious she was beside herself because I had laid the truth of the situation on her.

"I don't want to talk about it anymore, Rob. I'll expect you and Philip to do your best to locate it and return it to me. What will the pastor think?"

"Hey, Mrs. Colwell," Philip spoke up, "the pastor can shove it. He's the one that left his car here and went to hide out in the embassy. We weren't here when he dropped it off, and we assumed no responsibility for guarding it. Talk to Max."

She turned to me to put down Philip. "Okay, let's all drop it. Philip and I will look for Max tomorrow, but that in no way implies any responsibility on our part for its loss. If it is lost."

Luz Marina left shortly in a huff, calling over her shoulder, "You should know that the Iraqis have announced they will execute any Kuwaitis caught harboring Westerners."

Chapter 12

Death of a Major

Awakening the next morning, my mind instantly riveted on Luz Marina's report of the Iraqi announcement to execute any Kuwaitis caught harboring Westerners. Philip and I had discussed the ramifications of the report before hitting the sack. Anyway you cut it, they were not pleasant for either us or the Kuwaitis.

Up front, the Iraqi threat meant any Kuwaiti, no matter how friendly, could be expected to turn us in to the invaders to save his own ass and that of his family. Here on out, I would think they would want to avoid us like the plague. Who could blame them? We were walking bombs. Why should they be in our vicinity when the explosion came?

Turnabout, we had to believe that any social intercourse with the Kuwaitis only placed our well-being, if not our lives, in jeopardy. If they were to turn in the people whom they might be hiding, what was to stop them from fingering Westerners? People who had no genuine ties to the Kuwaitis, but whose existence and whereabouts were known to them. Nothing like currying favor with the new leaders.

Realistically, I knew there was no way Philip and I could continue to elude the Iraqis without the support of the Kuwaitis—even if only on a peripheral basis. Christ, it was their city, their environment. They were the source of all our necessities, one way or the other. We would just have to trust them.

For several days I had been talking on the phone with another dear friend, Aubyn Hill, a Jamaican, who had been employed with a Kuwaiti bank, about ways we might get out of the country. He and his wife, a Sri Lankan, and their two young children lived out on the Fifth Ring Road in Mishrif.

I mention Aubyn because of the news about the Iraqis' intention to kill Kuwaitis harboring Westerners. That very morning he had told me his Kuwaiti landlord was after him to leave his rented apartment immediately because he was afraid of Iraqi retribution.

Quite rightly, Aubyn said he was not about to leave and went to the Iraqi authorities, who said they had no interest in him. In fact, he probably would be allowed to leave sooner or later. Within days, Aubyn, along with his wife and two kids, simply drove across the Saudi border to the Jordanian border and crossed over without incident. He was one of the few friends who let me know in advance that he was leaving Kuwait.

Philip and I, the two survivors of the original group still at the Colwells, reviewed our situation and decided the first thing we should do was to try and locate the Hansens as well as Max and Mary McGee. We still could not bring ourselves to believe they had gone off without us.

Our search for them was made more difficult by the fact that we had no wheels. My BMW was out in the desert somewhere—probably stolen. The Hansens' car was with them, wherever that was, and Max had driven the pastor's car back to the hotel with Mary McGee. There was nothing for us to do but to walk and hitchhike downtown.

First, though, I made another series of calls around town to talk to people who knew the Hansens well. None of them had a clue about their whereabouts. A call to Max's hotel brought only the cryptic response that he was "not available." On that note, we took off for Max's hotel in the Al-Salmiya section.

When we reached the hotel an assistant manager informed us that Max had checked out and Mary had gone with him. They had left some of their personal belongings because they had debarked in such a hurry.

"Yeh," I told Philip, "but they didn't leave the pastor's car, and Luz Marina's going to be bonkers."

God bless Philip. He always had a way with words to put things into the proper perspective. "Screw her," he said succinctly.

Now what? Not yet willing to give up the search, we went discreetly about the Al-Salmiya district. We stopped now and then to talk to some acquaintances who might have had some knowledge about the whereabouts of the Hansens or our other two erstwhile friends. Didn't turn up a thing. They had apparently gone right down the rabbit's hole and disappeared into their own wonderland. (1)

We went around the city that day without once being stopped by any Iraqi soldiers. They were everywhere, thousands of them. Their military vehicles were parked one behind the other along the length of the streets.

Luz Marina returned to the house in the early afternoon for the embassy messages and was remarkably indifferent to our news about Max and the pastor's car.

"Max has obviously stolen it and is trying to get across the border. I'll make a report to the embassy people and inform the pastor. Let's just forget it."

After Luz Marina had left, Philip and I went back to monitoring the calls and listening to the BBC. About the only thing new on the BBC—except for the Iraqi threat against the Kuwaitis harboring Westerners—was a report about U.S. naval forces in the Persian Gulf. The U.S. was going to authorize its warships to intercept any ships going to or coming from Iraq and Kuwait, especially tankers and freighters which could be carrying weapons. That was fine, but it didn't help us in our situation.

"I think we're going to have to get out of here, Philip," I said. "Look at the situation. We're Westerners in a predominantly Kuwaiti neighborhood. How long before some Judas in the crowd turns us into the bad guys? There's just the two of us now that the Hansens, Max, and the lovely Mary McGee have bugged out. We'll be handling these phones day and night while contending at the same time with the slings and arrows of the pretender to the ambassador, the one and only Luz Marina . . . . "

"And," Philip added, "we have no wheels. Paul Kennedy is the only one now with a car, and he's back at the Al-Muthanna. I think all signs point to our return to the Al-Muthanna. Right?"

Agreeing that we would discuss the situation later at dinner, I went off to the health center with a Kuwaiti neighbor, Essam, in his car. While I feigned ignorance, I knew Essam was one of the early organizers of the Kuwaiti Resistance. He made no effort to disguise the fact he was delivering anti-Iraqi materials to colleagues as we went around the First Ring Road and up Jaber Al-Mubarak Street to the government health center at the corner of Abdulla Al-Ahmad Street.

I figured whatever he was up to was his business. Still, I could envision myself being shot out of hand were we to meet any Iraqi soldiers, who might insist on searching Essam's car. I was comforted by the knowledge that Essam was one stout-hearted Kuwaiti, who would never betray us.

I kept mum, but my heart would beat a bit faster every time he stopped to make a delivery to one of his Resistance pals. In those early days, he could be delivering a batch of posters of the Emir or the Crown Prince or fact sheets on public health, poison gas. Small things initially. At least it was a beginning.

The Resistance took many courses early on. It was not just direct military retaliation against the invaders, although that was already occurring. There was resistance of a passive nature—civil disobedience, perhaps the furtive distribution of food, drugs, and money to the neediest. The Resistance was also active—refusing to register as a citizen of Iraq as Saddam Hussein was demanding or declining to switch Kuwaiti registration plates on vehicles for Iraqi ones.

While I remained silent and acted ignorant about the Kuwaiti Resistance, I still felt great respect for Essam and his fellows for taking the first of many actions against the Iraqis.

Essam waited for me when I first went by Mike Clark's place near the U.S. Embassy. Mike was a Brit, who worked for their embassy. He and I used to play a lot of tennis together in the pre-invasion days. I remembered then how he had sort of hinted that something big was on just a few days before the actual invasion on August 2nd.

Mike was usually a good source for cold beer. He brewed it himself and could have as much as 60 litres on hand. Tough for me. The house was tightly locked up, and there wasn't a soul about.

I next went to the Specialist Dental Center, where Essam dropped me off and left to continue his Resistance activities. I wished him luck and thought again how low all our fortunes had fallen in the past several weeks.

The clinic was in dismal shape with only a few dentists on hand. All of them were Palestinians, handling only emergency patients. We greeted each other warmly, but I was aware that the Palestinians were great admirers of Saddam Hussein and were suspected of turning Westerners over to the Iraqis. Some were even reported to be working actively for the Iraqi secret police.

I inquired about one of my favorite colleagues, Dr. Jawad Behbehani, a member of one of the rich merchant families in Kuwait. Lo and behold, wearing casual clothes, he showed up at that very moment in the clinic, but he appeared to be very depressed.

Apparently not wanting to talk within the Palestinians' hearing, he led me outside where we sat down under a large date tree that had been recently planted on a grass plot. It was very hot, and we welcomed the shade.

I waited patiently for him to speak because I knew him to be a well-educated man and a person I could talk to without fear of being quoted elsewhere. He was about 45, a graduate of the Forsyth Dental Center in Boston, Harvard University, and Guys Hospital in London.

In the three years I had known him, we had carried on many lengthy conversations about myriad subjects, including his country's government leaders. I was reminded that our recent discussions had covered the renewed political activity (civil protests involving at times up to 10,000 Kuwaitis) that had occurred in the three to four months leading up to the invasion.

Many people had been arrested, including community leaders, by the Emir's police. Usually they were only held overnight in the hope of cooling them off and getting them to think straight about the government and its policies. The arrests showed the populace who was in control but in a benign way.

There had been some talk that Saddam Hussein used these reports of unrest and protests in Kuwait as a raison d'etre to invade the country and make it Iraq's 19th province. He implied that the dissidents had appealed to Saddam to join them in democratizing Kuwait. It was like a rabbit inviting a crocodile into its nest to help neaten up.

Getting a grip on himself, Dr. Behbehani told me that he had returned to Kuwait just a few days before the invasion after a delightful vacation in California. Only days after August 2nd, the Iraqis had come to his newly-built villa in the Al-Shuwaik district beyond the Al-Jahra Gate and looted it of all the furnishings and valuables. Finished; they trashed every room in the villa.

"It's not the end of the world, Rob. Perhaps if I hadn't gone out, they wouldn't have dared to enter as they did. To what purpose did they ransack my home? Most of the furnishings were smashed to no end. Can you imagine what the rest looks like? And where will the Iraqis take my things? Few of them will ever reach Iraq."

Even as he talked with me, I could see he was already getting over his loss. Those belongings could always be replaced. The thing that was really bothering him was the presence of strangers in his homeland—the realization that his country had been invaded and the sanctity of his home violated.

Late afternoon was approaching, and I asked whether he could give me a ride down to the Al-Muthanna complex to check out my apartment. On the way I told him I was very low on cash. He gave me 70 dollars worth of Kuwaiti dinars, which would cover me for a few days. He explained that was all he had with him, but he would call me within the next day or so and bring me as much money as I needed for the immediate future.

Our conversation came to an abrupt halt as we neared the intersection of Al-Hilali and Abdulla Al-Salim Streets. There, hanging from the tip of a telescopic crane, was the body of a military man.

As we drove slowly by, I could see that the soldier had been dead for a few days. His body was bloated and gave off a strong odor of rotting flesh. His arms had been tied behind him, and I could see up close that the rope wasn't around his neck but bound around his wrists.

Imagine the horrific pain when the man was hauled aloft by his wrists held fast behind him. The strain on his shoulder and shoulder blades as they were ratcheted upwards would break them in short order—undoubtedly collapsing his lungs.

A big handwritten sign was displayed in front of the dead man to explain that he was an Iraqi major, who had been executed for looting. The same fate would befall anyone else caught committing such a crime.

Dr. Behbehani and I didn't believe for a minute the man was an Iraqi officer, never mind a major. Hell, they would have to hang their entire army if they started executing majors for looting.

Whoever he was, his crime apparently was the theft of a $16 pair of cheap Adidas sneakers, which he was still wearing with the price tag affixed to the exposed soles.

We proceeded at a very slow speed through the intersection because it was thronged with the curious. Hundreds of them were taking photos and making videotapes of the corpse. Our pace permitted me to see that the victim had been shot at least once in the stomach. Maybe one of his executioners had had a spot of humanity and opted to help speed him on his way.

I bade Dr. Behbehani goodbye at the sidewalk entrance to the complex after first looking about for any Iraqis who might have been assigned to guard duty there. I entered the ground floor quickly and made it to the elevator and upstairs to my apartment without incident.

I was shortly on the phone to Philip to tell him I was at the apartment. I reiterated the reasons we had discussed about making it our hideout once again. He agreed. I told him I would make arrangements for Paul Kennedy to pick him up in his car later that day.

Kennedy was quite amenable to my request. We agreed that the best time was right about sunset when the Iraqis were praying or eating and generally more relaxed. I stayed at the apartment, straightening up and checking our resources and food stuffs while Kennedy made the rendezvous with Philip.

Kennedy carried it off without a hitch. Philip and I expressed our gratitude for his service. I was especially relieved that the young man was back with me in the apartment. I felt responsible for him—being family and all and sort of my guest since coming to Kuwait.

Kennedy had gone by the corpse hanging from the crane at the corner, and Philip and he talked about it. The sight of it had obviously shaken up Philip, making him truly face the seriousness of our situation.

"Yeh, Rob, play time is over. It's all for real here on out," he said in almost a whisper. "I have to tell you. I've got to get out of here."

Later that night, I dreamt about the dead man swinging from the crane out on Al-Hilali Street. He was twisting ever so slowly in the desert breeze, and I strained to see his face. I woke suddenly in a cold sweat—afraid that I had recognized it.

Chapter 13

Regrouping

Since I didn't keep a daily journal, I believe it was about this time that the United States decided to intercept ships going to or from Iraq and Kuwait. It was the start of the UN plan to levy economic sanctions.

Philip and I thought that the sanctions weren't a bad idea, but we could see by looking at a map of the Mideast that they would be tough to enforce against the land borders of Turkey, Jordan, and Iran. Those borders would be like a sieve to smugglers.

Philip suggested that the United States would make better use of the ships if they just sailed up to Kuwait City and landed the Marines.

"We should set up a *"cordon sanitaire,"* I volunteered. "Just tell Saddam that the coast road from Kuwait City to the Saudi border is a neutral zone and that all foreigners will be permitted to leave the country along it without any interference. If he interferes, he could have himself a nice big war."

Philip smiled. "Yeh, I like that idea. Sweet and to the point. You ought to pass it along to the embassy people."

I gave him a look to indicate that he was out of his mind "Those people don't know what day it is. Didn't you hear that guy who came by for the messages at the Colwells talk about the big party for the charge d'affaires at the embassy the night before the invasion? They were all there. It was the straight poop. I know. I was there. All the know-it-all diplomatic types. Lots of Kuwaitis and Marines, too. Drinking and having a hell of a time. There wasn't one word said about the possibility of an invasion. It was less than an hour before it happened. What do they know?"

Philip shook his head in disbelief. "I thought embassy people were supposed to have their ears to the ground, looking for information. You mean to tell me that there are no CIA types with your embassy?"

"Damned if I know. People I know over there always deny it. Not that I buy it. This region of the world is too critical not to have our spies handy."

"Well, at least President Bush isn't wasting any time showing Saddam he means business," Philip said. "He's forming a hell of a coalition to fight the Iraqis and get them the hell out of Kuwait."

I was not convinced. "I'd be very surprised if he gets the Arabs to line up with western forces. Can you see Arabs fighting Arabs? Highly unlikely. The Arabs might fear and hate Saddam, but he's still one of them."

In turn, Philip was not convinced by me. "I'm not sure about that, Rob. There's *realpolitiks* involved here. The U.S. is offering Egypt, Saudi Arabia, Syria, and the rest a golden opportunity to knock off the bully on the block. The Iranians will love it."

Wearying of the subject, I asked Philip whether he had picked up any more red-hot rumors in his comings and goings.

A big smile lit up his face. "Yeh, a couple. Did you hear the one about half the Iraqi armored vehicles have been immobilized because their troops have been kicking the wheels?"

I sort of half-smiled.

"What about the Iraqis asking the Russians to stamp 'This End Up' on the next shipments of artillery shells?"

Encouraged to continue, he informed me that the Greeks, as a contribution, were sending shipments of sand to help fill U.S. Army sandbags. Meantime, they couldn't send any tanks because they were waiting for supplies of anti-freeze.

When he paused, I asked whether he had heard how the Iraqis new tanks had four gears, one forward and three in reverse. And what about Saddam Hussein being shot between the eyes by an assassin? Not to worry though because the bullet missed his brain by six feet.

We were both getting silly, but it felt good to know that in spite of our current situation we were still able to laugh. I really got going when Philip recited some famous quotes from the invasion.

England's Margaret Thatcher on August 2nd was quoted as saying: "What are those wogs up to now?"

The Emir of Kuwait on entering his helicopter before fleeing to Saudi Arabia the same day: "Stand fast. I'll be back in half an hour with help."

American citizens on invasion day: "Don't worry, guys. George will have us out of here in a day or so."

Saddam Hussein to senior army officers during the planning for the invasion of Kuwait and Saudi Arabia: "Do Kuwait first—a couple of days won't make any difference."

Saddam Hussein at the same time as above: "Oh, and while you're there, see if you can get me one of those watches like George Bush wears."

"The one about the Kuwaiti border guard to his buddy," Philip interjected. "That's a riot. They were observing the Iraqi army's build-up. The guard said to his buddy, 'Go on, give them the finger. They can't do anything to us . . . .'"

We chuckled in unison over that one and then became silent, each regarding the other with somber faces. Okay, so we had a few laughs, but where were we?

"Not to throw a damper on our joviality, Rob," Philip said softly, "but I assume you've heard that the Iraqis have threatened to use Westerners in Iraq and Kuwait as human shields."

I expressed surprise about the report. He added that Paul Kennedy had mentioned it off—handedly on the ride back from the Colwells.

"That's just what the crazy bastards will do, too," I exclaimed. Stake us out, in front of their goddamn nuclear, chemical, or biological plants and leave it up to the good old U.S.A. to kill us or not."

"If you ask me, our people will kill us on the basis that the end justifies the means. What's a few hundred or so civilian deaths in gaining the big prize? The President doesn't even acknowledge that Westerners held by the Iraqis are hostages. Bottom line, Rob, in the great scheme of things, we are expendable."

The truth of Philip's observation hit home hard. It made me more determined than ever before not to be taken prisoner by the Iraqis. Never to surrender. I was an American, and there was no way I was going to become a hostage for Saddam Hussein at one of his man-killing factories.

Philip was just as adamant about remaining free of the Iraqis' clutches. "We have to develop a plan of survival. We have to build up a support system—especially since we would be fools to be coming and going from this building."

I considered what he said and pretty much concurred. Our first attempt at building some sort of group—cell—to foil capture had failed. The Hansens were God only knew where. Max and Mary had obviously fled in some fashion. None of them had informed us of their intentions.

We needed to form a new group, but it had to be a solid one of individuals agreeing to bend their wills and goals for the general well-being of all members. Most importantly, we needed people we could trust, who knew the meaning of loyalty and sacrifice, who shared our hopes of surviving until the nightmare ended.

"And when might that be?" Philip inquired.

I had no answer. Only guesses, estimates. "Weeks, months, longer. Who's got a crystal ball? Maybe less if we can devise a plan to get out of Kuwait. Best we plan to hunker down for the long haul and begin to secure the bare necessities as soon as possible."

While Philip and I remained in Apartment 826 of the Al-Muthanna complex, John Levins, who lived diagonally across the hall from me, acted as sort of a scout for us. There was just no way we could keep him from constantly coming and going. That being the case, he was directed to pick up any available information and foodstuffs on a day-to-day basis.

Paul Kennedy was still upstairs. He would venture out too, but not on a regular basis like John. Kennedy's big interest was his car, whose location and condition he checked daily by slipping into the garage.

At the time, many people were roaming about the complex, continuing to loot any apartments they could break in to and to take their pick of hundreds of cars parked on the garage's three levels.

Over a period of several weeks, the vehicles gradually disappeared until there were very few left. Plainclothes Iraqi secret police, submachine guns slung over their shoulders, could be seen breaking into these cars for anything worth stealing.

Kennedy's car, surprisingly, was always found in the same spot and untouched every day. No one had even bothered to break into it. He figured since the car was parked in a flooded section of the garage, people were deterred from approaching it by splashing through six inches of water.

Between what we had on hand in the way of condiments and fruit juices and what John and Paul were still able to buy and scrounge—if not steal themselves—we managed to keep enough food in our stomachs to ward off malnutrition. However, we knew such a system would not keep us alive for weeks or months.

I had gathered enough food supplies at the Colwells' house to last a week or more. At the time, I no longer had a car and foolishly had forgotten to have Paul Kennedy get some supplies when he went to pick up Philip.

I realized I had made a bad mistake in leaving the food there. Hell, it was probably gone by then—eaten or stolen. I made a mental note to ask Kennedy to go by the house again, but I knew he was very reluctant to take his car out on the street. Irish or not, the Iraqis didn't hesitate to pull westerners out of their vehicles and drive away in them

Philip and I would spend hours thinking of ways to make the apartment more secure and to build up our supplies of food, medicine, and other essentials. In the end, however, it would always come down to the realization that we couldn't do it on our own—especially since Americans were the most highly-prized of Saddam Hussein's captives.

We shared our concerns with John Levins and Paul Kennedy. They agreed to look out for any trustworthy types still about whom we could recruit for the new group. Westerners would be preferred, but any Arab who could make a contribution of money for food and other necessities would also be welcomed.

It was not long after this decision had been reached that there was a knock at the door. Our visitor identified himself through the closed door as Aleppo, a Filipino, who lived with his wife and five of his countrymen on the fourth floor of my section of the complex.

Aleppo informed me that an elderly western couple on the tenth floor had told him I might be in need of food. He had worked with the man, Ken Hoyle, at IBM in Kuwait City. Since it was much easier for him to get about the city, he had been bringing Ken and his wife, Magda, food almost daily.

I was both surprised and moved by the Hoyles' thoughtfulness—especially since I didn't really know them. For a while, Aleppo would come by with a couple of eggs and some pita bread, a chicken now and then, litres of milk, a bag of rice, and some cereals.

It was very helpful on a daily basis, but there was never enough left over for us to begin building a surplus for rainy days. John and Paul weren't doing much better either. Whatever food they obtained, it wasn't much more than could feed the four of us on any given day.

The group had to expand in order to gain the resources of money and contacts to secure the food, medicines, and other vital necessities to keep us among the living. Who could we bring into the group to help us meet that key objective? Aleppo and his wife, maybe his fellow countrymen, and the Hoyles immediately headed the list.

We learned from Aleppo that the Hoyles were both in their mid-60s. He was British, a prisoner of war in World War II. Magda was Czech and had survived the Nazi invasion in 1936 and the Russian invasion at the end of the war. Now she was involved in the middle of another one.

According to Aleppo, Ken Hoyle had been employed for most of his professional career with IBM and then had retired with Magda to the island of Cyprus. To their delight, he was called out of his retirement to become a consultant for IBM in Kuwait City. The money was excellent, and they loved the change of scenery—at least until August 2nd.

I must mention that they had a dog—a little French poodle named Samson. Unfortunately, in time, Samson would become a problem because of his need to answer nature's calls twice a day and the Hoyles' insistence on taking him outside from their tenth floor apartment to do so.

Over a period of a week or more, the membership of our new group gradually took shape. We hastened to put it into place because our need for a steady supply of food and other items was becoming desperate.

John, on his frequent missions through the complex, had met an English couple, Chris and Mary Chambers, who lived in an apartment two stories below me. Chris was a nervous personality and Mary was the tougher of the two, constantly taking charge of their affairs and keeping Chris in line.

Their next door neighbor was another Englishman named Cliff. I never did learn his last name. Perhaps he never gave it to us although I would be surprised if John Levins hadn't picked it up—what with his relentless penchant for compiling lists of names at every opportunity.

I was never able to make John understand how dangerous such lists would be were they to fall into the hands of unfriendly Arabs and the Iraqis. Repeatedly, I asked him to forget such lists; he was endangering people. I might as well have been talking to a wooden Indian for all the reaction I got out of him.

In any event, Cliff was a former publican in the home country. That is, he owned a pub, but gossip had it that he had drunk up most of his profits and had lost the business. He had come to Kuwait to be a surveyor of some sort. His drinking would present us with another problem.

The group was shaping up to become quite British because our last two potential recruits were two young English fellows. One was Dave Hough, about 31, and then Neil Beevor, no more than 25. Both were good company, fun, and very laid back—seldom losing their tempers and always very direct in everything they said and did.

John had discovered them in one of his forays into the Plaza Hotel, which was part of the Al-Muthanna complex and located around the corner to the right off Fahd Al-Salim Street. This was the hotel the Iraqi secret police had taken over for its headquarters in Kuwait. More and more of their agents were moving into billets in the hotel every day.

Meanwhile, Dave and Neil had befriended an Iraqi army major, who gave his assurance to tell them and any other foreign guests when and if the secret police was planning to apprehend them. The Egyptian manager was also very friendly with them and the others. He asked them all to check out and then check back in again under assumed names with eastern European documentation, which he had arranged for them to secure.

Dave and Neil and the other guests did so over several days. Soon only eastern Europeans were registered at the hotel. In accomplishing this sleight of hand, many of the foreigners had given up their own passports but not the young Brits.

Despite this switch in identities, the young men figured it was time to leave the hotel when the Iraqi major told them the secret police had asked the management for a list of everyone registered as a guest. The move was fairly easy because the hotel's chef had taken an apartment in our complex but had never moved into it. He had opted instead to stay in the hotel and gave the keys to his place to Dave and Neil.

John said they would make a great addition to the group. Philip and I agreed. We said we would arrange to meet them to get at least superficially acquainted and provide them with some of our thoughts about forming the group.

While the apartment was a convenient windfall for Dave and Neil—it was even furnished—it unfortunately didn't come with any foodstuffs at all. For a while, the chef, apparently feeling some responsibility for the young men, left food for the two of them outside a particular door in the complex each evening. Usually, it was something already cooked. They got one meal and some leftovers out of what he provided.

Shortly after the English moved into the complex, the chef's luck ran out. I forget his nationality, but the Iraqis took him away, and we never heard of him again. We always believed he had never said a word about Dave and Neil taking over his apartment. Good man.

John Levins tried to swell our ranks with a young American couple and their two young children, but he had no luck in moving them into the complex. They were paralyzed by fear and indecision. They had only been in Kuwait for a brief time when the invasion occurred. The man didn't know the country or anyone of any substance in it. Despite John's persistence to join us, they stayed in the hotel and soon were rounded up by the secret police and taken with other hostages to Baghdad. That was the last we heard of them.

As the days passed, the new group was taking final form with the regulars—Philip and myself, Paul Kennedy, and John Levins—as the nucleus. Then we had Aleppo and his fellow Filipinos, Ken and Magda Hoyle, Cliff of the no-last-name, Chris and Mary Chambers, and Neil and David.

I should also include Jane Anderson, who had been keeping a low profile but was now expressing an interest in moving into the new group. By way of background, Jane was about 24, university-educated, and fluent in Arabic. Her father was a top British diplomat, maybe even an ambassador, but I have forgotten the country to which he was posted.

She had a very pretty face, a tendency to put on extra pounds, and a most admirable directness in the way she dealt with people. She could tell you that you were an airhead to your face without ever raising her voice or showing the slightest bit of emotion. A job with the Swedish home furnishings firm Ikea had brought Jane to Kuwait early on.

John Levins, my Australian friend, who was constantly in and out of my doghouse—although I doubted it mattered much to him—was the group's gadfly and foremost forager. He was in his early 30s, I believe.

The Irishman, Paul Kennedy, was a bird of another feather. He was about 45, a native of Dublin, who was employed as a consultant by the National Bank of Kuwait. He tended to create an air of mystery about himself, implying deeds of derring-do in his past and connections with the CIA as well as with the IRA, PLO, and other groups.

You must remember that this new group had not taken final form as yet. We regulars—Philip, Jane, John, Paul Kennedy, and I—had collected the names and were discussing the pros and cons of each potential member among ourselves.

John, in his maddening fashion, continued to make up lists of people whom we might want to consider for membership. We started to scream at him to leave off the lists. Was he out of his birdbrain, out of his mind? Putting anyone whose name was on any of his stupid lists in jeopardy? What if the Iraqis got hold of the lists? Had he considered the damage the lists could cause to innocent people?

Undeterred, John continued to glide through the ransacked complex like some fast-moving green mamba, hardly ever encountering Iraqis because of his fleetness of foot and quick thinking. He was a constant thorn in our side, an unending source of worry and concern, a moving target who could lead us all into captivity because of his need to prove his courage and elan.

On some of his trips through the complex, he met an occasional Arab, whom he thought might make a good member. Unfair or not, we tended to shy away from inviting Arabs to join us. One exception was the only Kuwaiti family, who—to my knowledge—was still living in the building. He was a businessman whose name was Mohammed Al-Awadi, the black sheep scion of one of the country's most affluent families.

Al-Awadi, his wife, and their three sons had returned from living in England only days before the invasion. Now they were lying low in a one-bedroom apartment diagonally across the hall from Ken and Magda Hoyle. Big and small, rich and poor, we all had been laid low by the arrival of the Iraqis with their bloody plans for Kuwait.

Another exception was an Arab named Imad. John didn't know his last name but said he lived above us, had studied in the States for years, and knew how to fix all kinds of mechanical things. He was to bring him around later to meet us.

Directly across the hall from the Hoyles was a Syrian couple, who were in their early 70s. Magda could hear them through the door trying to convince the Kuwaiti businessman he would get in trouble associating with westerners. The Syrians had the look of Judas about them, and we shied far away from them, warning John to do the same. The Hoyles already held them in high suspicion.

We were especially wary of the Syrians. There was talk the Iraqis had promised Syrians and Palestinians, residing in Kuwait, that they would be allowed to stay on in their apartments rent-free. The quid pro quo, naturally, was that the Syrians and Palestinians would keep the Iraqis apprised of any suspicious people in their neighborhoods, especially foreigners.

Morris Family at Smithsonian Museum, Washington, D.C. in July 1990. Morris returned to Kuwait. Jill, Anna and Trish went to Trinidad, West Indies, where they were caught up in a Muslim coup attempt in the last week of July 1990.

Morris and friends enjoying Eid holiday at Al Khiran southern Kuwait, by the Saudi border.

Kuwaiti residents being rounded up below Morris' apartment, 7 AM Aug 2, 1990.

Captured residents being searched by Iraqi Military below Morris' apartment, 7:15 AM Aug 2, 1990.

Iraqi helicopters in shootout over Hawally District. Courtesy of Dr. Robert Hansen.

Iraqi helicopters on line to Al Muthanna Building. Courtesy of Dr. Robert Hansen.

Al Muthanna Apartment Complex. Arrow points to Morris' apartment. The apartment directly above was destroyed by tank artillery fire soon after Morris had vacated the building.

Map of streets around Morris' apartment building.

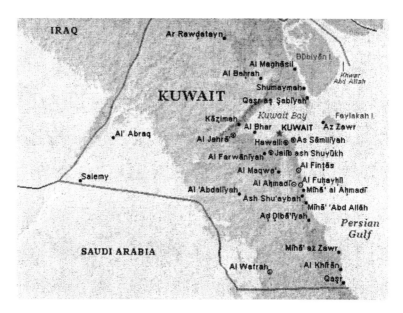

Map of Kuwait. Morris' escape attempts were to the Salmy border post, to Al Abdaliyah area, and to Al Khiran.

Morris and Daher at Frankfurt-am-Main Airport preparing to travel to USA. Courtesy of WorldWide Photo.

Pan Am charter from Frankfurt arriving at Andrews Air Force Base, Maryland with hostages, Dec 10, 1990.

Morris, Daher and families upon hostages' arrival at Andrews Air force Base, near Washington, D.C. Dec. 10, 1990.

Morris' arrival at Boston's Logan Airport from Andrews Air Force Base. Courtesy of The Patriot Ledger Newspaper, Quincy, Massachusetts.

Arrival in Boston, photo and article courtesy of The Boston Globe.

DETAILS OF A 'HORRIFIC' TIME

By Doreen E. Iudica
GLOBE STAFF

A Milton dentist living in Kuwait returned to Boston last night after spending four "horrific" months hiding in his Kuwait City apartment complex from what he called "barbaric" Iraqi soldiers who "pillaged and raped their way through the country."

Robert Morris, 47, arrived at Logan Airport with his wife, Jill, and their two young daughters and shouted "Merry Christmas!" and "God Bless America!" to about a dozen family members and friends who greeted them with hugs and kisses.

"It's so good to be home," he said. "It's been a horrific experience."

Morris, a South Boston native, had been working in Kuwait City for 3½ years training dentists for the Kuwait Ministry of Health. His wife and two children were in her native Trinidad when Iraqi troops invaded the country last August.

On Aug. 2, when the troops stormed into Kuwait

ACCOUNT, Page 15

Armand Hammer, capitalist titan, dead a

By E. Scott Reckard
ASSOCIATED PRESS

LOS ANGELES – Armand Hammer, the socialist's son who became a titan of American capitalism and a tireless crusader for world peace and a cancer cure, died last night. He was 92.

He died at his home after a brief illness, said Frank Ashley, a spokesman for Hammer's Occidental Petroleum Corp.

The affable Hammer was a self-made millionaire by the time he graduated from Columbia University medical school at age 23. Throughout a life of international wheeling and dealing, he was on a first-name basis with world leaders from Vladimir Lenin to Ronald Reagan.

His empire rested in Occidental, based in Los Angeles. He bought the tottering company for $100,000 in 1957, during a try at retirement, then turned it into the nation's seventh-largest oil company.

Ray Irani, Occidental president and chief operating officer, became the new chairman immediately, the company said.

Hammer's death came one night before he was to ce mitzvah, 79 years lat ded ceremony and was born a Jew, but I fly did not observe re

Hammer was times and had one his first wife. His t ces, died in 1969.

Funeral arrange immediately known.

Contraceptive implant receives FDA approval

By Judy Foreman
GLOBE STAFF

The US Food and Drug Administration yesterday approved the first new contraceptive for the American market in about 30 years, an implantable device known as Norplant that provides birth control for up to five years.

The device, which consists of six match-sized capsules inserted under the skin of a woman's upper arm in a minor surgical procedure, releases low doses of the hormone levonorgestrel at a constant rate. The hormone, a synthetic version of the natural hormone progesterone long used in birth control pills, is believed to be safe; it prevents ovulation, and thereby, prevents contraception.

While in place, the device is considered 99 percent effective in women weighing 150 pounds or less. Soon after the device is removed, fertility returns to normal.

Family planning and women's health specialists heartily applauded the FDA's action, which brings to American women a method of contraception that has been used for years by half a million women in 46 countries. The United States is the 17th country to approve the drug formally for marketing.

Norplant was developed by the nonprofit New Yor tion Council and will Wyeth-Ayerst Labor

NOR

Cuts in budget leave family with grim prospec

By Ray Richard
GLOBE STAFF

Four-year-olds don't know much about government budgets, but they

TO HELP GLOBE SANTA – Mail your donation to Globe Santa, Box 1525, Boston, MA 02104, or deliver it weekdays to the Globe Corner Bookstore at the intersection of

mother of 4-year-old Joey tells how government budget cuts have left her family's refrigerator almost bare, harmed her son emotionally and physically and hampered her at-

Santa's friends

In Tribute to Davis Taylor – Boston Century Club
Jack and Jaclyn Kirwan
In loving memory of Agnes Driscoll
in memory of Mis and Pa O'Neall
Will Haydock, age 3¼

Article cont...courtesy of The Boston Globe.

■ ACCOUNT
Continued from Page 1

City, Morris said, he moved quickly and was able to escape capture until the third day of the invasion when he and 60 other American and British nationals were taken hostage. Shortly after, however, Morris and four others were able to talk their captors into setting them free, and they returned to his apartment complex.

From the window of his hiding place in the boarded-up building, Morris recalled seeing Iraqi soldiers killing Kuwaiti citizens at random, raping Asian and other women, and looting shops.

"These people are not civilized, they are barbarians," Morris told a group of reporters. "In my opinion, what's happening over there is genocide."

While Iraqi secret police and soldiers patrolled the outside of the apartment complex, Morris and several other foreign nationals stayed inside the sealed-off structure using coded knocks and passwords to communicate and living as quietly and as sanely as possible.

"We broke the elevators so they wouldn't work. We couldn't turn the lights on and we eventually blacked

to help secure Morris' escape. But it was not until Saddam Hussein ordered the release of all American hostages that Morris was able to come out of hiding and travel to Baghdad for the first leg of his journey home.

Two other Massachusetts hostages, Glenn Colemen of Marlborough and Richard G. Sementelli of Newton, also returned home from Kuwait last night.

Exhausted and 25 pounds thinner, Morris said it felt "wonderful" to be home, but wanted Americans to know that Kuwait "is not just an oil patch."

"They are a tribe of people, a culture of people and they do not deserve what is happening to them," Morris said.

Morris and his family will stay with relatives in Milton, where he lived for two years before moving to Kuwait.

"We were very concerned that he get out of that country before the fighting began," said Morris' sister, Dorothy. "We were getting desperate, and we prayed a lot. But now, thank God, we're ecstatic and grateful that he's home. This is our Christmas gift tonight."

Article cont...courtesy of The Boston Globe

World

The Terror Of Hiding In Kuwait

ROBERT MORRIS spent 120 days in isolation, fearing the Iraqi soldiers and wondering whether he would outlast Saddam Hussein. Now he worries about the fate of the Kuwaitis.

By ROBERT AJEMIAN BOSTON

Q. How did you avoid being discovered by the Iraqis?
A. We lived in secrecy. It was exhausting, but we kept strict rules. Windows were always covered with heavy blankets so that people outside saw no body motion inside. At night all lights stayed off. We used only the glow from a TV set fixed on mute. We had to beware of everything we did. In an empty building, something as simple as dropped silverware makes a racket. To cut noise I took showers at 3 o'clock in the morning. Even our cooking smells in outside hallways became a danger signal.

Q. How many were in your group?
A. We were nine: six British, an Irishman, an Australian and me. We all lived in adjacent apartments.

Q. You could stay in touch with one another?
A. Our phones kept working. We worked out systems for calling one another, three rings, hang up, then three more rings. The person called never spoke first. To take our telephones into more soundproof rooms, we extended phone lines with lamp wire. At safer hours we slipped up and down corridors to meet together in different apartments. On the hall floor outside my apartment, I positioned a piece of broken mirror against the wall so that the entire length of the corridor was visible from my partly open door. It was a group rule that everyone checked the mirror before stepping into the hall. When we made visits, knocks on the door required still another code.

Q. You identified different sounds fast?
A. In that silence our hearing became acute. Footsteps of group members were unlike those of strangers. We discovered that bare feet on concrete floors made more sound than soft soles. As an early warning, we wedged an empty Coke can against the fire door outside my apartment. Whenever strangers entered, the Coke can cracked like a gun. Immediately we'd warn the group that strangers were on the floors.

Q. Did many Iraqis come to the door?
A. Looters constantly prowled the building. Most of the 450 apartments had been vacated in a hurry and were still full of household goods. It was like a big store. To hear a sudden pounding on the front door was terrifying. We had towels stuffed along the door bottoms to help muffle inside sounds. And we laid small rugs in front of the doors to let us tiptoe close and look out through glass peepholes. We taped over the peepholes. In each tape we made a tiny opening with a pin, like a camera, so we could see out but remain unseen.
One day there was a banging on the door. I crept up and looked through the pinhole. Two heavyset men in dirty Arab dress stood there. One of the faces seemed to stare right at me. They were studying the nameplate on the door. I had posted the name of an Egyptian friend, Amr-Al-Arabi. They muttered something to each other and left. I was elated.

Q. The Iraqis offered a cash reward for every foreigner uncovered?
A. That unnerved us. Also we kept hearing awful stories about doctors shot at hospitals, about incubators confiscated and babies left to die. We heard that Kuwaitis who hid Westerners were strung up and castrated in front of their own families. Some Arabs offered refuge to foreigners for long periods and then suddenly turned them in to the police. The stories made us more tense.

Q. Some Arabs helped you?
A. Downstairs in our building was a Syrian, Imad, who saved us. For four months he brought us food and water. He warned us when soldiers came. He installed double-bolt locks on our doors. He mailed our letters. Years ago, Imad went to engineering school at George Washington University. He's very pro-American. If he were caught hiding us, he faced execution. But he never wavered. Imad is a saint.

Q. Did you ever wonder if he might turn you in?
A. I'm ashamed to say I did, several times. Imad had no money. I remembered the Anne Frank story. Her family was hidden for years and then betrayed. In Kuwait we heard so many stories of betrayal. Group members who ran off with cars or stole money or panicked.

Q. Your building remained a good target?
A. To discourage Iraqi visitors, we got the idea of immobilizing the building's elevators. Imad agreed to knock out six of the seven lifts. He removed some parts, and the elevators stopped running. It was wonderful. Upstairs we took doorknobs off fire doors so looters couldn't move around so easily. We carried the knobs around in our pockets.

Q. What about food and water?
A. At first we believed the crisis would end fast. As the months dragged on and the U.S. forces sat and waited, we began to worry about starving. We decided to store all the food we could get our hands on. Together our group had several thousand dollars in cash. So Imad began to buy up more supplies. He delivered food between midnight and 2 o'clock. On my computer we began to keep track of our provisions. Now we could tell how many cans of tuna we had, how many kilos of dry beans. We even factored in how much protein we had, how many calories. That computer gave us great comfort. By October we figured we had enough for nine months.
We filled our bathtubs with drinking water. Every bottle

One day there was a banging on the door. I crept up and looked through the pinhole. Two heavyset men in dirty Arab dress stood there. One of the faces seemed to stare right at me.

we owned was filled with water—75 grape-juice bottles, garbage cans, plastic clothes baskets.

Q. Did your group stay on good terms?
A. Not always. We had some bad arguments. Often we turned on those who created noise. Two of our group, the Australian and the Irishman, took way too many risks. After a few months they acquired a hero complex. They wanted to make trips out of the building. The rest of us protested that it would draw too much attention. Imad was very much opposed. After several weeks, the two of them insisted. So we made them sign a paper saying they could not return. They left and somehow got to other houses.

Q. What about keeping spirits up?
A. We had dramatic mood swings. Little things crushed us. When we heard about Jesse Jackson's taking out a number of people, all of us were filled with hate and anger. Who picked the lucky ones? we asked ourselves. Why them and not others? News that George Bush would not permit the presence of hostages to influence his foreign policy saddened us. I was a combat veteran who had served in Vietnam. I wanted to count for something. Even the news that the President would spend Thanksgiving with the troops, such a short distance away, depressed me. You begin to feel abandoned. Your mind turns soggy.

Q. How did you deal with endless time?
A. The process of survival itself chews up enormous time. It's so absolutely fatiguing. You spend so much time and energy trying to avoid mistakes. One of us rephrased an old saying that we put at the top of our written rules. "Yesterday's gone. Tomorrow will come if we survive today."

Q. You kept up with the news?
A. We had a radio and listened to the BBC every hour, also Voice of America, which broadcast messages from home. I heard a dozen messages from my own family. News of the military buildup lifted us too. We thought Bush was really going to invade. We even sealed off a safe room with tape in case of poison gas. All of us wanted Bush to hit the Iraqis. When nothing happened, we began to feel Saddam Hussein would outlast us.

Q. And now that the hostages are out?
A. It's great, of course. Now the Kuwaitis are the ones in danger. I know them well. I'd been there three years teaching dentistry. The Kuwaitis are imperious. They exploit people. They're spoiled with wealth. One is certainly entitled to ask why soldiers should fight and die for them. But no people deserve this kind of horror. Last week we heard that Kuwaiti doctors, some of them friends of mine, were systematically being shipped to Iraq. I don't think they'll ever be seen again.

Q. Is your mind still back in that apartment?
A. I still can't relax. I developed such rigid habits in that place. But this afternoon I'm really happy. One of our group just telephoned and said Imad was granted a humanitarian visa by the U.S. We all told our embassies about him. He risked his life for us. And now he's free himself. What a marvelous piece of justice. ■

Article and photo courtesy of Time Magazine.

Ex-hostages Morris, Ernie Alexander and Paul Pawlowski meeting with Senator John Kerry in Washington, D.C.

Morris and Senator Edward Kennedy meeting in Washington, D.C.

Oil well fires set by retreating Iraqi Army.

Destroyed Iraqi Artillery in Kuwait Desert.

Highway of Death, " the Turkey Shoot", northern Kuwait. Courtesy of Michael Clark, F.O., Britain.

Highway of Death, " the Turkey Shoot", northern Kuwait. Courtesy of Michael Clark, F.O., Britain.

Chapter 14

Hanging Separately

It wasn't long after we began forming our new group when the Iraqis announced that all Westerners in Kuwait were to immediately assemble at one of three hotels in the city. The hotels involved in the round-up were the Meridien across Al-Hilali Street, the Hilton International out near the U. S. Embassy, and the Regency on the Gulf Road in Salwa.

It was not made exactly clear why the Iraqis wanted the Westerners to assemble. They implied that it involved paperwork. Others said the Iraqis wanted to distribute ration cards. The naive believed they were to be flown home.

For my part, I was adamant I wasn't going anywhere near the assembly points. Having been captured once by the Iraqis, I had no desire to be in their hands again. Philip agreed with me. If they wanted us, let them come find us and take us away. All I could think about were the millions of Europeans, who had assembled with open hearts and trust at the request of the Nazis during World War II, only to be shipped off to extermination camps.

Who could say the Iraqis weren't going to try the same? Why should we assemble for the Iraqis, who had savaged Kuwait and destroyed our way of life? Why would anyone want to trust their life, their security, and that of their family and friends to such monsters?

I wasn't about to be so foolish. Incredibly, scores of Westerners did assemble at the time and date stipulated at one of the three hotels and were taken as hostages. I couldn't believe they had been so stupid. So trusting. They knew Westerners were being rounded up at every opportunity. They knew they were being sent as hostages to serve as human shields at Iraqi military facilities. Yet, they went to this fate like pilgrims filing to Mecca. I raged against them and their foolishness.

"Rob, cool it, for Christ's sake," Philip cautioned. "You'll have a stroke. And for what? They don't want to listen. Don't want to see the truth. Screw them! People have to do what they feel is best for themselves. We didn't make the world, remember. We only live in it for a bit."

Stroking my beard, I muttered, "Hey, the husband and wife want to give themselves up, that's one thing. But putting their kids into the hands of those thugs? Mother Mary give me strength."

In the following days, it appeared to us that the Iraqis and their Palestinian goon squads went all out to round up any stray westerners, who had eluded the nets they had cast at the hotel assemblies. Below us on Al-Hilali Street, we witnessed the occasional seizure of a Westerner. How stupid could they be? Walking around in the daylight hours and dressed so obviously different from the Arabs? We also received reports of other arrests, some of them forcibly, leaving their victims badly beaten and bleeding when last seen in the rear of a military vehicle.

At odd times of the day and night we heard explosions, always in the distance like out along the gulf superhighways. Rumor had it that the Kuwaitis had set up a rag-tag fighting group within the Resistance and were conducting small-scale raids against the invaders. These reports were followed by many others dealing with the torture and execution of many of these heroic Kuwaitis.

To counter the Resistance, the Iraqis were said to have established militia units of Palestinians, who knew the city. In turn, the Kuwaitis had recruited Filipinos and Thais to buttress their manpower. The Thais included many former members of the famed Thai Ranger units, who were particularly adept at garroting their enemies. The only weapon required was a piece of piano wire wrapped at both ends around two small pieces of wood.

Somewhere around the first week in September, I lost my telephone service. The line just went dead. I had lost the long distance service a day or two into the invasion, and now I was unable to make a local call from my own apartment.

Philip and I became dependent on John for a telephone. It was a bit inconvenient having to go back and forth to his place across the hall, always wondering when you might bump into an Iraqi squad or a turncoat Palestinian.

With the loss of the telephone, Philip became more depressed. It seemed we were constantly losing every battle in the war. He felt terribly confined and expressed a need to get out of the apartment, out of Kuwait, out of the goddamned Middle East, and to go home to Canada. He talked a lot about getting up to Baghdad, going to his embassy, and procuring the necessary papers to take a flight home.

I was depressed myself about my whole g.d. life, and his depression only seemed to intensify mine. I had to argue with myself to get out of bed in the morning and clean up and get ready for another day. I couldn't let myself wallow in self-pity. Philip depended on me, and I depended on him, but I had the greater responsibility.

"All right, we've got to snap out of this black mood and get the group organized," I announced with the intention of trying to get Philip's mind off himself.

We had an initial meeting with Philip and myself, John, Paul Kennedy, and the two young Brits, Dave and Neil. Most of the talk was devoted to the need to come together and set up a system to obtain food and other necessities and to implement an internal security plan.

My impression was that Dave and Neil were two splendid fellows, charming and gracious, and a wonderful addition to the new group. However, I was unexpectedly taken aback when Dave said he and Neil would welcome our assistance in obtaining supplies, but he, for one, had no interest in discussing anything to do with security.

"Frankly, chaps, I just came by to enjoy a pleasant day and to spend some time in your company. That's all."

John began to stutter. Kennedy just looked at Dave as if he knew all Limeys were crazy. What did you expect? I was puzzled. How could he not want to talk about our collective security? What could be more important to us, individually and as a group?

"It's just too upsetting, Rob, to talk about what could happen to us," Dave persisted. "Really, what difference does it make anyway? If I get picked up, they'll just take me up to Baghdad. Once there, I'll be released in a day or two. We know the U.S. Marines and the Brits are coming in, and the Iraqis know it. They're going to be good chaps and release us. You'll see."

In making us privy to his thinking, he remained a model of self-control and affability. It was amazing how forceful he could be without raising his voice a note. For a time, I could only regard him in stunned silence.

John, however, was continuing his argument, his stutter becoming more pronounced. I have to admit that he did handle himself well in these types of discussions. I remembered he had once told me he had been a college debater. I thought that strange, what with his stutter and the way he could talk and act so illogically at times.

I pointed out to Dave and Neil that we had to face up to reality, and reality was that we were all in danger. Like it or not, we endangered each other, and we should own up to that fact. In effect, anytime we did something thoughtless or foolish—John looked at the ceiling—we could be putting not only ourselves but others at risk.

"There's a lot of little things we can do, Dave, that require little time and effort and yet could greatly improve our chances of remaining undetected."

Catching his questioning glance, I said, "Curtains, heavy ones, whatever it takes, across every window to seal in any light that might be seen from the outside. The Iraqis are cute. They watch the windows from the outside at night. When they see any glimmer of light showing, they check out the apartment. If they come up with a Westerner, he's hauled off."

I listed a few more precautions we could take, some which Philip and I had already implemented. They dealt with lights seen under the corridor doors, loud talking, heavy walking in leather-soled shoes, and noises generated by running baths, showers, and washing dishes. "Simple things, Dave. A few simple steps. They're for your own good."

"Yes, I understand, Rob, but frankly Neil and I came by because you mentioned something about dinner. Can we get on to that now? I'm famished and would greatly appreciate anything you have to offer."

I gnashed my teeth in silence. How could such an obviously intelligent young man act so indifferently to the dangers all around him? And Neil's attitude was the mirror of Dave's.

They left later in the evening without giving any indication they intended to do anything in the way of improving their security. Dave would only reiterate that if he got picked up, so be it. He would muddle through.

While the meeting with Dave and Neil didn't achieve what we had intended, we remained undaunted and held a series of similar meetings with the others whom we had designated as potential members of the new group. Our basic argument for the group was out of Ben Franklin's handbook: "We either hang together, or we hang separately." Something like that anyway.

Meanwhile, food or the lack of it was a constant problem. Only Aleppo continued to bring food to Philip and me, and that was always in minimum amounts. The two of us began to lose weight. Fortunately, my colitis was no longer a pressing problem.

We got lucky briefly for a few days. A group of Indians on my floor in an adjacent section had received permission to leave Kuwait and arranged for us to receive their remaining food supplies. It was generously given and gratefully accepted. God bless the Indians.

Occasionally, another Arab friend, Amr Al-Arabi, an Egyptian and a computer expert, who used to live downstairs in my building would drop by with some food for Philip and me. He and his wife, Rolla, a Lebanese citizen, had moved out of the complex to live with Al-Arabi's brother on the other side of the Second Ring

Road. Rolla was pregnant and wore traditional Arab dress, but Al-Arabi still worried constantly about her being raped by the Iraqis.

Rolla's father was an old friend from my early days in Kuwait City. He was a businessman whose company I enjoyed. It was through him that I had met Rolla, who introduced me later to her new husband, Amr Al-Arabi. Her father had retired sometime before to Miami, and Rolla held a green card from the United States.

Al-Arabi would come around to visit and to check on the status of his apartment. So far it hadn't been broken into and ransacked, but he figured it was just a matter of time. He had been removing his belongings as discreetly as possible.

Al-Arabi had a handsome nameplate on his apartment door and looking at it gave me the idea to lift it later. I was sure its disappearance would be of little importance to him.

It was about that time that Prime Minister Thatcher of Britain accused Saddam Hussein of being a coward for hiding behind the skirts of the western women whom he was holding as hostages. In response, Hussein said he was going to free all women and child hostages.

The only effect this had on our burgeoning group dealt with Magda Hoyle and Mary Chambers. At the time they expressed a willingness to remain with their respective husbands. Jane Anderson said she would have to think about it.

As the days passed into September, the weather became very hot and sticky. I was eternally grateful we never lost the power to keep the air conditioner humming in splendid fashion. Imad, the quiet U.S. trained Arab, was very helpful in keeping the central cooling system working.

Not too long afterward, Al-Arabi and Rolla came by to say they were leaving the country and going to Egypt and possibly on to the States. I was very anxious to get a personal letter, a note—anything—out of the country to Jill and asked Al-Arabi whether he would take it along and post it in Cairo or wherever so that she would be sure to receive it.

All of us would seize on anyone who we thought was friendly and leaving Kuwait to take our letters out with them. It was about our only way to communicate with the outside then because the U.S. Embassy wasn't forwarding messages through its diplomatic communication channels.

Al-Arabi was eager to comply with my request. I thanked him profusely and bid a sad bon voyage to Rolla. Before leaving, he brought us a share of their food. It was not that much really because he had to divvy up the food with his brother, who was staying in Kuwait.

We had one last laugh when he saw his nameplate on my door. He thought it was a great idea and insisted that he didn't mind in the least.

We felt even more lonely after Al-Arabi and Rolla had left the city. So many people we had known were now gone. The Hansens and Max and Mary McGee. The Sudanese doctor. The Iraqi married to the Kuwaiti. The Iraqi, who had invited the Hansens to his flat. Most recently, the Indians upstairs, the Thai women who had roomed with Kennedy, and some of the Filipinos.

While keeping my depression at a level I could handle, I wondered whatever had happened to my Kuwaiti friend and colleague, Dr. Jawad Behbehani. He had said he would return the day after we viewed the executed Iraqi major, but he never had.

During the latter part of September, I began to write a series of letters for my hometown newspaper, *The Boston Globe*, to relate what it was like to live underground and in hiding during the Iraqi occupation. The letters, addressed to my wife, Jill, were smuggled out by people returning to the West, who posted them in Amman, Jordan. (1)

Chapter 15

Terror Call

What was to be the new group slowly coalesced and got its act together in a "circle-the-wagon" approach over the following two to three weeks. It was amazing to me how much pushing and shoving, begging and threatening, bribing and whining was required to stimulate people to organize in their own behalf.

Even when you thought you had them all working together, they would carelessly breach security regulations—which we had all agreed to—individually or in twos and threes. I was reminded once more that people just don't think at times—even when their own lives are at stake. They could be so goddamn careless and thoughtless, forgetting that their actions could not only be the end of them but also of the innocent among us who were attempting to hold fast to the rules and regulations.

Security was the key concern for us since we were only a few Westerners in a roiling sea of Iraqis with a license from their government to steal, rape, and kill. It was no time to rock the boat and do anything foolish.

We agreed we would use whatever materials were available to black out our apartments so no light could be seen from the outside. New locks and bolts were fastened to the doors. We fashioned tiny peepholes in them to check on any callers. To confuse the Iraqis or any other would-be house robbers and looters, some of us changed the numbers on our doors. Some, like myself, replaced our name plates with those of Arabs, who had fled elsewhere.

Since noise was another big problem, we agreed we would cover all the floors with rugs and carpets and began to break into deserted apartments to obtain them. We justified our direct action on the fact that the Iraqis and various Arabs were way ahead of us. We could make better use of these and other necessary items than they.

We began walking about in our premises in soft-soled shoes or sneakers. Only John Levins continued to stomp like a Cape buffalo through the hallways. He had to be deaf not to hear the racket he made.

Our kitchens were located with one wall buttressing the outside corridor wall, which meant that kitchen noises had to be cut way down. Anyone sneaking about the hallways could easily detect the sounds of pots and pans banging, dishes clattering, and water running.

The same was true about the bathrooms. We began to take showers quietly and only late at night. I got in the habit of showering between 2 and 3 a.m. Again, my friend, John, had a problem in this area. He became very averse to bathing at all and began to emit a very strong body odor.

Dave and Neil began to realize how important the weight we had placed on security measures was and came around in no time flat, becoming most adept at adapting to those we had recommended.

Surprisingly, to me anyway, Paul Kennedy showed he was far ahead of us in implementing ways to keep us invisible from the Iraqis. In making his support for total security known at our meetings, he began to hint further at some sort of mysterious background. He even intimated he had connections with the Palestinian Liberation Organization and the Irish Republican Army.

I didn't say much in return. We all had our own fantasies. Still, I had to wonder why in the world he thought the PLO or the IRA would do anything for us lost souls buried deep in the bowels of ravaged Kuwait City. I always had the feeling he just liked to tell stories that would make him out to be some heroic soldier-of-fortune type, sort of a Colonel Bo Gritz type—someone to whom we all could look for survival.

One time he openly stated he had been in Thailand years before to hunt for American MIAs, missing-in-action personnel from the Vietnam War. From Thailand, he said, his people would go into Laos to search for the MIAs.

I had been in Vietnam during the war, and this story always shocked me because I had no awareness that there were U.S. MIAs there. In fact, it was widely disputed by the early 80's that any MIAs were missing. When he repeated the story, I told him about my doubts, but he remained nonplussed and refused to elaborate. (1)

Unlike me, John Levins was always challenging Kennedy about many of his claims, and they often came close to blows. Kennedy had a good Irish temper, and he was stronger and better built. I dreaded the day when I wouldn't be around to keep them from each other's throat.

The telephone answering machines that recorded taped messages brought John and Paul near to blows on more than one occasion. One time, John's machine was broken, and he had told all his "friends" in the city to leave messages for him on one of Paul's two machines.

Paul, of course, quickly learned of this and burst into a meeting we were having with John and berated him with every four-letter word known to English-speaking people. Why was John giving out Paul's telephone number to everyone? Why was John telling everyone he was living in the Al-Muthanna complex? Paul knew this for a fact because he had many of the same sources as John.

John said that since his machine was broken, Paul should lend him one of his. Paul said no way because he needed the second one for his "top-secret business." When we pressed him to explain that arcane phrase, he would never give us a straight answer but hint instead of clandestine activities with the IRA,

PLO, or whoever. Maybe even the CIA. He was always suggesting he was working with the Iraqis and the Palestinians on a plan to get all the Irish out of Kuwait and safely to Jordan.

The meeting degenerated when Paul refused to release the second machine to John and continued to call him every obscenity in the book. I called on him repeatedly to calm down, but he ignored me as though I wasn't even present. Afterwards Cliff, the publican, said he would not attend any more meetings involving John and Paul because they always "acted like two children" and he wanted no part of them.

Despite their fierce altercation, John and Paul went to an upper floor that night to break into an apartment in the hope of finding another answering machine. They jammed a trusty, sharp screwdriver into the door frame and burst in only to find the apartment occupied by some 13 Filipinos, whom we never knew were there.

No sooner had the door banged open than several of the Filipinos slammed it shut in the astonished faces of John and Paul. Inside, another Filipino quickly telephoned the Arab security force to alert them about the would-be robbers. They came in a rush to catch them, but Paul disappeared almost instantly.

John was slower to react and was seen running through the corridors by one of the Arabs, a Lebanese fellow, who lived next door to Neil and Dave. He apparently knew who John was. He later informed our Syrian contact, Imad, that the one Australian, temporarily living in the building, had scared off the robber.

Imad, who had melded slowly into our group, could only roll his eyes in wonderment. He insisted to us that the security rules be amended to make future participants in such undertakings divulge their intentions to the group first for its approval.

On the second day of each month, which marked the monthly anniversary of the Iraqi invasion on August 2, 1990, the Kuwaiti Resistance would plan some memorable action to grab the attention of the enemy soldiers. On one occasion, knowing the U.S. photography satellites would be passing overhead, Resistance fighters went up on many roofs in the city and fired off their weapons in one long, sustained burst, figuring the muzzle bursts and tracers would be duly photographed.

Simultaneously, they would shout to Allah to give them the strength of arms and convictions to throw the cruel Iraqis out of their country. They were also known to exhort the United States via the satellites to come and help them, believing the space vehicles could pick up and record the sound of their voices.

Food, of course, was always a key concern. We agreed we had to take concerted action to put in a surplus of it to keep us properly fed in the weeks and months ahead. Friends were still providing us with food, but it was mostly on a daily basis. We needed to build up a big stockpile so that we wouldn't be dependent on these people, many of whom were leaving on almost a weekly basis.

Water, too, was absolutely necessary to our survival. We agreed that each of us would become responsible for our own requirements. To store it, we filled one of the two bathtubs in each apartment with water. Even the bidets were used to store water.

Everyone in Kuwait City kept the traditional grape juice bottles. You could find 50 to 60 of them in every house in the country. Whenever possible, we boiled the water and poured it into sterilized containers—especially the many grape juice bottles.

Since we had gone into deep hiding, it was very important we stayed healthy. From everything we had heard, the Iraqis were seizing anyone showing up at a hospital for treatment. We agreed we couldn't go to a hospital unless it was an emergency because we knew we would be taken. We had to do everything to remain healthy.

Whenever possible, we stressed we had to eat good food; drink only sterilized water; exercise by any means possible; avoid bad teeth, stomach problems, and any and all of the obvious ailments laymen usually couldn't contend with themselves.

As a dentist, I was particularly conscious of the trouble toothaches could cause. I urged them to keep their teeth immaculate. To brush after every meal. To gargle and rinse with whatever was handy. Most of all, to use dental floss.

It was then that we made a big effort to put in several months' supply of dental floss without success. All we came up with were a few salesmen's samples—probably enough to only last for two weeks in normal times. We were to make it last for all of us for months by washing our individual pieces after each use and hanging them out to dry. A couple inches of floss can go a long way.

Medications were needed in a solid supply to help ward off illness and to treat its effects. Paul Kennedy came forward with a large supply of medications bequeathed him by the Thai women on their departure. The women had kept the medications to sell out of their apartment as a means of obtaining extra income.

Because of my medical background, I knew the drugs were a Godsend. They were not illegal drugs but the best legal medications, including antibiotics and antifungals; ointments for burns, rashes, insect bites; pills for headaches and stomach aches, indigestion, capsules for bowel and lower-tract infections. All in all, we listed more than 30 different types of drugs and happily had a fine quantity of each.

We added to these medications by getting into Dr. Hansen's apartment and taking his medical supplies. They were another excellent find, alleviating further concern. I felt Dr. Hansen would be delighted to learn of our confiscation.

We still had several gaping holes in our medical needs. We needed supplies of bandages, bottles of alcohol—the medicinal kind—bacitracin, and items of that nature. We could always make bandages from sheeting, but we needed adhesive tape of all sizes. John and Kennedy were put on the scent to find anyone who could supply us with these needed items.

I should mention that on one of our so-called raids into abandoned apartments, we found a beautiful Persian cat whom we named Dingleberry. He was so friendly and attentive Dave brought him into his apartment as a household pet. He reminded us of Garfield, the cartoon cat, because of his size and appetite.

In moving throughout the complex in search of supplies, we sought at all times to avoid any contact with strangers, especially any Iraqi soldiers, who were still trying to find items to steal, and others of their ilk who were hunting for westerners—particularly of the U.S. and U.K. stripe. We knew the soldiers and their civilian supporters were constantly conducting forays into the huge complex with its 450 apartments.

We not only could spy on them entering and leaving like lines of working ants, but we could also hear their passage through the corridors. They were forever yelling at one another from various elevator shafts and stairways.

In Jeff Gilbert's apartment—he was a consultant from Cambridge, Massachusetts—we were repeatedly reminded that other people were going in and out. The place was never ransacked, but the bottles from his wine cellar kept turning up empty on a glass-stained table. In time, the cellar was bereft of a single bottle.

Strangely, despite all the noise the Iraqis made in ferreting about the building, a sound never reached us to indicate any individual apartment was being looted. We would only realize it upon sighting a forced, broken door and looking inside to determine the losses.

On one trip through section seven, adjacent to my section eight on the eighth floor, we discovered that six apartments in a row had been ransacked. The doors were smashed, the interiors ransacked, and most of the furnishings gone. Yet, we had never heard a sound to indicate the intrusion.

Over time, the group also came up with rules on how to use the telephone in a secure manner. When calling out, we would first let it ring three times, hang up, and immediately dial back. When the phone was answered, the caller would speak first and always in English.

If my phone rang—it was back in service—I would let it ring without picking it up. When it rang again within moments, I would answer it without saying "hello" or any other word and wait silently for the caller to identify himself in English. Occasionally, we would pick up the phone and hear a voice in Arabic. They would receive no response from us but continued to jabber away excitedly in the hope of our speaking. Without a word, we would hang up.

It was no easy task to keep the rules governing the use of the telephone constantly in mind. We are all creatures of habit, and one of our most ingrained ones is to say "hello" on answering the phone. Try to pick up the phone sometime and not say a word.

One day I forgot completely. I was alone, and my mind was a million miles away. The phone rang. I reached over and without a thought picked it up and said, "Hello, Dr. Morris."

I was swept with panic when a female voice inquired in Arabic whether I still lived in apartment 826. I was too shaken to answer, and she repeated the question in broken English. What was I to say? I had already answered the phone at that address. She must have known it was me.

A male voice came on the line and asked again in English whether I was still at the same address. I recognized his voice. He was a Palestinian and an employee of the Kuwait Ministry of Housing. He was the very person who had originally arranged for me to have the apartment.

All I could think of while he kept repeating the question in his poor English was now the enemy knew where I was. We had heard numerous stories about the traitorous activities of the Palestinians and how they were turning in westerners. True or not, we were inclined to believe them, although they only added to our fears. Now there was this call from a Palestinian, who knew me and that I was now still at the Al-Muthanna complex.

I wanted to scream into the mouthpiece: "Why do you want to know? Are you going to turn me in to the Iraqis?" I was struck mute with terror and slammed down the phone.

I convened the inner members of the new group together in a hurry to ask for their advice about what course of action I should take. Philip was there, John, Paul Kennedy, and Jane Anderson. Everybody had a different piece of advice.

Philip suggested I hide out in one of the abandoned apartments for a few days to see whether anything developed.

John thought I was overreacting. The caller was just a bureaucrat, ignoring the invasion and probably updating his files. Lighten up, Jane offered. Stay out of sight for a bit.

Kennedy was somewhat of the same mind but said that I should consider going into even deeper hiding. "Come to my place. I've plenty of room. Three bedrooms. Lay low for a few days. See what turns up."

I looked at Philip, and he nodded his head as if he thought that was a good idea. But what about him? If they came for me and he was on the premises, why wouldn't they grab him?

"I doubt it, Rob. I'll point out I'm a Canadian."

"We'll have to talk about it, Philip."

It was all so sinister in my mind. The call in the middle of the day. First the woman's voice and then the Palestinian's. Nothing warm or friendly in his voice. Son-of-a-bitch was probably trying to ingratiate himself with the Iraqis by giving them an American hostage.

I sat there alone, racking my brain for a solution to this latest problem. What to do? I visualized myself being taken into custody, being beaten, tortured even. A series of horrible pictures flashed through my mind. I saw myself strapped to a cement pillar in front of an Iraqi chemical factory. Waiting, just waiting for the U.S. bombers to come over and wipe me and the factory off the map. Quickly, that picture was replaced by one of me standing in my grave, awaiting the impact of AK-47 fire.

I cursed myself, berating myself for such thoughts. Here I was a free man in hiding with a loyal coterie of friends, and I was already visualizing myself being executed. I had to act. Had to decide what to do.

I called my friend, Dr. Jawad Behbehani, who had given me the ride into town past the body of the Iraqi major. While he was coming to the phone, my mind was a kaleidoscope of images, mostly of the dead looter.

Jawad was very apologetic about not having come by with the additional dinars. He said he and his wife were arrested by the Iraqis as they were entering the Al-Muthanna complex. Mrs.

Behbehani didn't have the proper ID cards, and the Iraqis put them through a terrible ordeal.

He had then decided that he could not try again to come to Al-Hilali Street and visit me. He said the entrance was guarded by soldiers, and the streets throughout the downtown area were swarming with them. He asked that I didn't think too harshly of him.

I assured him that I was very grateful for his attempt to reach me and expressed my sympathy for the trouble the Iraqis had put him through. He replied he would somehow try to get some dinars and food to me when things quieted down a bit for him and his wife.

I told him about the quixotic phone call from the Palestinian in the Housing Ministry and urged him to check into it. By way of hedging my bets, I called Jawad's director, Dr. Ibraheem Al-Muhallal, with whom I had always had a good rapport in peacetime, and made the same request of him.

During our conversation, I felt the panic creeping back into my voice. "Find out why this man is calling me. Is he turning people in? What do you think I should do?"

He advised me to move as quickly as possible out of my apartment and hide in another apartment. I was to check with him periodically to determine what, if anything, he had found out. If necessary, he would call me with any urgent information.

Paul Kennedy confirmed I could stay as long as I wanted in one of his bedrooms. I would remain there during most of the daytime hours and eat my meals, when it was deemed safe, with members of the group. Usually that would be Kennedy, John Philip, Jane, and the Hoyles. Hopefully, I would hear good news from Jawad or Dr. Al-Muhallal and soon be back in Apartment 826, now numbered 824.

I was anxious to move before any Iraqis came to take me into custody, but I had to consider Philip's welfare. I just couldn't go and leave him to any Iraqis looking for me. He had a simple solution. He would move into the Chambers' extra bedroom. He had become very friendly with the English couple, taking meals and playing whist with them and Cliff well into the evening.

The Chambers were all for the idea, and Philip packed a small overnight bag in unison with me. Off we went to our temporary apartments for the next ten days. We agreed to keep in touch on the phone and by personal contact at appropriate times.

I went truly into deep cover—not informing anyone outside the group where I could be located. It was as if I had become a Trappist monk and was living in my solitary cell without any human intercourse. Most of the time it seemed like that, but I had plenty to read and television to watch and Kennedy to talk with at mealtimes.

Regarding the television, we finally realized we could adjust and auto-tune the sets to catch English-language news programs and shows from Riyadh, Bahrain, Tehran, and even Baghdad. It was a big change to view this programming after the interminable showing of the Kuwaiti propaganda films during the opening days of the occupation. It was like being seated before a huge window on the world, and everything was being unfolded in color before our eyes. We certainly felt a little bit more like a part of the human race than we had before.

However, the news reports were very disappointing at times. The Iraqis remained unflinchingly in Kuwait despite the bluster of the Coalition members and the relentless buildup of their forces in Saudi Arabia. Bush and Gorbachev met in Helsinki to condemn the invasion, but it didn't help our cause. Bush would address the American public but never said much about our predicament.

He wouldn't even use the word "hostage" in talking about us. It wasn't until about the 70th day after the invasion that he used the word "hostage" to describe us. We couldn't believe our ears and howled in derision and appreciation—if you can figure out that strange coupling.

While held fast to Kennedy's pad until I heard something definite about the Palestinian and what he was up to, I thought very intensely about our security and what other steps we could take to tighten it. Though I was generally pleased about the way the group members had come around on the issue, Kennedy was almost a fanatic on security. He accepted all our recommendations and came up with some of his own. Imad contributed several excellent ideas as well.

I was especially pleased about the way Dave and Neil had come around and become ardent supporters of the security program. They didn't change their pleasant personas, laid back and all, but they did transform their thinking and attitude and turned their apartment into one of the most secure in the group.

Eventually, they transformed the entrance to their apartment in a clever fashion to resemble a door to a utility room. They removed the apartment number and the door bell—putting a panel over the empty slot—and took down the outside hallway light. On the door, they placed "No Smoking" and "Electrical Room" signs. Even if someone tried to force the door, it wouldn't budge. They had double-bolted and secured it in other ways.

Other group members also changed their apartment numbers and name plates around to confuse any hunters. Unused doors and doors to certain elevator shafts and staircases were welded shut. Imad took the lead with his acetylene torch. Now and then, we could hear the Iraqis and their cohorts cursing and yelling when they came up against a door that wouldn't open

Chris noticed that coded numbers previously given to the apartments by the Ministry of Housing had been scrawled in large script with a magic marker on the hallway walls. Several of us used Clorox and other bleaches to rub off the numbers.

Another thing we would do when going to visit a group member was to go through the phone procedure to say we were on our way. We had also timed how long it took to get to each other's apartment. Within seconds of that time, our host would unlock the door so we could push it open and step in quickly, closing it immediately. If we were late, we would find the door locked and have to pass by the apartment and return to our own.

Bastards! I thought. They are all around us. My fears intensified but so did my determination to beat them at their own game. Everyone had agreed previously that towels should be rolled and laid down against the bottom of the doors to stifle noise and prevent any light from showing in the hallways.

Aleppo, the friendly Filipino from downstairs, informed us that he and his wife were leaving with a busload of their countrymen for Iraq, where they hoped to take the road to the border and cross into Jordan. Many of these buses—filled with Filipinos, Thais, and other Asians—were ambushed by the Iraqis, who proceeded to rob them and rape the women. Any man who opposed them was shot.

I was very fond of Aleppo. He had been a loyal, trusted friend who had provided us with food and information many times. I was very fearful for his safety and that of the other Filipinos because of the horror stories we had been hearing about the bus convoys.

Kennedy had become very friendly with some Filipinos, whom he claimed were members of the Kuwaiti Resistance. He implied that, through them, he was also tied to the Resistance and that he could obtain weapons for our group if we were interested.

I was very cool to the idea but met with the others to discuss the offer. We decided to refuse the weapons. It was bad enough to be wanted by the Iraqis. Imagine what our fate would have been if we were taken with weapons in our possession?

I had no problem handling weapons because of my experience in the Navy and with the Marine Corps. In fact, in Vietnam, though a dentist, I was assigned an M-16 and a .45-caliber automatic pistol. Heavy stuff. Yet, I was convinced there was no place for them, given our situation. They would just give the Iraqis another excuse to kill us out of hand.

Chapter 16

Contacting the Media

Ten days went by while I waited anxiously for a response to my queries from Jawad and Dr. Al-Muhallal, interminably hunkered down in the bedroom. Kennedy had a full box of coated almonds and another of small cigars in the room. I tried not to be tempted by them. In the end, I ate my way through the box of candy, which had been so evocative of my childhood, and smoked all the cigars.

Not hearing from either of my Arab colleagues, I called them both in a fretful mood. Jawad was most apologetic but had to admit he had been unable to learn anything. Dr. Muhallal was very difficult to reach because he apparently had several apartments in the city. It was never very clear to anyone in which he could be located at any given time. He kept moving about to stymie the Iraqis searching for him.

In any case, it didn't matter. His response was not very helpful because he claimed he was unable to get any information. Here he was—the big boss; the main, main man, the chief of staff; a member of a very important Kuwaiti family and he told me he couldn't get a line on the Palestinian from the Ministry of Housing and learn what, if anything, he was up to.

I was p.o.'d, and I made little effort to hide my feelings. For all I knew, my life was threatened by this Palestinian, trying to make a name for himself with his Iraqi masters. My colleagues, with whom I had worked for more than three years, couldn't determine the truth of the situation. Bull shit!

I took the bull by the horn after ten days and informed Philip I was returning to the apartment and would take my chances with the Iraqis. Kennedy had been a good host, but I wanted to get back to my own surroundings. No one had any impression the Iraqis had come looking specifically for me. Maybe the episode was due more to my imagination than any evil intent on the part of the Palestinian employee from the Ministry of Housing. (1)

Hoping that the matter was behind me, I called a meeting of the group to discuss the pressing need for food and how we could build up our reserves. We were still depending mostly on friends outside to make occasional contributions, arranging for small purchases on our own, and raiding vacant apartments like old-time barbarians.

At least the booze picture was brighter. Iraq was a secular country, and Iraqis drank liquor. Following the invasion, the more enterprising among them came to Kuwait and set up small grog shops to take care of their own people and anyone else who wanted to pay a stiff price for whiskey, beer, or wine.

One of our routines by then was to go around to each other's apartments in the evening and share a cocktail or beer. About every third day, we would get together to partake of a communal meal. We believed the food could be stretched farther by cooking for more than one person at a time.

Paul Kennedy and John were very important in obtaining food for the group since they could move about more freely than the rest of us. However, this ability alone wasn't enough. It was also important to be well-connected. Those who had food were not about to give it away to anyone, especially strangers who couldn't pay the price.

With this in mind, Cliff became invaluable to us because of his ties to several food vendors. Previously, he had been of little help to us, spending his days drinking alone in his apartment. He had gone along with most of the security rules, but he had shown little inclination to interact with the group except to join us at dinner.

His attitude was that the "occupation thing" would soon end, and he was not about to get all worked up over it in the meantime. The Iraqis would leave, or the Americans and the Brits would attack. He felt everything would go back to normal and that we should not put too much pressure on ourselves with a host of onerous rules and regulations. Such stuff should be left to the military. Moreover, while he awaited the coming day of freedom, he would stick fast to his digs and indulge himself with his favorite alcohol, much like any good publican back in England.

Fortunately, we were able to convince him it might be months before we were rescued and that he better begin to think of ways to stock the larder. It was bad enough he had to drink all day— and God only knew what trouble he would get into—but there would be no food for him unless he got off his duff and helped us find additional sources.

Once he had his head clear, Cliff wasted little time in contacting his friend, Carol—an Englishwoman married to a Syrian—who operated a small grocery store only a short distance from our building. With $700, or about 200 dinars of his own money, Cliff arranged for Carol and her husband, who drove a Volvo, to deliver a big load of canned goods.

The couple rolled quietly into the garage, where we met them and quickly unloaded the many boxes and whisked them onto a waiting elevator. In his apartment, Cliff generously shared the canned goods equally with each member of the group. We were one happy bunch of people for a while, and Cliff was the star of the hour.

In such a group with so many diverse nationalities— American, Brit, Australian, Irish, and Filipino—nothing ever went smoothly for long. All of us had been under much pressure and strain since August 2nd, some more than others. Kennedy was constantly worrying about our future—fearing capture, torture, even execution—always hoping for the best but never knowing what would happen.

Added to all of the above, we were now experiencing bouts of depression, varying degrees of claustrophobia, and advancing and receding waves of paranoia. I began to wonder who among us might flip out first. Go around the bend. Pull some stunt that would attract attention to the building, our apartments, our very selves. Many times it would be just a small thing that would get one or more of us terribly upset to the point of arguing about trivialities and screaming over nonsense.

At one time, I had an opportunity to purchase 20 kilos of frozen french fries but then realized I didn't have enough room in my refrigerator for them. I went by Cliff's apartment to inquire whether he had any space for the fries. Frankly, both of us had put away several cocktails by then, and I badly flubbed trying to explain my need for the frozen fries. Cliff was convinced I had bought the fries for him without first checking with him and I was now insisting that he pay up.

In a very belligerent voice, he bellowed, 'Who the hell gave you permission to buy those fries for me? 20 kilos, for Christ's sake. Enough for an army.'"

Mary Chambers, who had been having a drink with him when I arrived, suggested it was nothing to argue about and why didn't we just forget it? While Cliff was mulling over this idea, I slipped into the john to relieve myself.

Mary and Cliff became very concerned that I was most upset and that such a situation was not good for the group. He owned up to the fact that maybe he shouldn't have been so nasty about the fries. At least I had been thinking of him, he noted. With that, I stepped out of the bathroom, and their faces brightened immediately. I smiled back to show them I had already forgotten his criticism and the matter was of little concern to me.

I explained I had not bought the fries for him but merely wanted to know whether he could store them for a while. Cliff's ruddy features brightened anew when he realized he did not have to pay for them.

Some of the New Zealanders were a big help off and on. My wife, Jill, had worked as a teacher at the Kuwait English School, a primary and secondary school, which employed the British method of teaching. One of her colleagues was Karen Lane. Her husband, Alistair Lane, was a manager of the Kuwait Danish Dairy, which was still operating and producing Long Life milk. Learning about our group and our need for food, Alistair Lane would hide milk and other dairy products in the trunk of his car and take the cache to his home supply lockers. We would call and list our needs, and the items would shortly be delivered to us at the right place and time.

With his help and that of other New Zealanders, who were not Iraqi targets because of their country's neutrality, we built up large supplies of milk as well as fruit juices from the dairy.

As we approached the end of September or thereabouts, we heard a report on Radio Australia that our old pal, Max, was passing himself off back in Australia as a hero who had saved a small group of Westerners from the grasp of the Iraqis. With Pastor Maurice's car, he told how he and Mary had driven across the desert to Riyadh, Saudi Arabia, where they left the vehicle in the parking lot of the Australian Embassy and disappeared.

According to Radio Australia, Max had been begged by the Westerners to save them from the Iraqis. Only he and Mary could lead them across the desert. Mary McGee, in fact, was not mentioned by name, but we bet dollars to doughnuts that she had accompanied him on the nail-biting flight.

Luz Marina told us later that Pastor Maurice was taking legal action against Max for the theft of his car. The Aussies had traced the vehicle's registration back to the U.S. Embassy in Kuwait City, who then contacted the minister.

About the same time, we bade farewell to Mary Chambers and Jane Anderson, who had decided to accept the Iraqis' offer of safe conduct for all western women still in Kuwait and Iraq. They met a British Embassy representative at a prearranged rendezvous and went by bus to the Kuwait International airport. From there, the women jetted to Baghdad and soon afterwards flew onto Amman and freedom. After their departure, our group consisted of Philip and myself, John Levins and Paul Kennedy, Dave and Neil, the Hoyles, Cliff the publican, and Chris Chambers along with a smattering of Filipinos on the periphery.

Even with the departure of the two women, the food situation continued to worsen. Ten to twelve people, even on short rations, can put away a lot of calories in a day. We pressed our collective brains to the task of finding a solution.

I recalled that my friend Mohammed Attai was in the wholesale distribution business. Happily for us, he was a big distributor of foodstuffs throughout Kuwait. I kicked myself for not thinking of him earlier. When I contacted Mohammed, he readily agreed to provide us with whatever we needed. John was selected to go to Mohammed's warehouse with our list.

John drove back into the garage's top level in one of Mohammed's vehicles—loaded with cans of tuna fish and sardines, bags of dried beans and rice, and tins of coffee. Most of the supplies were the basic staples that could keep anyone going for a long time.

Best of all, Mohammed refused to take any money for the food he supplied us with on a periodic basis. Unfortunately, his assistance did not last long because the Iraqis trashed his warehouse, stealing its contents valued at some ten million dollars.

In addition to supplying us with badly needed food, Mohammed had also given us $700 U.S. I knew he would have given us ten times that amount if I had asked. Maybe I should have, but I didn't. Money never proved to be the problem that food did during our ordeal.

An Indian couple, Arnoo and his wife, Shireen, friends of John, began to slip into the apartment to bring us small offerings of food. They said they were maintaining their food supplies by raiding apartments abandoned by friends, who had lived on Al-Hilali Street near the Meridien Hotel.

Anytime one of the Indian families left Kuwait to return home, Arnoo and Shireen would clean out their refrigerators and pantries and bring us a share of their acquisitions. Unlike Mohammed's supplies, much of their contributions were top-of-the-line, including at times ten kilos of Dutch veal and ten of Dutch beef, which made excellent roasts. Even the spices for the roasts and other selections of meats were included. They also gave us video tapes and an occasional bottle of whiskey. We became very friendly with them and would visit back and forth late at night.

Paul Kennedy began to insist we had to break into a lot more of the abandoned apartments before the Iraqis and their fellow looters beat us to them. His suggestion made sense to me, and we sold the idea to the group.

Crouching in darkened hallways at the quietest times of the day or night—mid-morning was an excellent time as was mid-afternoon when most of the building's remaining occupants were not at home—we would insert a sharp screwdriver into the lock and turn it, simultaneously throwing our weight against the door to spring it open. In time, we became expert at opening the doors by bouncing or springing the door frames and went in and out of many apartments like so many Jimmy Valentines, the old-time burglar.

Although food was our main priority, we also began to take some other essential things like telephone answering machines and microwaves. We kept records though of the ownership of these items so that some day they might be returned.

Quixotically, as we increased our food supply from our forays into the vacant apartments, we developed the need for more refrigerators. We had no room for the perishables in our own individual refrigerators. We could not just let such food rot in front of us—not when it was so badly needed. We knew the problem and recognized the solution.

We became adept at removing refrigerators from the unoccupied apartments of friends, moving in silence through the hallways to the apartments of group members. Several of the group soon had as many as three refrigerators humming away in various rooms in the apartments—usually loaded with meat, dairy products, vegetables, fruits, and liquids.

When Arnoo and Shireen informed us they were going north to take the road to Amman, Jordan, John Levins and I decided to make videotapes for our families and the various media. We asked the Indians to smuggle them out for us.

They readily agreed, and John and I began to make our tapes. For the videotapes, we set up a bright back light, used various screens to shadow our faces, and shot with a video camera we had found in another Indian couple's trashed apartment.

Nothing ever goes easy—especially when you are desperate to succeed. On the tape to my media, I ran a test. There I was—standing full face in my Kuwait City apartment—readily identifiable. It had to be erased so the Iraqis couldn't track me down later. Try as we might, we could not delete that one-second portion of the tape. We would have to forget it, hoping that friendly editors in the West would have the good sense to erase it themselves.

My media tape ran about three minutes and focused on our current situation, our hopes and aspirations to see U.S. forces attack the city. Lots about the raping and looting and the general destruction and murders. We mostly emphasized how important it was for us to see U.S. government presence as quickly as possible.

In my tape to Jill and my daughters, I had to borrow eyeglasses to read what I had written to them. It was about seven minutes long, and I used most of the time to generally relate what had happened to Philip and myself from the beginning. Everything of importance was touched upon—even my failure to escape and get Philip to freedom.

In telling them about these events, I became quite emotional and overwhelmed by it all at times—to the point where we had to re-shoot the tape three times before I could finish it. By then, John was beside himself with similar feelings—but ones mixed with exasperation.

Toward the end of the tape, I told Jill I had learned one hard and fast lesson from my experience and that was how much I loved her and how much she meant to me—how my only hope and prayer was to return to her loving arms and be held fast there forever. I had known her for 15 years. She was my wife and the mother of our two daughters. If nothing else, I learned the importance of her love in my life during my ordeal in Kuwait.

John, for his part, prepared a list of questions I was to ask him as if he were an important figure being interviewed at a major news conference. I sort of smirked a bit but got into the swing of it. He had, after all, been very patient and understanding when taping my messages. He was a true ham and rose to the occasion, responding to the queries of the unseen interviewer with a strong voice, sans stutter, filled with the proper determination and elan.

In essence, John told his Australian audience how the military could attack Kuwait and destroy the Iraqi army. For a few bright, shining moments, in his mind anyway, he was General Schwarzkopf personified. No people were to be better briefed on the situation at that point than those who would view John's video.

Shortly before midnight the same day, we stole through the hallways down to the Indians' apartment and gave the tapes to Arnoo and Shireen. We impressed upon them the need for great care. We didn't want them to be caught with the tapes. A viewing of them by the Iraqis could quickly lead to their arrest and worse.

Arnoo said we were not to worry. As soon as they boarded the bus, they would take the tapes from their handbags and hide them somewhere in the interior. Even if they were found at a roadblock or border crossing, he expressed doubt that the guards would be supplied with VCRs to view the tapes.

One copy of my media tape was directed to the Kuwaiti Resistance in Amman, whose whereabouts Arnoo would seek out. He was to do this, and the tape would then go onto the Kuwaiti Resistance in London. In turn, its members were to send copies of it to the BBC and ITN (International Television News).

The Kuwaitis in London screened it first for any breaches of security. In doing so, their editor, an Irishman named Mike, carefully erased my full-faced figure shown at the very beginning of the tape.

My videotape was shown by both the BBC and ITN and made a big smash according to what I was to hear later. I had many friends in England, who saw the tape. Several of them called my sister, Joanne, in Boston, to tell her about it.

One of them said he knew it was me despite my efforts to hide my features in the shadows. As he said: "He could never disguise that nose of his."

Weeks later, we would also hear that my tape was shown on Dan Rather's news show on CBS, ABC's Nightline, CNN, Canadian television, and others. Unfortunately, what I thought was a good idea to send a video message, had a devastating emotional effect on my older daughter, Anna, who was sitting alone in the living room in Boston when the CBS' 6 O'clock News came on. When my face and voice came on, she lost control, became hysterical and ran to her room crying. At this point, Jill had no inkling of what happened.

I would also learn that several audio tapes and many letters I had written to Jill were never received. Surprisingly, the majority of the letters I wrote to *The Boston Globe*, in care of Jill, did arrive in due course. How do you figure it?

In the beginning, most members of the group were dead set against our taping endeavors. They felt strongly that such tapes breached security. Not much later, most of the members were asking John and me to make similar tapes of them for their families and the media. It was up to them to find ways to smuggle their tapes out of Kuwait.

Besides taking our videotape to Jordan, Shireen and Arnoo showed extraordinary courage in trying to free our friend, Clem Hall, who was a prisoner in the Regency Hotel. We had arranged an elaborate scheme to remove him from the dining room, to the indoor tennis courts, out onto Gulf Road where a Resistance driver would be waiting at a prearranged time. However, the Iraqi secret police stopped Shireen from ever reaching our friend.

Chapter 17

On My Own

Sometime in mid-October, I received a message from Jawad Behbehani that I should expect a call from a Kuwaiti, who would try to arrange telephone contact between Jill and me. I became tremendously excited but wondered how this could be done. Jawad said he had no idea. Why didn't I just wait for the call to find out?

A few anxiety-ridden days passed while I held fast to my apartment, not going anywhere because I might miss the Kuwaiti's call. It finally came. Jawad had informed the caller how to telephone me vis-a-vis our security guidelines.

"How are you going to put me in touch with my wife?" I asked the caller almost immediately.

He said he was in Kuwait. While he had me on the phone, he would use another phone to call a colleague on his car phone just across the Saudi border. My wife would be on a open line to a third colleague in that particular country, who would in turn use a second phone to call the man in the car on the border.

The latter man would then hold together two phones with their incoming calls. In theory, Jill and I would be able to talk with each other. It was all very confusing, but I assured the Kuwaiti I was very anxious to give it a try. When could we do it?

"Why not right now?" he replied.

I became ecstatic thinking about speaking to Jill within moments. It would be such happiness. There was so much we had to say to each other. So many things to tell each other.

"Sorry," the voice said on the phone. "I don't have your wife right now, but would you please talk with Tom Brokaw, he's a news anchor at NBC?"

I was flabbergasted. Here I was so keyed up to talk with my wife, trying to make a quick mental list of the things I wanted to tell here. Now this Kuwaiti said I was going to talk to Tom Brokaw. Hey, Tom Brokaw!! Any other time would be great—especially if he could help us get our story out to the world. Right then, though, I wanted to talk with Jill.

Whoever the interviewer was on the international hookup, hhe didn't sound like Tom Brokaw. However, he was very professional, very concerned, and asked many pertinent questions.

I replied to his queries and then finally asked, "When are the Marines coming? When are they going to get us out of this place?"

He seemed rather taken aback and asked me to repeat my questions. I don't know whether he hadn't heard me, or because I sounded emotional, he wanted to be sure to record my remarks properly.

I repeated my queries, and by then, I was convinced that the interviewer was indeed Tom Brokaw. He wound up the conversation by thanking me and saying, "All our prayers are with you, and I hope that you will soon be free and safely home with your family. God bless you." (1)

I rang off—disappointed that I had been unable to talk with Jill but happy that Tom Brokaw would broadcast at least part of the interview. The family would learn that I was still all right.

Not too long after that, while the group was practically in seclusion deep within our various camouflaged apartments, Dr. Behbehani contacted me again to say I could expect a call from Jill on the same telephone network.

I became very impatient and said I wanted to call the Kuwaiti myself. He replied, "No, you can't do that. It's a secret system.

He'll call you. I can't say when. It could be in an hour, a day, or a week or more. You must be patient."

Easy enough for him to say but not for me to appreciate. I did wait around for hours but then went down to the young Brits apartment for a group dinner. John, who had not been invited, came rushing down at some point—making a racket like a rusty tin man—to say there was a message on the answering machine from Dr. Behbehani, instructing me to stand by for a call from the Kuwaiti.

I rushed upstairs, disregarding several security rules in my mad dash, and waited only a few minutes before calling Dr. Behbehani at home. He said that he could not contact the man. "He only calls me. Please understand. We never call him. I wouldn't know how to."

He strongly urged me to hang on and be patient. I did so for three straight days—never going out of the apartment, always being within easy reach of the phone. The call never came then or later. (2)

When I was alone, isolated, especially after Philip had left for Baghdad, I had these interminable hours to consider my situation. The hours seemed to stretch to the horizon like a line of telephone poles wired together across the flat plains of Nebraska—all in one straight, endless rank that extended to the Pacific Ocean.

During much of that time, I would look at the few photos remaining in the apartment and recall happy moments. One of the most remembered ones was the night I had met Jill at a friendly Irishman's home in Port of Spain and had experienced love at first sight. I had been in the Trinidanian capital for only a few weeks—a bachelor on my first assignment with the World Health Organization—when I received an invitation to attend a calypso party at Sean Sullivan's lovely house on a hill overlooking Paria Bay. I thought it was a very romantic setting—even before I went inside—and Frank Joslyn, my counterpart with the government, introduced me to this beautiful woman. I don't know whether it was the setting, the night and the Latin music, the perfumed frangipani, or what, but Jill and I were immediately drawn to each other.

Jill, then an employee of AMOCO, and I dated on every possible occasion. After two years, we agreed "that the right thing to do was to get married," and we did.

It was a beautiful period—interlude—in my life. I would relive it repeatedly to escape the reality of my present life in deep hiding from the Iraqis.

Through all those days of emotional ups and downs, fits of depression, and constant bouts of fear stemming from the daily incursions into the complex by the Iraqis, we worked tirelessly to build up our food supplies.

By then, we had a number of sources to achieve that goal. There were the occasional gifts of food from friendly Kuwaitis and Arabs; heftier amounts from the New Zealanders and Aussies, still functioning in some capacity under the Iraqi occupation; and the items we secured ourselves by raiding unoccupied apartments. The latter course was risky because of the Iraqi threat to hang looters.

With my ALR computer and Lotus 1-2-3 program, I began to plan exactly what our group would need in the way of food and medicine for a period of four months or more. I ended up with a list of some 150 basic food items I felt would be necessary to ensure our health and well-being.

With the computer, I was able to determine the amount of calories and grams each of us would need on a daily basis, multiply it by the number of days, and come up with the totals. Once that was figured out, I had to determine the amount of calories and grams we would get from different staples—say a can of peas, tuna fish or soups, flour, bread, rice, frozen and fresh foods.

Canned goods figured very big in our food planning because they were less perishable than fresh foods. Eventually, we would have cases stashed away in the group's different apartments—in ceilings, behind walls, in sofas and chairs.

No one was more high-tech or more far out on the so-called razor's edge than our group in obtaining food and recording it in my computer. With the help of many generous people—black marketeers, thieves, Resistance members, friends, and even casual acquaintances—we would reach a maximum supply of 245 days by mid-November, enough to last us until June 1991.

Every last bit and byte of information about our food stocks had been put into the computer and forwarded to memory. We had an instant read-out on the screen about the status. As food was used and replaced, we duly noted it in the computer. Neil Beevor, the young Brit, was a big help in keeping our medical supply records computerized on a daily basis.

Along with food and medicine, we had an urgent need for a big supply of insect spray because the building was becoming overrun with cockroaches among many such pests. As though knowing we were unarmed to defend against them, the cockroaches boldly scurried over the walls and dashed about the floors. Our carpets and rugs were filled with the loathsome bugs. You couldn't walk in the hallways without insects dropping onto your head and being crunched underfoot.

Since the maintenance crews had disappeared during the first days of the occupation, the insects quickly asserted themselves in every crack and cranny of the complex. They feasted like the proverbial locusts of the fields on the garbage deposited in the hallway trash containers.

Every one of the disposals was soon overflowing—not only with bags of trash and garbage but with black and gray cloaks of swarming insects. There were chutes to drop the trash to the basement, but we were cautioned not to use them. They too quickly became fire hazards.

However, many tenants did use the chutes and inevitably self-combustion set off fires. One brought the firemen, but the fire was confined to the lower floors. There were other fires which we doused ourselves. Just one more worry for us.

The firemen were always accompanied by Iraqi soldiers, whom we feared might begin searching for suspected arsonists. We also worried about thick smoke forcing us out of the building and into the waiting arms of the Iraqis. In fact, there was one bad fire that sent clouds of smoke billowing through the hallways, but we managed to hold fast to our apartments by placing wet towels around the doors.

In time, our repeated requests for insect spray were answered, and we had boxes of the stuff to use in our campaign to defeat the bugs in our apartments and to a lesser degree in the hallways. To completely remove any trace of them in the public areas was to tip the enemy to people hiding behind the strangely marked doors.

Quixotically, our group tightened and became more unified, but no one leader emerged as you usually find in such an endeavor. I think this was true because no one member wanted the responsibility.

What we had instead were members providing leadership in our different areas of activity. One would be very interested in security matters—like Paul Kennedy—so he was in charge of coordinating and enforcing efforts to maintain the best possible security. Imad also had a deep interest in security and gradually assumed the leadership in this key area for the group.

John Levins was very big in getting out of the building at every excuse and in asserting the leadership required to keep the group stocked with food. It was a very natural undertaking for him in any case, because, as an Australian, he had access to the streets and also counted many contacts in the food industry among his friends.

Many of them still had keys to a number of the city's sealed warehouses and food outlets. With him no doubt leading the charge, they would raid a Pizza Hut warehouse and come away with 50 pounds of salami and pepperoni. We would use these meats as bacon in the morning.

In one raid, I recall that 50 pounds of fast food hamburger was obtained, divided up equally, and distributed for storage in the group's many refrigerators. A great deal of this hamburger was used to prepare different pasta dishes. One favorite was Spaghetti Bolognese.

Another person assumed the leadership in obtaining and maintaining our medical supplies. These also were distributed equally in every category—from aspirin to cough depressant—to each member. No supplies of any kind were ever concentrated in any one apartment. They could all be lost by an Iraqi raid on that particular apartment.

While John was very helpful in obtaining food, he continued to act irrationally in other areas. Once, on his own computer, he listed the members of the group by name, nationality, address in Kuwait City and in their home country.

On learning this, we accused him of breaching security. Paul Kennedy was especially incensed—almost coming to blows with John once again. Security was Kennedy's forte, and he despised John for his constant lapses, taking it almost as a personal affront to his leadership in this area.

Reluctantly, John agreed to erase the detailed list from his computer, but he wanted to do another list with only our first names. We protested once more. He then compiled another list of the membership by using only our initials. This still was not acceptable to the group.

Ultimately, we compiled ten firm security rules. Each member was required to read them, agree to them or leave the group, and then sign his name at the bottom of the page. When all had read and signed, the paper was destroyed. We felt that in completing this ritual, all were duty bound to honor the rules. Though we had destroyed the written agreement, we collectively held that there was an informal gentlemen's agreement existing among us.

John signed the agreement along with the rest of us. Almost immediately, in his own bumbling way, he began to breach the rules. You could talk to him until you were blue in the face about how illogical he was, but he never seemed to get it. I put it down to the fact that he had had no formal higher education, especially in basic philosophy, where a solid course in logic might have turned him into a steady, dependable fellow.

He could be so damnable likeable at times, even imaginative in some of his actions; e.g., the quick thinking that had gotten us out of the hands of the Iraqis in the Sheraton Hotel. He would then spoil all the good will he had earned by pulling some asinine trick that could have blown our cover.

He never seemed to realize that his need to be a free spirit—by moving in and out of the building at any time of the day or night—posed a threat to all of us. Australian or not, most people on the outside didn't know his nationality. All they saw was a westerner coming and going from the building at will. It didn't require a vivid imagination to understand that sooner or later the Iraqis would follow him back into the building and find out who his friends were and what he was up to.

I temporarily put thoughts of John on a back burner because Philip had announced that he was getting out. He was going up to Baghdad and flying on from there to Amman.

Sure you are, I thought. How did he expect to pull that off? Actually, I prayed that Philip could get away. He had become progressively more depressed about his situation and was drinking daily, mostly Scotch he had secured from outside sources.

I continued to feel guilty about his situation. I was responsible for him, and I had failed miserably to effect an escape on several occasions. The Hansens had pulled it off. So had Max and Mary McGee and many others. Why couldn't I?

Philip explained he had obtained another passport from the Canadian Embassy to replace the stolen one. So what? I shrugged. It could possibly get him to Baghdad, but it wouldn't necessarily get him on a plane to Amman. Canadians were being held in Baghdad along with Americans and Brits.

"The embassy here received a telex saying there would be a United Nations *laissez-passer* document for me at the embassy in Baghdad. Once I've got that, I'm on my way. A copy of the telex should also help me to get up to Baghdad."

Good for him, I thought ruefully. His father was a UN employee and, of course, had obviously pulled some strings to get his son out of the country. Yeh, good for him. He's away, and I'm stuck in this cesspool.

I couldn't help but remember my efforts from early in August to get a United Nations passport. At least I had worked for the

UN for years in the past. You know that old loyalty thing. I never got one then or later when I tried again.

Philip wasted no time in preparing to leave on a flight from Kuwait City to Baghdad. We embraced and shed a few tears, and I sent him off with my good wishes and a host of messages for my family.

With his departure, I went into a real funk of depression. Philip was family. He had been with me in this mess since the beginning—since the first Iraqi shell had exploded in the cemetery across the street. We had shared so many experiences since then. He was a solid link to Jill, and now he was gone. I had to face how many more weeks and months of isolation before the Iraqis either grabbed me or the Coalition freed the city. (3)

President Bush had announced earlier that he had ordered an additional 150,000 to 200,000 American troops to the Gulf, upping the total to more than 400,000. Later it would go to over half a million. It was a formidable force, made even more so by the reinforcements sent by other member states of the Coalition.

I had to wonder though when the U.S. planned to use the troops against Saddam Hussein and his army. It wasn't as if they were going to fight World War III. Obviously, the good guys had bought the bad guys' story about how tough they were.

With Philip gone, I was the only North American left in the group. Actually, I was the only North American in the complex and, to my knowledge, one of a few still in Kuwait City. I felt at high risk.

That being the case, I decided to get rid of everything that would underline my U.S. citizenship or at least hide incriminating materials from any would-be searchers. A lot of old mail, paid bills, and a few unpaid bills were disposed of by tearing them up and burning them in a wastepaper basket.

It was tough discarding many of the certificates and documents because they held fond memories of the family for me. One of the best places to hide such stuff was in the vents of the air conditioning system. I would get up on a chair, loosen just two screws to let a vent down, and stuff in handfuls of papers. A few twists of the screwdriver, and the vent was sealed tightly again.

My passport posed a special problem for me from early on. On the one hand, I was determined to keep it to prove my nationality to the right people. On the other hand, it could be a death warrant for me if I were caught with it on my person by the wrong Iraqis.

From mid-August on, I had hidden it in many different places, always fearful that the Iraqis would easily find it. Finally, I hid it in a small well behind a ventilation shaft in the ceiling in Anna's bedroom, and let it be. Someone would have to know it was there before they would ever find it.

It was then that I began to think seriously about how I could get out of the country with different documentation—perhaps another country's passport, *laissez-passer*, whatever it took.

Chapter 18

Close Call

By the middle of October, I felt totally depressed and demoralized, mostly because I had a sense that no one seemed to be concerned about us. I wasn't receiving any messages from the Voice of America at the time, no letters from home, and the American government had little, if anything, to say about us.

I kept remembering the U.S. assault on Grenada to quell the threat the Cubans and rebels posed for American medical students at St. George University Medical School. And Panama, too, where the Americans went in after a U.S. naval officer and his wife were accosted in Panama City. Here we were—thousands of Westerners—either prisoners or hiding from the Iraqis—and the U.S. didn't appear to be taking any initiative to rescue us.

The effect of this apparent inaction was psychologically damaging on us. On one hand, we had taken it upon ourselves to survive a day at a time, but on the other, we had heard of many Westerners deliberately putting themselves in jeopardy as though they wanted to be caught or shot—just to get the waiting and the hiding over with at last.

My British friend, Chris Thrupp, had to run for it when the Iraqis surrounded his apartment house in the Al-Jabriya district and began picking up all the Westerners. It was a close call, but happily Chris had gotten away clean. The Iraqis had waited until evening and watched for any lights to go on. Then they raided those apartments to apprehend the Westerners hiding out in the building.

All too soon, we determined that Westerners were being picked up because they were being turned in by informers. The secret police could never have taken so many into custody without cooperation.

We had to conclude that it was not just unfriendly Arabs like the Palestinians, who were turning Westerners in to the Iraqis. Even friendly types like the Filipinos, Egyptians, Sri Lankans, Thais, and Kuwaitis could be motivated to inform on Westerners out of fear of being executed for withholding information on their whereabouts.

The Kuwaitis did betray some Westerners early on because they had been warned they would be subject to summary execution for harboring any. However, the Resistance soon passed the word that those Kuwaitis would face retribution from their own people if they continued to betray westerners. We heard later that Palestinians were responsible for the betrayal of most Westerners because the Iraqis had put a price on our heads. The sum could run from $300 to $1000 depending on the exchange rate at the time.

The Palestinians were responsible for turning in my good friend, Clem Hall, an Air Force veteran, and at the time an employee of a Kuwaiti defense firm. Another one of my tennis partners, he and I would call one another every three days to check on each other's well-being.

One day when I called Clem, his roommate, a Yugoslavian reporter, said the Iraqis had grabbed him. He was betrayed by Palestinians, who had catered his New Year's Eve party.

Bastards, I thought. Whom could you trust? These were people with whom he had done business, helping them meet their bottom line, and paying them good money—and they informed on him anyway.

There was quite a large colony of Westerners living in lovely villas in the Mishrif district off the Sixth Ring Road, who fell into the Iraqi net with one quick, vicious cast. Apparently, the Iraqis had shut off the phones in the district, put some kind of a tap on them, and then restored the service. I don't know how it worked exactly, but when the westerners used the phones again, the Iraqis were shortly pounding on their doors. One of Dave's best friends, a British military attaché, was caught in this roundup. He did his damnedest to escape, running through back yards and jumping over fences but the Iraqis caught up with him. Dave had communicated every day with him. When we lost someone we all dropped into a deep funk.

However, sometimes we had a good laugh when events did a turn. The attaché was taken to the Regency Hotel with Clem Hall and other prisoners to be processed for the trip to Baghdad and to be used as human shields. He somehow was put on a plane without a guard to be picked up again by security in Baghdad. When in Baghdad he mingled with many Germans who were on the plane and were still free to move about. Unbelievably, no Iraqi secret police were there to pick him up. He quickly jumped into a German Embassy limousine with the others and was taken to the German Embassy. Suddenly, he was a German with a passport and out of Iraq in a few days, safe in the West.

Wondering whether our phones could be tapped, we contacted Fred Skolberg, a Canadian, who had been employed by the Kuwaiti telecommunications people in pre-invasion days. Fortunately, Fred had been in charge of the system that was used to tap phones. However, the system was not operational in Kuwait City because Fred had not completed the project and refused to report to work. He warned us, however, that the Iraqis could tap the phones in a time-consuming and ineffectual mechanical way, which caused a clicking noise. If such occurred, we would immediately hang up.

Fred had lived in our apartment building but had moved out after his wife was attacked by Iraqi soldiers and almost raped. Fred had sent his wife up to Baghdad to fly home while he stayed in Kuwait. On his way to one of his periodic visits with us, he had been picked up and questioned for three hours before being released. The Iraqis really didn't have much interest in holding male Canadians although they wouldn't allow them to leave the country.

Fred told us that one day the Iraqis had raided the apartment where he had been living with an Englishman and his Iranian wife. The Brit decided he should hide. They boosted him up into the air conditioning duct in the bathroom, giving him a blanket to keep him warm.

As the Iraqis checked their identities, Fred told them the woman's husband had disappeared and he was staying there to protect her. While Fred watched, the Iraqis looted the apartment of the valuables they could carry away. They had become very rough with him when they found an old Zenith tube radio and thought it was a broadcasting system. He had had to explain the presence of air tanks, diving masks, knives and weaponry books—pleading that the vanished Brit had been a scuba diver and weapons buff.

After several hours of intense questioning—something Fred was familiar with because of past interrogations—the Iraqis had concluded he was not a U.S. Seal or other American underground Special Forces type.

Fred and the woman had groaned inwardly when several of the soldiers went into the bathroom and had actually stood on a chair to open the vent and look into the air conditioning duct. They had looked at each other in wonderment. How come the Brit hadn't been spotted? Maybe he had slid farther along inside the duct—if that was possible.

The officer in charge announced he was going down to the local headquarters to check on Fred's story and would leave them in the custody of two guards. This was too much for the Iranian woman, who dearly loved her husband. She became possessed of panicky thoughts of his freezing to death in the duct.

She told Fred she was emotionally spent and was going to turn her husband in to the soldiers. She didn't have the strength to worry about him any longer and was about to collapse from the strain. Fred said he understood. He informed the Iraqis that although the Brit was hiding nearby, they would never find him. He and the woman would bring him around in the morning if the Iraqis would permit the woman and her husband to spend one last night together.

Surprisingly, they approved but noted that the building would be surrounded until daybreak when the Brit was to turn himself in. They had warned Fred not to play any tricks or he would face dire consequences.

As soon as the Iraqis had shut the door, Fred and the woman rushed to release the Brit from his hiding place. "I have to tell you, Rob, the poor bugger was a bowl of jelly. Stuck up in that cold duct for twelve hours! Fearing every moment that he was going to be found and taken away and God knows what else."

The Brit was so shaken and so discomforted by his experience that he had urinated in his pants. He almost fell, and his legs were so wobbly that Fred and the woman had had to carry him from the bathroom to the bed. In any event, the couple had a final night together, happy in each other's arms. He was a more composed and determined fellow in the morning as he left for Iraq.

Listening to Fred tell his story, I felt a deep kinship for the man and particularly his condition when he was removed from the duct because I had had a similar experience only a few days earlier. I had been downstairs visiting a Filipino family when there was a sudden knock on the door and a loud Iraqi voice demanded that the door be opened.

The head of the family had motioned for me to duck into a bedroom filled with cots and small beds, piled up with spreads and blankets. At times, some six or more Filipinos slept in this bedroom. The Filipino had told the Iraqi at the door that he had no knowledge of any Westerners in the building. Here I was trapped in his apartment!

For more than an hour and a half, I had had to remain unmoving under the bedding while the Iraqi had bullied the Filipino by telling him all the terrible things he could do to him and the others. They were completely at his mercy, he said. He could easily sell the women to the Iraqi soldiers. Indeed, he could sell them all to Arab slavers for a good price.

While he went on, ranting about how the Filipinos better cooperate with him or he would sell them all off, it suddenly occurred to me that I might not have locked the door to the bedroom. I was already very apprehensive that the Iraqi would come into the bedroom, looking for any woman hiding there. He had stood just outside the door for a time.

I could just see his face when he found me. Expecting to rape a luscious Filipino woman, and instead he finds a bearded male Westerner! He would have had the secret police on me fast.

I struggled to keep myself from shaking and giving myself away and hardly breathed. Just go, you son-of-a-bitch, I prayed, and I'll skip up to my apartment in a flash. My luck held, at least on a small scale, and the Iraqi left without coming into the bedroom. I bid the Filipino a quick adieu minutes later and fled for the upper reaches of the building.

The Iraqis were more successful in capturing a Frenchman, who jumped from the second floor of the Regency Hotel to escape them. He bounced off an awning and ran down the beach but was seized and badly beaten in front of other Westerners.

The secret police used the Regency Hotel as a temporary prison, where they held their captives for four or five days before shipping them to Baghdad. It was a handsome five-star hotel on Salwa Beach, but the hostages were kept indoors until they were shipped off in groups of 30 for the trip by bus to Baghdad.

An Englishman, who had hidden for 70 days right next door to the Regency in an apartment house, finally decided he had to get out when he was reduced to subsisting on rancid butter. With English aplomb, he strolled out of his doorway, bid the Iraqi soldiers "good day," and went straight across Gulf Road to a designated house.

He had called the occupants minutes earlier to say when he would be there. At the exact moment, they opened the gate, and he strolled through to go under cover with them.

Chapter 19

The Green Line

Back in Boston, Jill and my family never faltered in their efforts to get the UN, Trinidad, or the Irish government to provide me with a passport, a *laissez-passer* or whatever temporary document would allow me to travel to Baghdad and then fly to the West. Sadly, bureaucrats raised roadblocks almost willfully at every turn.

Finally, Jill, acting on a friend's suggestion, made an appointment with U.S. Senator John Kerry of Massachusetts and at a meeting in his office presented my case. The senator expressed dismay at the lack of cooperation her efforts had received as of that date and pledged he would personally contact the Irish ambassador in Washington, D.C., and demand I be given Irish papers—papers I was entitled to because of my grandfather McGoldrick's birth in County Sligo.

I was informed about Kerry's reaction and waited hopefully for any hint or sign that he had set a fire under the buns of the Irish government. God bless him. He had!

Paul Kennedy, of all people, informed me in early October that a messenger with the Irish Government had entered Kuwait and would shortly pay me a visit. I was not so surprised that Kennedy had brought the news because he was the "warden"— civilian leader of sorts—for the Irish living in Kuwait City. Mr. Irishman called me soon after and asked a series of questions.

We set a time and date for him to meet with me in the apartment. Paul Kennedy slipped him into the complex and up the one working elevator to the eighth floor where I responded to the pre-arranged knocks on the door.

My meeting with the Irish official lasted only a few minutes—if you can believe it. There were a few questions about myself and my family and my grandfather McGoldrick.

Was my name really Robert Emmet Morris? Robert Emmet, the Irish revolutionary, who gave one of if not the greatest speech from the dock before the British hanged him. It was so Irish. I must be Irish. Where was my grandfather born? I must have been getting weary of the questioning by then because I said Suffolk instead of Sligo. Suffolk, of course, is the county in which Boston is located in the States. There is no County Suffolk in Ireland.

Finally, Mr. Irishman finished with all the Q & As and handed over the Irish documents that had been prepared for me. It should be understood that I was not given an Irish passport but rather an Irish *laissez-passer*. It was a very good step in the right direction since I was trying to shed my American persona.

All the time, Kennedy had been hovering nearby. As soon as we had finished with our business, he had hustled the messenger into a small back room. "We're about some business, Rob. Nothing that concerns you."

Kennedy's need to have a private meeting didn't faze me at all since it was a frequent habit of his to meet secretly with one stranger after another. The meetings would be with Thais, Indians, Palestinians, etc., and run on interminably. When the meetings were over, he would emerge, and with a wink or a nod or some gesture or other, he would indicate his meetings were of a very top-secret nature. He would always mumble something about "colleagues . . . fellow travelers . . . mates . . . ."

It was all so much horse shit—as though the people he was meeting with so often were IRA hit men, black marketeers, smugglers, resistance fighters, M5 or M16 agents, or even "Company" men. I usually didn't pay any attention to whom he met with, figuring it was all so much crap. There was no way Kennedy was going to impress me with his fun and games.

At one point, he came out of the meeting and implied he had been one hundred percent responsible for getting the Irish government to issue me the document. His claim was truly laughable because John Levins had just come into the apartment, heard about the transaction, and immediately asserted that he was the prime force behind the issuance of the *laissez-passer*. I only laughed. I knew full well that Senator Kerry was the man solely responsible for getting the Irish government to move on my behalf.

It must be kept in mind that the Irish *laissez-passer* was not a passport. Having it, though, provided me with mental relief because it identified me as an Irish citizen, a highly desirable category to be in because the Iraqis were not rounding up Irishmen.

At that time, there was no way I could physically use it to fly out of Baghdad because an Iraqi exit visa was required. The Iraqis were not in a hurry to issue visas to westerners unless they had a specific plan to gain another propaganda victory.

I was quick to realize, too, that there were still plenty of people walking around Kuwait City, who knew I was an American—no matter what papers I might be carrying. In fact, most of my co-workers at our training center had been Palestinians.

Following his meeting with Kennedy, the messenger came out of the back room and was immediately pounced on by other members of the group. Surely, they all complained, they also had the right to an Irish *laissez-passer*.

Chris Chambers noted that his wife was Irish. Neil said that his girlfriend, with whom he had been living and whom he planned to marry, was of Irish lineage—but that argument wasn't good enough. I remember that Dave didn't press for an Irish document. The messenger then had Chris swear to uphold the Irish constitution and then gave him the requested *laissez-passer*.

As an American of Irish descent, I found it ironic that the Brits, who probably had little love for the Irish out of guilt for all the wrongs England had done the little country for centuries, hadn't hesitated a moment to voice their so-called Irish connections and try to grab the Irish *laissez-passer*.

While all this negotiating was going on, I noticed Imad, whom we now knew was a Syrian, sitting quietly on the other side of the dimly lit room. He was taking it all in. Up to that point, Imad had been helpful on several occasions, but he was not an "inside" member of the group—a Westerner, if you will. His presence was a clear breach of our security rules.

I cursed under my breath. A breach, nothing! His being there at all was a major breach. What the hell had we been thinking about? How did we know he wouldn't betray us to the Iraqis? He could get dinars for each one of us. Christ, we had to tighten up on our security!

Well, the proverbial crap hit the fan the very next day. In less than 24 hours—according to Kennedy—the word was out on the street that Irish documents were available from my apartment. Talk about a major grapevine in a ravaged city. It was speedy and accurate and posed a dangerous threat to us.

Of course, we already knew who was responsible. Once again, several of us had heard John Levins telling people on my telephone that they could get Irish papers from the westerners in the Al-Muthanna complex. He just sat there, flapping his mouth, making no effort to muffle his voice. We heard him provide this information as if he was chatting about the weather to one caller and then to another. We couldn't believe our ears.

I bellowed to John to get off the phone, and the group literally tore into him with Paul Kennedy leading the assault and pounding him with some of the most intense oral abuse I had ever heard. He called him every possible name and swore that he was going to cripple him, if not kill him, for his stupidity and irresponsibility.

"Do you always have to be the big know-it-all, idiot? The only one who can get anything done? Is the esteem and admiration of the bloody beggars around here so important to you that you'll shout your mouth off just to get attention? To take credit for things you had nothing to do with?"

Kennedy claimed he was told that reports about the Irish documents were on the street within minutes of the messenger's departure. How could John shoot his mouth off so? Where were his brains? Kennedy made the point that if the Palestinians knew the Irish papers were being handed out indiscriminately, they would be useless. Anyone carrying them, who was stopped by the Iraqis, would soon be arrested. I am convinced that if the group hadn't been present, Kennedy would have killed John or, at the very least, crippled him. Once again, he threatened to kneecap him, his favorite IRA terminology.

To be quite honest, there was a part of me that said let him do it. My family had busted its backside to help me get the documentation to show that I was Irish, and John had immediately broadcast the information to the city.

Actually, the Irish *laissez-passer* and the local ID card provided by the Resistance—which indicated I was Irish and a doctor of medical engineering (the title was incorrect, but I let it stand)—were flimsy documentation. However, since I was trying to cast off my U.S. nationality, I very much appreciated both.

I had no immediate intention of emerging from deep hiding and testing the *laissez-passer* and Kuwaiti ID card with the Iraqis. I had folded them carefully and slipped them into my old leather wallet. Maybe when I truly needed them or their value had been proven to me—at least in being able to travel to Baghdad without hindrance—I would show the documents. Until such time, they would remain in my wallet.

Sometimes—when I would sit by a window and crack it open a hair to stare at the Iraqi soldiers passing along on the street below—I would think of other soldiers in another time and place thousands of miles away in Vietnam. Memories long suppressed. Repeatedly, my mind focused on the day my dental assistant Chauncey Bates and I—accompanied by six marines as our armed guards—wheeled up to a mountain village to provide free care to the inhabitants. I volunteered for this duty frequently, probably out of some suppressed guilt.

On that particular day, some 150 villagers crowded into the large village council hut to await my ministrations. It was hot and steamy as always, and my ears were filled with the sing-song voices and light laughter of the Vietnamese as I took them in turn to treat their betel nut-stained teeth. The six Marines had moved downhill to a coke stand some three hundred yards away.

I never thought much about the enemy when I was assigned this type of duty. Charlie, the enemy, was somewhere out there. I knew that, but he had more important things to do than harass me.

Suddenly, within a few minutes, the hut emptied. As though given a silent command, the villagers had all filed out with hardly a sound among them—at least none that caught our attention. In bewilderment, my assistant and I looked about the dirt-floor hut for even a single patient. There wasn't a villager to be seen or heard.

But, we were not alone. My heart thumped, and my mouth went dry. Only a few feet away, two uniformed North Vietnamese soldiers stood staring at us. Oh, shit! I thought. They will either kill us right now or start us up the Ho Chi Minh Trail to toss us into a bamboo tiger cage. I would have plenty of years to wish they had killed me—fast and painlessly.

For a few moments, no one moved or spoke. I couldn't take my eyes off the barrels of the AK-47s they kept aimed at us. Instinctively, I knew it was time to act.

"Okay, we're getting out of here, right now, Corpsman. Forget the instruments. Just follow me out of here and no bullshit about it."

For one final second, I looked at my adversaries, whose dark eyes gazed unflinchingly into mine. In my mind, the enemy soldiers were like two hooded cobras, raised up and prepared to strike. We would soon find out if that was what they intended to do to us.

I turned slowly about and walked toward our jeep just outside the hut—all the time expecting to hear a split second of automatic fire and feel a burst of bullets in my back. I hoped the corpsman wasn't frozen in fear and unable to move out of the hut. I passed through the entrance and walked out to the jeep. Where the hell were the Marine guards? Screwing off? Or dead? With both of us in the jeep, I started the engine and slammed my foot to the accelerator. After we had traveled about 100 yards, I glanced back to see the two North Vietnamese soldiers watching us from the hut. If they had chosen, they could still have shot us at that distance, but they made no move to do so.

"Damn it, Doc," the corpsman screamed, "We're going to get away with it! I don't believe it. Why didn't they just waste us?"

"Forget it," I replied. "Who cares why they didn't? They didn't. That's the important thing. What I want to know is where are the fucking grunts who were supposed to be watching our asses?"

We found them about another 400 yards down the road, screwing off around a coke machine, plugged into an electric generator on the periphery of the village. Can you believe it? In the middle of a stinking war, and there was a Coke machine?

We screamed, "Charlie, Charlie, he's in the village! Grab your weapons, and let's get the hell out of here—fast!"

Without another word, the Marines leaped into their jeep and followed us in a crazy, careening dash to clear the area. Once away, I blistered those Marines for taking off from the council hut and leaving us bare-assed to confront the enemy. Puke sonsofabitch! Who was going to pay for all those government instruments, easily worth several thousand dollars? Not me, I swore.

Twenty years later, and I could still see those dark brown eyes beaming at me. I still wonder why they didn't kill us on the spot. All those years I could have been dead. All those years I could have been held in captivity or died at some point in captivity. Who can explain it?

Chapter 20

Capture of the Hoyles

There was no end to the looters who constantly prowled throughout the huge Al-Muthanna complex. They apparently still thought of it as a big department store that held rooms full of household goods awaiting discovery.

At various times, the Iraqis would make a concerted effort to uncover any foreigners who might still be hiding in the building. One time, they went room by room across the 13th floor, not one apartment escaping their attention. Happily for us, that was the height of their planned program to sweep the complex. They immediately went back to their old habit of hit-and-miss in checking out apartments.

It was terrifying to hear the sudden pounding on the door. I would creep up and look through the peephole. It was a tiny opening made with a pin inserted into a piece of adhesive that had been taped over the regular glass peephole. One day I looked through the hole and saw two heavyset men in dirty Arab dress standing there. One of the faces seemed to stare right back at me.

They were puzzled by the nameplate of my Egyptian friend, Amr Al-Arabi, which I had affixed to the door. They kept studying it and muttering something to each other. They apparently decided it wasn't a good idea to break into the apartment of a co-religionist by that name and left. I was both relieved and elated. The nameplate had served its purpose well

Whenever we thought it was safe, we slipped up and down the hallways to each other's apartments to share a little company, talk, and food. In the silence induced by our isolation, our hearing became very acute. In time, we could distinguish between the footsteps of group members and strangers. We soon learned that bare feet on concrete floors surprisingly made more noise that soft-soled shoes or sneakers.

To tighten my own security, I positioned a piece of broken mirror glass on the floor and against the hallway wall outside my entrance so that the entire length of the corridor was visible from my partly opened door. It was a group rule that everyone had to check the mirror before stepping into the hallway. By then we had also devised secret door knocks when visiting each other.

I also wedged an empty Coke can against the fire door in the hallway outside my apartment. Whenever strangers came through the door, it opened with a crack like a gun shot against the aluminum can.

With Philip's departure, the group's membership had dropped down to John Levins and Paul Kennedy, Neil Beevor and Dave Hough, Ken and Magda Hoyle, Chris Chambers and Cliff of the no-last-name, a few Filipinos—whom we seldom saw anymore because they were paralyzed by fear of the Iraqis—myself and Imad.

We knew by then that Imad was a 33-year-old Syrian who had graduated from George Washington University in the District of Columbia with a degree in engineering. It was my impression that John or Paul had known him slightly since he lived somewhere up above us. I never asked for his apartment number. If I didn't know it, I couldn't divulge it if I were picked up.

I'm not even clear when or how he started to join us at our meetings. It was very early on, but he hardly ever spoke—just listened and nodded his head a lot. He was very quiet, almost mysterious. Being Syrian, I had to wonder later why he had taken up with a bunch of Westerners. When I heard he had no money because of the Iraqi occupation and the loss of his job as an engineer in Kuwait City—I wondered whether he would turn us in for money.

I remembered the story of Anne Frank, the Jewish girl, who hid from the Gestapo in an Amsterdam attic for 2 years during World War II, only to be ultimately betrayed—allegedly for money—by the Dutch who had hidden her. We constantly heard stories of betrayal. There were even stories about Westerners who stole cars, purloined money, or panicked and betrayed compatriots.

At one point, John informed me that a Canadian warden had stolen some $500,000 in Resistance funds. It was only a rumor but so devastating to our morale. I knew the Canadian well and refused to accept John's statement. Another story circulating was of a Turk who volunteered to take people out of the country for $10,000. With half-payment in hand he would bundle you into his truck and, as he said, would head across the desert. Well, in fact, he would circle the city for a couple of hours and drop the unwary Westerner off at the Regency Hotel to become another human shield in Iraq.

The first time Imad made an impression on me was when he had shown up at the door about two o'clock in the morning and asked whether he could be of any help to us. He returned shortly with 50 kilos of potatoes. Initially, our relationship with Imad was a peripheral one. He was at best a very shadowy figure, who would be around one minute and gone the next. Why he would suddenly disappear was never fully explained. In truth, it probably wasn't any of our business.

I guess what I am saying is that, in the beginning, he was a suspicious character in my eyes. However, little by little, it became obvious to us that Imad was very pro-American. What the hell? He had studied for four years in the nation's capital—something of the old red, white, and blue must have rubbed off.

As I got to know him better, talked with him, and observed his activities on behalf of the group, he was beginning to assert a leadership role in many of our endeavors. I became ashamed of myself for suspecting him of being capable of turning us in to the Iraqis.

Because of his engineering expertise, Imad came up with many ideas on how to stymie the Iraqis in their periodic forays through the building in search of Westerners. If he had been caught helping us, he faced execution.

I am proud to say Imad never wavered in his support. He placed double-bolt locks on our doors. He instructed us on how to remove doorknobs to keep looters from moving easily about. We carried the knobs around in our pockets to use when needed.

Imad was one of the leading lights in coming up with the idea to immobilize the elevators throughout the complex as a way to discourage looters and impede Iraqi hunters. He personally knocked out six of the building's seven elevators. He removed several key parts from each lift, and they stopped running. The Iraqis never did get them fixed and had to make use of the one working elevator if they wanted to get to the roof or to any of the upper floors.

As we moved into the middle of October, I considered Imad a jewel in the way he was holding the group together and providing support in every way possible. He would warn us when the soldiers were coming. He smuggled our letters out of Kuwait. He helped in a big way to bring us food and water and worked with me in keeping our computer tabulation of resources up to date.

We put our remaining cash of $2000 in Imad's hands to make the most of our food purchases, although he did provide John and Paul with the funds they needed to make payments to their sources in the food business. Imad's food purchases were always delivered to us between midnight and two a.m.

After Philip left for Baghdad, I kept busy by interacting with group members, exercising, reading, watching television and video films, reading the Bible, and listening to the short-wave radio. We could get the Voice of America, BBC, Radio Australia, Radio Moscow, and a mix of others depending on the atmospherics. We seldom heard any references on the short-wave radio about the westerners still holding out in Kuwait.

There was no mention of us at all on Voice of America until many weeks had passed. We assumed, correctly or not, that we were forgotten, unimportant, and not part of the American equation in resolving the Gulf crisis. We thought back to Tehran—

when the Iranians had grabbed the U.S. Embassy and held some 52 Americans captive for more than a year—and about how they were constantly in the news.

There were thousands of hostages, or "guests" as the Iraqis described us, in both Iraq proper and occupied Kuwait. There was violence on an incomparable scale vis-a-vis the Iranian situation, and yet, we heard nothing to indicate that our country cared a wit about us.

Mail was another sore point. We never received any letters from home at any time although I knew Jill and other family members had to be writing to me. Only John Levins was receiving mail through the so-called Australian pipeline.

From the BBC, we learned about the many support groups organized on behalf of the United Kingdom's hostages, about welfare assistance being provided to their families in the home country, and how loan payments were being suspended for the duration. We never heard about anything of a similar nature being undertaken by the United States government on behalf of its hostages.

Finally, the embassy—very reluctantly on its part agreed to forward one message a week to the States for any Americans still hiding out in Kuwait. They also made food and cash available in small amounts, but only a few of the Americans ever learned about this assistance.

After almost three months of lying low, hiding on a 24-hour basis from the Iraqis and their stool pigeons, the group decided that we could use the services of a reliable physician. Paul Kennedy was pressed into service to contact a Kuwaiti doctor who was married to an Irish nurse and was the father of two children.

The physician, now a member of the Kuwaiti Resistance, was brought in through the garage to Kennedy's ninth floor apartment. We were all assembled there, but Chris, Ken Hoyle, and myself had specific problems. I was still bothered occasionally by the colitis; Chris by high blood pressure, which was controllable by the proper pill intake; and Ken by bronchial asthma.

Ken's problem was the most serious because the prognosis was death were he to be afflicted with a severe attack while without medication. However, he would know when an attack was coming on. He could then be rushed to the hospital, where he would be an easy target for the Iraqis as would anyone who had accompanied him.

We had talked about this problem among ourselves earlier, noting the need for an Arab to take him to the hospital. Imad expressed his willingness to perform this task if needed. However, like the rest of us, he became more cautious as time went on and had made it apparent about the time of the doctor's visit that he was no longer available for that duty.

The doctor and his wife were no sooner inside Kennedy's apartment when she said in a voice limned with a soft Irish brogue that we could all use a haircut. She was too late. We had decided weeks before to let our hair grow until freed. Many of us also had beards, but we kept them neatly trimmed.

The Kuwaiti doctor spent about two hours listening to our alleged and factual complaints and treating our various ailments. From Resistance resources, we were also given added supplies of medicines, bandages, various spray-on ointments, and Bacitracin, which would be very beneficial were we to be cut by flying glass.

The doctor gave us a running commentary about what was happening around the city and the country itself under the Iraqi occupation. He confirmed many of the stories we had heard through the grapevine about atrocities and executions. He horrified us all by one account after another in this vein, including the story about a young Kuwaiti physician, who was fatally shot right in front of his wife for carrying saline drips in his car. One bullet in the head was the typical method of execution.

He smiled proudly when he related how the Resistance had ambushed the top Iraqi secret police official and blown off his head. In turn, the Iraqis had seized a Lebanese man, who had attempted to plant a time bomb in the Plaza Hotel, which was attached to the Al-Muthanna complex and was also the headquarters of the secret police. He had been quickly executed.

In light of these horror stories and many more, the group held a series of covert meetings to decide on ways to further tighten up security. We already had many security rules, but John Levins was repeatedly breaking them, and now the Hoyles were walking their dog in the open. It was as though they thought themselves invisible—that they could go outside almost at will because they were immortal and nothing would come of it.

As usual, the violators of the rules pledged to renew their sense of security, not only for their sakes but for ours, too. Maybe they had a death wish or whatever. Fine, but don't take us with you. Incredibly, John would soon be up to his old tricks of blatantly breaching the rules.

Ken and Magda Hoyle were returning to their apartment after an outing with their poodle, Samson, when they were accosted by a Jordanian truck driver. He was in the building to move out the furniture of the Syrian couple, who had lived directly across the hallway from the Hoyles. He verbally accused them of being English, of being from Britain, but they contended they were Czechoslovakian. The Jordanian didn't buy it. He put his wrists together to indicate that the Hoyles would soon be in handcuffs.

The Syrians were the same people who had been telling their next door neighbors, the Kuwaiti family of Al-Awadi, not to have anything to do with the Hoyles. It was too risky for them, the Syrians had warned. The Hoyles were westerners and would soon be taken away by the Iraqis.

The Syrians had expressed a preference for Saddam Hussein because the Iraqis said they were going to give all non-Kuwaitis in the country ownership of their rented apartments. Under Kuwaiti law, foreigners were never permitted to own property.

One day when Dave, the Hoyles, and I were playing bridge in my apartment, Al-Awadi called me, using our secret code, and said the secret police had just been at his door to demand to know who lived in the Hoyles' apartment. He claimed he was a new resident and had no idea. Without hesitation, the police had broken down the Hoyles door and went inside, pushing Samson aside. Now they were just sitting there, awaiting the return of the occupants.

The Hoyles wanted to go back to their place at once to check on Samson's safety, but we held them back. A hurry-up meeting was called, bringing Paul and John on the run. Even before they arrived, the Hoyles had pushed their way out of my apartment and hurried away to check on Samson. I was really ticked off. What the hell were they thinking of? Their actions were very selfish and terribly risky for all of us.

I knew in a way that I was being hypercritical, but self-preservation will do that to you—particularly since I was well informed about the Iraqi atrocities. I was also a bit surprised because Ken and Magda were easily the most mature and easiest to get along with among anyone in the group. Of course, they were taken into custody as soon as they arrived at their apartment and whisked away to detention rooms at the Regency Hotel.

We also had security rules governing how anyone who got picked up was to contact the group. I must say Ken and Magda held fast to those rules. No way was anyone to contact the group if they thought the phone was bugged. If you could call out, call only from the lobby where the Iraqis could not see the number you were dialing.

A few hours later, they did call very briefly to say they were returning to their apartment to get some clothes and personal things. Obviously, they would be returning in the company of secret police officers. We alerted Imad and the Kuwaiti neighbor, Al-Awadi, to watch out for them. The Hoyles had not said a word about the rest of us.

Imad shadowed the Hoyles and their escorts from the time they entered the building until they left. Al-Awadi listened to their voices when they were in their apartment. Imad reported back personally, Al-Awadi by phone.

We never saw either Ken or Magda again. According to Imad, they returned to the Regency Hotel with Samson in tow and ten days later flew to Baghdad. After that, we lost track of them. (1)

I imagined frequently that Samson was the only "French dog hostage" at a strategic site in Iraq.

Chapter 21

Running Amok

The secret police returned to the building the very next day after rounding up Ken and Magda and put their Arab informers through the third degree. A few Arabs lived in the complex and were responsible for its security under an agreement we knew they had made with the Iraqis.

Unfortunately for them, our security was so exemplary that they didn't know of the group's existence. Ken and Magda had either been seen by the secret police while walking Sampson outdoors, or the elderly Syrian couple, in collusion with the Jordanian truck driver, had betrayed them. These Syrians were not members of the Arab security force.

The leader of the Arab security force was an Iraqi, an educated man, who was permanently angry because either the Palestinians or the Iraqi soldiers had stolen his expensive automobile from the garage. He was so upset with his own people we doubted he would tell them about us even if he knew.

Imad swore that the Iraqi had no idea we were in deep hiding in the Al-Muthanna complex. He had made it his business to try to be in the company of the Iraqi whenever he was visited by the secret police so he would know exactly what they were up to at any moment.

Ignoring Imad, who was playing his Gunga Din role, the secret police thugs grabbed the Iraqi and began slapping him around, kicking him in the butt and thighs.

"You told us there were no westerners in the building! There were! Why didn't you tell us?" they bellowed in his face.

Imad said later the Iraqi did have some awareness that Ken and Magda lived in the building because he had seen them once on an elevator before Imad had short-circuited all but one of them. For some reason, the Iraqi never thought of them as Westerners and continued to deny that he knew of any westerners at all.

Imad, catching the gist of the conversation and not wanting to get caught up in the slugfest, slipped quietly into the shadows as though he were of no importance and then disappeared. He always had the knack for doing this—turning first into an innocent bystander, next a gray shadow, and finally an invisible ghost. When necessary, he would just mumble he had work to do and leave. Hardly anyone paid him any attention.

He was a first class engineer and could fix or disable any piece of equipment in the building. Yet, he passed himself off successfully as a lowly worker whose day was never long enough to finish all his work.

Our worst nightmare came true when the secret police sent some of their agents to take up residence in the Hoyles' apartment. Imad brought the news, and we were thunderstruck. Our greatest fear became an obsession that these policemen would undertake a thorough sweep of every floor in the building. How best would we be able to evade their omnipotent tentacles?

We held a series of furtive meetings to discuss ways to tighten security even more now that members of the secret police were our neighbors. We undertook further camouflage of our entranceways, reassured one another we would obey all the rules involving light and sound, exercised the greatest caution in using the telephone, stuck fast to all codes, and maneuvered between apartments with laudatory caution.

We beseeched John to shape up and be more responsible in his activities and movements about the complex. Paul berated him for past errors and breaches of security and threatened him physically were he to screw up our cover.

Falling back into his IRA persona, Paul said on more than one occasion, "I'll kneecap you if it's the last thing I do, you stupid son-of-a-bitch, if you bloody pull a cock-up!"

John, never a blushing violet when it came to the issue of his masculinity and dignity, gave it as well as he took it in such squabbles. Inevitably, we would have to step in to keep them from pounding each other. In time, Imad became the referee of their donnybrooks.

Of great concern to us was the possibility that John was still storing information about us in his computer. We had caught him at it before and had insisted he erase the material. Imad contended that John had printed out a copy of the security rules with our initials on it and left it with Ken and Magda. He had a sense he had recently seen the list on the coffee table in the Hoyles' apartment. We groaned in unison, picturing the Iraqi secret policemen scrutinizing the printout and trying to decipher its meaning.

John was completely unpredictable, immature, and without common sense. I recalled that earlier he had printed out a list of all our names and addresses and sent them by mail to a plethora of people to let them know our whereabouts. Fine. Who else had seen the list?

Even earlier, he had slipped a piece of paper with his name and apartment number under every door in the complex. The recipients were told he was their natural leader, and they should report to him for assignments.

John's personal habits didn't help to make him any more lovable. He continued to refuse to bathe, saying he would do so only when the Yanks and the Brits charged into the city. Exasperated, we periodically forced him into the shower to soak.

His apartment was a pigpen. We had to spray it constantly to keep the cockroaches and their colleagues at bay. Moreover, he was so helpless—or perhaps so manipulative—we also sterilized his drinking water, washed his clothes, and cooked his food. He once tried to cook eggs by seasoning them with cloves. It was his last effort as a chef.

We made it very clear to him that he was considered a disruptive factor by the entire group. I especially was becoming very turned off by him because he lived diagonally across from me and spent more time with me than any other member of the group.

John would listen quietly to lengthy critical recitations about his activities and then suddenly turn on us in a burst of anger to say, "Bloody off, mates. I'm tired of you using me for a punching bag. It's not fair. I'm always thinking of ways to help the group. Bloody thanks I get for it."

What was just about the final straw—the proverbial one that breaks the camel's back and, in this case, the group's back—came when I heard a loud rumbling noise one morning out in the hallway by my door.

It was *de rigeur* in such instances to call the other members and alert them to possible danger. John didn't answer his phone, but I thought nothing of it while I went on calling the others. I checked my tiny peephole. There was nothing to be seen, and I reported this by phone to the other group members. I continued to call John's number in the coded manner. No answer.

Hours went by, and I couldn't raise him. I didn't want to leave my place and check on him because I was fearful of walking into an Iraqi trap. It would be just like the bastards to wait in hiding for any poor sucker who rose to the bait.

At first, I couldn't believe John had left his apartment without notifying the group. Even if he had intended to just roam around within the confines of the building, he was obligated to let us know. Shortly after the seizure of the Hoyles, the group had gone to maximum security status, which made his unexplained absence even more galling.

The hours went slowly by while we wondered whether he had been picked up. Australian or not, the Iraqis were calling the shots and could arrest anyone at any time. Besides, you never knew from day to day when another nationality was going to be proscribed by them. We became convinced the damned fool had slipped out of the complex and had been nabbed. He would be the third member we had lost within days!

About 6 p.m., I heard a key in my lock, and the door swung back to reveal John standing there with an expression of baby innocence. In he sauntered without ever having called to alert me he was coming by. Another breach of security!

"You sonofabitch," I blasted him, "where the hell have you been? We've been worried to death about you, thinking you were picked up and being tortured and God knows what." All he could say was, "Oh, was I supposed to call?" "Don't pull that Joe Dummy act with me, John. You helped write the rules. You signed and agreed to them. Where have you been?"

I couldn't believe my ears. He said he had gone out to check on the Evangelical church to see whether any food was stored there.

When I asked to see the food, he replied, "I don't have any. There wasn't any there."

"How could you go out when we were under maximum security?"

"Oh, were we? It wasn't clear to me."

I tried for the next four hours to get John to think logically about what his misadventure had meant to us. How we had been put in fear of our lives because he might have been picked up and been tortured and given us away.

I had informed the group by phone about his return and my lengthy discussion with him. Some of them were of a mind even then that he had to go—out of the group, out of the building. He should be banned. Shunned.

I reported these comments to John without revealing who had said what. He still didn't get it. He had put us in jeopardy by leaving the building without good reason. Just wandering around inside the complex was dangerous enough now that the secret police were living in the building.

Imad came by and laid it right on the line to John by telling him he had been spotted leaving the building by the Iraqis. John expressed disbelief.

"You think I'm lying?" Imad pressed. "You went down to the garage on the basement floor, walked out the exit to the street, and then went around by the Plaza Hotel, where the secret police are. From there, you went through some back buildings, crossed over Fahd Al-Salim Street, and down to the church."

John looked like some little kid who had been caught with his hand in the cookie jar, but he still held fast to his position that he had not been spotted. Imad insisted he had been.

Even then, the secret police were still looking for an Iranian, who had been reported coming out of the building earlier in the day. John had a long, scraggly red beard and hadn't showered in weeks. He was about as unkempt as any human could possibly be.

"An Iranian with a red beard?" John scoffed.

I pointed out that Iranians do have red hair. Even some Saudis have reddish copper color hair. He could very well have been taken for an Iranian.

Imad had his number. You could see that John was becoming very attentive to what Imad was saying. He had compromised security. He had put the group in jeopardy. The Iraqis were hot on his trail. A look of genuine fear washed over his face. John became ashen.

Imad even told him he probably would have to leave the group, get out of the building, go far away from us. He had been taking unnecessary risks at our expense. Imad said I was the one most at risk because of John's foolhardiness since I lived the closest to him.

I told John I had only one objective: to survive and go home to my family. I didn't want John to screw up that objective in any way. In my mind, he was doing just that.

John became very serious, took the chip off his shoulder, dropped his mantle of machismo. We tried to explain the facts of life to him over dinner. There were just John, Imad, and myself. The last person I wanted there right then was Paul Kennedy, who undoubtedly would have done John in without any wasted motion.

During dinner, I tried anew to explain the systems of logic and how he could apply them to his thinking. He listened attentively. I was hopeful he was beginning to understand what I was saying. It was not to be. He eventually became defensive again and accused us of turning him into the group's punching bag. He implied that I particularly was becoming increasingly paranoid.

"You bet your ass I am, John, and it's all because of your inane abuse of the rules, your constant breaking of the rules, and your insistence that you can run amok without bringing a load of crap down on the rest of us."

Returning fire, all he could think to say was, "I was not spotted. I don't care what Imad says."

Calmly, softly, Imad fixed him with his deep brown eyes and asked, "How do you know you weren't spotted, John?"

John replied matter-of-factly, "Because I didn't see anyone. That's why."

I groaned, remembering all the time I had just wasted talking with him about thinking and acting logically. He was still convinced he hadn't been spotted by the secret police because he hadn't seen anyone spying on him. God give us strength for the fools these mortals be.

Imad looked at him with a mixture of incredulity and dismay. "That makes a lot of sense, John. Remarkable. You don't see the secret police—who are paid not to be seen—so then you haven't been seen by them. As Mr. Spock would say, 'That's eminently logical.'"

John's indiscretions were considered by the group without any final decision made immediately as to whether or not he should leave the Al-Muthanna complex. Get lost. Go away. Anywhere. He had his detractors, but surprisingly, he also had his defenders.

Meanwhile, we intensified our efforts to become as invisible as possible, praying and hoping that the Iraqis wouldn't carry out any floor-by-floor sweeps of the building. We visited less and less, only whispered when we did, and used only the light from the TV screen to see by.

Imad learned from his Iraqi friend that the secret police officers living in the Hoyles' apartment were specifically told when assigned to the building to search it apartment by apartment.

Luckily for us, these policemen only slept in the building and worked elsewhere the rest of the time.

The Iraqi told Imad that the policemen were too tired when they returned late in the evening to carry out any such searches. To avoid any official retribution or punishment, they filed false reports about the periodic hunts they conducted within the huge complex.

Just when I thought John was getting his act together, Paul Kennedy called and informed me that John could be heard blabbering away on his telephone in English in the hallway outside his doorway! It must have been about midnight. I had been watching TV. I went quickly to the door and listened with my ear pressed against it. Son-of-a-bitch, if he wasn't!

I cracked my door open, checked the broken piece of glass to scrutinize the hallway, and stuck my head out. "John, you horse's ass, get back inside now, and close that door. Call me! Pronto!"

Within a minute, the phone rang. "What the hell are you thinking of talking in English on the phone with your damned door wide open? Are you insane?"

John, undeterred by my barrage of questions, explained that his phone hookup had broken down and he had installed a new outlet in the tiny hallway inside his doorway.

"I'll be right over," I snapped.

Inside his apartment, I glared at him and harangued him about his latest stupidity. "How could you hook up the phone right next to the door? Why didn't you put it in another room? Why did you have to leave the door to the hallway open while you were on the phone? I'm the one at risk, not you. They come looking for whoever's talking in English, and they could find me out."

I continued to glare at him. I was so angry that I really considered taking a punch at him. "Don't you get it? You're an Australian. They're not looking for you. I'm an American. They are looking for me."

When I calmed down, I informed John he would have to move the phone, hang a heavy blanket over the interior hallway of his apartment to muffle any sound, and keep the effing door closed at all times. I wanted this done immediately. John assured me he would get on it right away, but once again, he let me down. It wasn't until eight days later, and only after we had had a series of violent arguments that he finally finished moving the phone and hanging the blanket.

I could not understand why he consistently breached security rules. Rules that we had drawn up in a democratic manner. Rules to which he had agreed and acknowledged by signing his name. Why did he think that somehow they only applied to the rest of us but not to him? What was so special about him? So sacrosanct? To me, he was an idiot most of the time.

John's rejoinder inevitably was that I was paranoid to begin with since I was solely fixed on the idea of getting out safely and returning to Jill and the children and that my paranoia was increasing by leaps and bounds. He cautioned I had better get hold of myself, or I would soon be going loopy.

His charge of paranoia hit close to the bone. As a doctor, I recognized paranoia, but I also realized that to a degree paranoia was inescapable by any of us, given our situation. I admitted to my paranoia but noted that it could have been reduced significantly and quickly if he began at once to adhere to our security rules. It was more than paranoia. I recognized my own symptoms of post traumatic stress, a condition I dismissed twenty years before; my constant fears, my sudden recalling of war experiences from 20 years before, the North Vietnamese in the hut with me, the explosions, the dead and dying in Vietnam. All these memories I had totally suppressed for 20 years, had never discussed with my family, not even my wife. Now they were bombarding me daily, and I didn't know how to handle it.

"Don't you realize, John, that it was bad enough before? Never knowing when the Iraqis and their pals would be sweeping the complex. Now we've got some of the goddamned secret police living in the building. We're like sheep staked out only a hundred feet from the wolf's den. What does it take to smarten you up, for Christ's sake?"

What did I get for an answer? "Not to worry, Rob. They're too busy robbing the other units to pay us any heed."

I shook my head in amazement. "Is that right, John? Well, did you ever consider that if they're trashing the apartments, sooner or later, they're going to hit one of the group's, and that person is going to talk? You can count on it. They know all the cute ways to make people talk and in a hurry."

John's face was blank. "So, we'll get the word and then skip out of here. There're lots of places to hide. I have the keys to that Frenchman's villa. We can always move in there. Very posh."

Chapter 22

Loose Cannons

On November 3rd, I received my first message from home on Voice of America (VOA). It came from my Holy Cross College roommate, Don Morrissey, who opened by saying, "This is Sport, calling Emmet from Holy Cross."

Like the messages on the BBC, we taped the VOA ones, too—not that there were many. Actually, I was really ticked off that it had taken so long for the VOA to begin sending messages to us during its broadcasts.

The BBC was far ahead of them in this regard. Still, the messages from home always made my day. They also left me a little teary-eyed and filled with thoughts of happy times and my loved ones so far away and so out of reach.

I remembered Jill sounded very poignant one time when she said softly, "I love you, and we'll be thinking of you." Then she gave way to my daughter, Anna, who said, "Daddy, if you've got my letter, please write me back. I miss you, and I love you . . . ."

She was followed by my little Patricia, then only four years old, who almost got me bawling when she gushed, "I'll see you, Daddy, when Christmas Day comes. My cousin, Jim (he was about five), is mean to me sometimes, but that's all right because he's good to me at other times. Love you."

One of my sisters reported the weather in Boston "feels more like winter now. I planted 15 bulbs last week, courtesy of Jim—

who, by the way, is turning 50 next week. Wish you could be here for his birthday party."

I wished so, too. Terribly.

It was impossible to pick up the VOA for more than 90 days because we couldn't tune into its frequency from Kuwait City. We just recently could hear the VOA and then only at about 1:30 a.m. when the atmospheric conditions were right. I had been raising hell with the embassy people in the city for months because of the VOA's failure to beam its signal properly into our range. I sent my family notes about this to get them to lean on the State Department and others to rectify the situation.

We were never enamoured of the VOA because it always sounded like a mouthpiece for the U.S. government. I was told that the VOA took some 70 days before it made any mention of hostages. It consistently featured long-winded interviews with a bunch of blowhards who usually didn't know what they were talking about, out-of-date music, ridiculous programs about trends in every facet of life, slanted crap about world events. It drove us crazy to hear all this esoteric bull shit with not a word about helping us to survive in an occupied country.

Voice of America was giving us arcane baloney when we were looking for solid advice on how to protect ourselves against poison gas, chemical warfare, high explosive shells, booby traps, informers, spies, and everything else we had to contend with relative to the Iraqis. The VOA's broadcasts could never compare to the BBC's Gulf Link, which began providing us with messages from home long before it did. We could also still hear Radio Moscow, Radio Netherlands, and Radio Australia, which was doing a fine job in sending messages to the Aussies in Kuwait.

It was about this time that Paul Kennedy and two of his Irish friends decided they would try to get up to Baghdad, using the *laissez-passer* and the ID cards similar to those provided to Chris and myself.

I thought it was a good idea, but Kennedy was informed that once he left the building—in effect breaching security although in a worthy cause—he was out. He could not come back into the building. I thought he would take umbrage at this decision. Instead, he said it didn't really matter because he had already decided to move out and go live with two of his Irish pals.

So off they went to the airport. Using the temporary documents, they were cleared for a flight to Baghdad. Upon arrival, they used the documents to register with the Iraqis for clearance to leave the country and requested the necessary exit visas. The Iraqis listed them for a flight out but said the exit visas were temporarily on hold.

Kennedy and his mates remained at the Al Rashid Hotel in Baghdad for nearly ten days doing God knows what—if the other Irish were as mercurial and mysterious as he at least feigned to be when in Kuwait City.

Back in Kuwait City, John began to raise a stink as soon as Kennedy had left the complex, complaining he also had a right to go out if Kennedy had been allowed to do so. When we pointed out that Kennedy was only allowed to leave on the understanding he would not be permitted to return, John expressed disbelief.

"No way. He'll be back!" he warned us. "You'll see. I know that Irish bastard. He'll be back. So why shouldn't I go out? I want to get up to Baghdad, too."

He was told in no uncertain terms he could leave anytime he desired, but if he left, he would never be allowed to come back into the building and rejoin the group. We explained we had worked hard to make the members as invisible as possible to the outside world, and his coming and going would only serve to attract attention to us.

"John," I cautioned, "you've breached security so often, broken rules you helped to draw up and agreed to—we just can't permit you to leave and return. It would be a major breach, one that could jeopardize every single one of us."

John wasn't buying our position at all. For the next four days, he lobbied us individually and as a group to agree to his leaving and being allowed to come back. I couldn't help but remember Kennedy's incisive reading of John: "You get an ice cream, and the creep, Levins, has to have an ice cream, too. He's like a kid. An idiot kid."

In the end, John lost because the group held fast to its decision. Okay, he said, he would leave and not return. Did he fully understand his position? Oh, yes. He was never to come back into the building once he had left.

He agreed to sign a statement spelling this out as well as the fact that he couldn't take his car. It had been left to him by a friend who had gone to Baghdad, and the car was still registered in the friend's name. If John were caught driving the car not registered to him, he could be arrested. Who knows what he would tell the Iraqis if that occurred?

John typed the agreement on his word processor for all of us to sign and then destroy. Undaunted, John insisted on putting every one of our names in full at the bottom to indicate where we were to sign it. This was anathema to us, and the agreement was torn up.

That was the last straw for us, and we called a group meeting to discuss the matter with John. Even Cliff, the English publican, agreed to be in attendance. He had sworn he would never attend another meeting with John after the one in which Kennedy had threatened to kill John and Cliff had called them both "children."

For several hours, each of us in his own way and out of his own life's experiences, attempted to prove to John once and for all that he was just one big walking-around security risk for us. We cited one instance after another of his breaches of security to underline our position.

Mainly, we cited his compulsion and obsession to move about when there was absolutely no reason for it—his hungering to get out around the building and the outdoors. His need, it seemed to us, to let himself be observed as though he were the conquering hero for all to see and be remembered. We, in effect, told John that he had a hero complex, that he hoped somehow to come out of the occupation as a true hero, to ride into Kuwait City aboard the first U.S. tank, and to be hailed universally for his courage.

He was informed the real fact of the matter was that no medals were going to be given out to any of us when the Emir and his crowd returned. The occupation was just one of those unfortunate things that innocent people get caught up in. None of us, including himself, had done anything of exceptional note and bravery.

The only argument he was able to make in his defense was to tell us how "terribly difficult and stressful" it was for him to be constantly on the phone—organizing buses for Westerners who were to be evacuated to Baghdad. He went on for about half an hour, relating how "challenging" this task was as though he were a genuine combat hero.

I had had about enough of his bull shit, and I looked him in the eye and told him he didn't know what difficulty is, what stress is, and what it is to be challenged under the worst possible conditions and still go on about one's duty. I had never mentioned anything specific about Vietnam, but by then, I had had a bellyful of his fanciful heroics.

"John, you're talking to someone who was in Vietnam, out on Hill 21, Marble Mountain, up north by the border. You're looking at one of two military dentists who were decorated for their actions that year in Vietnam. So, John, I can't get too worked up about your heroics. Why don't you just shut up at this point?"

And he did, for the rest of that day.

Three days later, John signed the agreement, which did not list our names. We immediately ripped it up. We bid John goodbye, wished him well, and urged him to keep in touch by phone. Then, once again, John broke the rules by taking his friend's car out of the garage and driving it away to the villa, where he intended to stay.

There was no keeping John in Kuwait City after Kennedy had made his trip to Baghdad. No way was Kennedy going to get an edge on John. When John left for Baghdad, he told friends he would be away for three days. In fact, he was there in the Iraqi capital for nine days, raising one ruckus after another in every embassy still open in Baghdad.

One friend with the Australian Embassy itself reportedly described him as "well-intentioned but manic, a man who only completes about ten percent of what he sets out to do."

On his return to Kuwait City, he passed along the information that the best way to get a UN passport was to go to its office in Baghdad as soon as possible.

When I talked to him on the phone shortly after his return, he said the UN could send an Iraqi to pick me up at a rendezvous of my choice. The Iraqi, of all people, would get me safely through to Baghdad.

"John, tell me quickly. You didn't tell anyone where I was hiding, did you?" I questioned him.

I was not to worry, he said. He had not informed either the UN people or his Iraqi contacts about my whereabouts. "You think I'm crazy? I'm the only one who can communicate with you as far as they're concerned. Trust me!"

All I could think of when I hung up was why didn't the UN in New York just issue me a *laissez-passer* instead of continuing to act so bureaucratically?

No sooner had we been rid of John, the walking time bomb, when Paul Kennedy returned from Baghdad and rang us up to say he was planning to return to his apartment. His announcement stunned us all, and a group meeting was called immediately.

"He can't come back here," Imad said flatly. "He was told if he went out, that was it. He could not return to the building. It's far too risky. He'll only draw attention to us, tip the Iraqis that there are westerners in the building. I'm in danger."

I fully agreed with Imad, who had assumed increasing leadership of the group—if for no other reason than that he thought so clearly and was so damned pragmatic about things. I had also observed that Imad was distancing himself from the group, the constant security breaches were a serious threat to his life. In fact, the secret police had recently approached Imad and quietly told him to turn over the Americans. Imad was shocked, but held his ground.(1)

"Imad's right," Dave said. "Kennedy does not come back. He signed the agreement when he left. He has a place to go to with his Irish mates. The fact that he says the Iraqis all know him makes no difference. He's been gone for days. Now they'll see him coming back inside. It'll only take one snake to betray us. Don't forget that secret police are living here. They'll be all over him like a blanket."

Kennedy was informed he was "persona non grata" with the group. Of course, he would always be thought of as a friend and as one who had made some fine contributions to the group's welfare. But a deal was a deal, and he had to live with it.

In the end, he argued he had a genuine Irish passport so the Iraqis were not about to bother him, apprehend him, or whatever. We countered that the Iraqis could proscribe anyone they wanted to and begin picking up the Irish, Danish, New Zealanders, Australians, or any other nationality which up to that time had been left alone.

I never really understood Kennedy. He always wanted to be about and give the impression he was involved in many clandestine activities. Now he was out, living in comfort and safety with Irish friends, but almost demanding that he be allowed to rejoin the group.

I soon learned how hard he could push when it came to achieving one of his desired objectives. My phone rang, and he was at the other end, ranting about what a bloody ass I was for keeping him out. Like it was my decision alone to keep him out.

"You shouldn't be so hard on me, Rob, especially since I've got some secret information for you. I can't give it to you over the phone."

I suggested that he tell me in our code talk, but he said it wasn't possible. He had to tell me in person. I wondered whether it was just a ploy to get into the building.

"You can't come into the building, Paul. You know the rules. Now give me the information. Whatever it is."

He insisted he could only give it to me in person and that he had to come into the building anyway to retrieve some of his personal things. He said he only wanted to come back overnight and would leave the next morning, but the group continued to maintain a solid front. Again, Imad was the point man in fighting against Kennedy's return. I couldn't blame Imad. He was the one who faced the greatest threat of execution if he were betrayed to the Iraqis.

I relayed the group's decision to Kennedy, who moaned that it was very important for him to be back in the group. In being left out, he felt that the group had branded him as "socially unacceptable," a stigma he could not handle.

I went back to the group and relayed his latest argument. We agreed he could still be part of the group but could not come into the building under any circumstances.

Kennedy became furious when informed that he was never to enter the building and charged me again with unilaterally making the decision to keep him out at all costs. I retorted he was being ridiculous. With that, he chilled my blood by announcing I would never get his secret information.

"If I don't get back inside, I won't tell you what the UN in Baghdad said about your passport. I won't give you a letter I've got for you from your wife, and I won't tell you what she said to me when I called her in Boston."

"You son-of-a-bitch," I yelled into the phone. "You can't do this! You've got to tell me! It was a group decision. You can't hold me responsible. Give me the information. You have to give it to me!"

Kennedy, however, refused to be moved and repeated that there was no way I was going to get the information—especially the news from Jill—unless I got him back into the building.

In a mixture of rage and depression, I slammed down the phone. Now what to do? The bastard was holding back information for me from the UN in Baghdad and, more importantly, a letter from Jill and what she had told him over the phone.

The Brits, Dave and Neil, were cool guys—not at all emotional like me and John and Kennedy. I called, and Neil answered. I said he had to help me with Kennedy. It was bad enough before—dealing with John's filth, stupidity, and breach of rules. Now I had Kennedy trying to blackmail me to let him come back into the building.

Neil listened patiently and agreed to take care of it. He called Kennedy immediately and told him he was being an unmitigated bastard for trying to blackmail me and also the group in his efforts to get back into the building. He explained I was not solely responsible for the decision to keep him out. It was a group decision—in fact, a unanimous decision.

Kennedy protested the use of the word "blackmail," saying he felt he had been socially ostracized, made to look foolish in public. All he wanted was to return to the building. He even went so far as to apologize for the commotion he was causing. Neil reminded Kennedy he had been told in no uncertain terms that if he left the building, he stayed out. He had stated his understanding at the time and had left. Now he had to live with his choice.

Neil said he should just forget it. He was not going to be allowed back. He should stop blackmailing me about the information he purportedly had picked up in Baghdad and hand it over at once. Kennedy was not going to get anywhere with such cruel tactics.

The discussion ended without either side giving ground. I was pissed. I called one of Kennedy's roommates that evening and told him what was going on. Without getting too specific, I said I was emotionally drained by Kennedy's actions because he was acting so deplorably. The roommate said he would look into it. Almost two weeks passed before Kennedy offered to tell me about the information he had garnered in Baghdad.

Unbeknownst to Kennedy, I had my own way to get information from Baghdad and home. He was a fool to think I would count strictly on him and not backstop his efforts. Through the U.S. Embassy in Kuwait City, which was becoming somewhat more responsive to its own citizens still holed up in the country, I forwarded a message, querying the status of the UN *laissez-passer* to the wife of the Australian ambassador to Iraq. John had contacted her when he was in the city about my ongoing efforts to obtain the documentation.

She was a great lady, constantly working on behalf of many of us and contacting selected UN people in Baghdad surreptitiously about our status. I would receive requests from her that the UN wanted head photos, sample signatures, and any other foolish thing they could think of to delay taking any real action in my case. She was tireless in attempting to get the UN to do something. She had to be careful in handling these requests for the *laissez-passer* because the UN office employed many Iraqis.

As for my hope to eventually obtain an Irish passport in lieu of the Irish *laissez-passer*, I learned again from Jill in a message sent by satellite to the embassy in Kuwait City that the Irish government was not going to issue it. Like the world would end if I was given one temporarily.

The only thing Kennedy was still holding over my head was the alleged letter he said he had from Jill and the gist of his conversation with her. Occasionally, I would call him to tell him how immoral he was to keep the information from me, but I made no real effort to press him for it. By that time, I was convinced he had no letter and had never talked to Jill on the phone in Boston. I heard later from Jill that she had never communicated with him.

Kennedy was definitely *persona non grata* with the group. He would never be allowed to come back into the building. John had been an unceasing pain in the ass. Kennedy was not only that but also a troublemaker and very argumentative. Not just argumentative, but malicious.

I truly believed that Kennedy was a deliberately malicious person. He had a dark side to him that constantly wanted to strike at people and bring them down low. How many times had he threatened to maim or kill John Levins?

And how mean-spirited could he be to say he had news for me from Jill? That was despicable. He even had the gall 12 days after he returned from Baghdad to tell me I could have the letter—a letter he could have given to Imad at anytime to bring to me.

Incredibly, the letter, of course, was not from Jill. It was written by Kennedy. I would not lower myself to repeat even a line of it.

Chapter 23

Man of Action

By mid-November, the group consisted of only Dave and Neil, Chris and Cliff, a few Filipinos, whom we saw less and less of each passing day, Imad, and myself. Imad came and went fleetingly but continued to look after our interests at all times. John would call in on most days, still very prickly because he wasn't allowed inside to even visit. Overall, he was happy to be living outside where he had complete freedom to carry on his heroics and move about without restrictions vis-a-vis the group.

I passed most of my time when tired of my own company with Dave, Neil, and Chris. We were like so many ghosts drifting swiftly and unseen along the hallways and up and down the staircases to each other's apartments to socialize for a time. We had all the codes, secret knocks, and security rules down pat by then. We had, in effect, become invisible to any prying eyes—whether Arabs, looters, or the secret police.

Chris continued to mystify us by keeping his secret cache of liquor hidden. No matter how hard we tried, we could never unearth it or get him to disclose its whereabouts. All we knew was that he always managed to get a pleasant glow on day after day. We wouldn't have minded so much if he had shared it with us once in a while.

Cliff was of the same bent as Chris when it came to the booze. We were convinced that he also had a bottomless source somewhere, but he never made it known to the rest of us either. He became more reclusive as time went by, and we saw less and less of him except when he would join us for an occasional meal.

I guess you could say by the middle of November we were "cruising"—just going along day after day, trying not to make waves, keeping an intensely low profile, never making any noise, never being spotted because we knew from the constantly alert Imad "who to watch out for."

Imad was the group's leader by that time for all intents and purposes because we were so beholden to him for our security, food, and well-being. He never failed to keep us supplied with fresh vegetables and, when he could obtain them, fresh meat and bread.

We usually saw him late at night during one of his security rounds when he would stop by for a quick chat and provide us with any worthwhile news. He seldom ate with us because he didn't like western food except for steak and chips. We drank pretty good, too, and as a Muslim, he wasn't in favor of alcohol.

He was not always the bearer of happy news. He brought us a warning about then that the Iraqis were discussing the possibility of placing an anti-aircraft battery on the roof of the Al-Muthanna complex. Such batteries had already been installed on adjacent structures along Al-Hilali Street.

"Any such installation could be a major problem for us," he warned. "There are many soldiers assigned to each battery, and more than likely they would be bivouacked right here in the Al-Muthanna. Who knows what apartments they might break into and appropriate for living quarters?"

"Shit. Would it never end?" I muttered.

The news prompted the convening of a group meeting to consider what action could be taken in the event the battery was actually placed on the Al-Muthanna's roof. It was most unwelcome news—not only for the potential danger it posed to us but also because we periodically went up to the roof for fresh air and sunshine.

Even without the Iraqis on the roof, there was danger involved. On emerging from the roof doorway, one had to move very quickly because there was an open space to cross where you could be spotted for a second by Iraqis in the upper levels of the Meridien and Plaza Hotels. That hazard notwithstanding, Cliff and the two young Brits enjoyed going up on the roof. They said the air and the sunshine were necessary for their well-being and mental health. They certainly were maintaining great tans.

As if the news of the Iraqi battery was not troubling enough, Imad shortly informed us that a very professional gang of thieves was looting the building on a systematic basis, obviously intent on getting into every apartment on every floor to determine what was still available for the taking.

I was stunned to learn that the leader of this gang was a doctor, a pediatrician from the Kuwait government's own maternity hospital. When I heard he was an Iraqi, I was not as surprised, just pissed that in his nocturnal misadventures he might come across one or more of us and report us to his pals in the secret police.

Imad was insistent we had to do something about this Iraqi thief. I thought, fine, Imad, but what? We even contacted the Resistance and informed them we wanted the man stopped. They responded that such action could expose our group. We were just to avoid him at all costs. In the end, we decided that Imad and his security people would keep a close eye on the doctor and try to warn him off if he started poking into our area of the complex.

In any case, Imad decided to increase security to thwart the Iraqi doctor's gang from surprising us during one of its nocturnal raids. He picked up another bunch of steel locks and double bolts. Late at night, he would drill the necessary holes and insert the new locks and bolts. We gained additional peace of mind with the installation of this new hardware.

Now there was no way you could bounce the door open with just a sharp screwdriver and muscle. To get into one of our apartments thereafter, thieves would have to break down the entire door. Imad also locked the fire door adjacent to our apartments with a master key, but we could still open it from inside the corridor.

Thank God for Imad. Here was a man of action. He never waited passively to be a victim. He was always positive, always pragmatic, and down to earth. Once the group decided on a course of action, he was on it right away.

I had become so accustomed to living in deep hiding that I had little trouble going to sleep. As the months passed, I began to go to bed later and later so I would sleep until noon. I felt that the longer I slept in the daylight hours, the quieter my area was during the time the secret police might be moving about the building.

Throughout November, we heard via the different national radio broadcasts about the build-up of the Coalition forces in Saudi Arabia and hoped each day that General Schwarzkopf would unleash his air power again the Iraqis. What was the hold-up? Come December 2nd, it would be four months since Kuwait had been invaded. Meanwhile, with Paul and John out of the group, there was far less tension among the survivors and no arguments.

Imad had arranged to pick up some 20 kilos of flour, which put Dave in seventh heaven as he immensely enjoyed making fresh bread daily. While he would use the cooking gas to bake his various breads, we did our regular cooking on two-plate electrical burners saving our individual supplies of cooking gas for any squeeze that might occur later.

At that point in time, I was checking in with the U.S. Embassy about two or three times weekly for any messages received by satellite. There were very few, and they hardly ever had any worthwhile information regarding ways to maintain ourselves while hiding out. We received most of the ideas and instructions on survival from the Resistance or from each other. We put the information into the computer, printing out copies which Imad would distribute throughout the western community.

The Resistance was also supplying us with money and had given each of us about $700. Of course, it was in Kuwaiti dinars, which were not very acceptable—along with the Iraqi occupation script—in paying for various items, mostly foodstuffs.

We also knew Kennedy had received money from the Irish Embassy to distribute to the Irish in the city. I was on the list as being Irish as part of my cover to avoid arrest, but Kennedy never gave me a dime. John was also very cozy when it came to money. We knew at one time he had been given quite a large sum from his Australian contacts, and supposedly, he was to distribute part of it to us. John would only give us small amounts of this money, claiming that the sum was intended strictly for the Australian community in Kuwait.

We also knew John was collecting money from people he drove to the airport. He would just ask them for their loose change, small bills—noting that the money would be no good to them in Iraq. One time, he allegedly shook down a group of Germans for several thousand dollars worth of Kuwaiti dinars without sharing a penny of it with us. He would always contend he had other people requiring his assistance.

As always, just when things seemed to be going swimmingly, and we felt we were completely invisible, Imad would be the messenger of bad news. We had escaped the emplacement of the anti-aircraft battery and the forays of the Iraqi pediatrician, but now he informed us the Iraqis intended to make a very thorough "census" of the building. We knew this was the code word for looking for westerners. They had already conducted censuses in the adjacent buildings. Now they were coming into the Al-Muthanna complex within 12 to 24 hours.

It was panic time again in the group. We initially felt that we soon would be in the Iraqis' clutches. What could we possibly do to evade them? We couldn't remain in our apartments because Imad had heard they would be hitting one floor at a time and opening each apartment in order. Guards were to be posted so no one could escape up or down the stairs.

Once again, Imad came to the rescue with his clear thinking and ingenuity. He said he had just the place for all of us to hide if the Iraqis did undertake such a census. It was a so-called electrical room, adjacent to Dave's apartment. It measured 20 by 20 with solid concrete walls. If that was unacceptable, he could stash us in a little-known, large room at the top of one of the elevator shafts on the roof.

We voiced initial enthusiasm about his plan. All we had to do was furnish these potential hideouts with mattresses, chairs, several refrigerators stocked with food and water, and seal them, when necessary, from the inside.

But a strange malaise suddenly came over some in the group. Almost as one, they had concluded the jig was up.

They had struggled too hard and too long to remain free, and now they were weary of it all. They were paralyzed with the loss of will and could not find the strength to do what was needed to be done. Screw the census! Let the Iraqis come! They were not going to try to hide any longer. Imad shook his head sadly about such a defeatist stance and went off.

Once again, fate, in another one of those quirky, inexplicable twists and turns, intervened to save us. The report of the impending census turned out to be false and was never undertaken. The source of the rumor was an Arab.

For some strange reason—which was never made clear to us—he had been spotted slinking through the building in search of a Kuwaiti. Once the Kuwaiti's apartment was located and searched, he said he would not return to the building.

Chapter 24

Thanksgiving

Despite the restrictions imposed on us in deep hiding, as a New Englander, I was determined to celebrate Thanksgiving on the fourth Thursday in November with a memorable feast for the group.

Although John was now outside the group and living in his French villa, I called to ask him to try and get us a big turkey as the centerpiece for the dinner. John, however, was still outraged that we had refused to permit him to return to live in the building and caustically claimed that he had "more important things to do than to look for a bloody turkey."

Screw you, too, I thought, and immediately contacted Jawad Behbehani to ask whether he could find us a turkey. It was his impression, he said, that they were in short supply, but he would look around. While I naturally wanted a traditional turkey for the feast, I was reminded that we had about 30 frozen chickens stashed away.

I fixed on the following menu: Chicken, stuffing, gravy, corn and peas (canned), home made mashed potatoes (Chris' specialty), fresh bread (Dave's specialty), apple and blueberry pies (from canned fruit), and libations consisting of homemade wine, beer, and whiskey—followed by several Italian coffees and an Arab pastry.

Dr. Behbehani reported no luck in his quest for a turkey, but I had already reconciled myself to that eventuality. Then John called at nine o'clock on the morning of Thanksgiving Day to say that he was going to get a turkey at the Sultan Center shop on the Gulf Road.

"John," I said, "even if you were able to get the turkey, they'd only have the frozen kind, and there's no way we could get it thawed out in time to cook it for dinner today. But thanks anyway."

In truth, I was sorry that John couldn't come to the dinner. He had been my family's guest for Thanksgiving the past three years. Being a bit of a sentimentalist, I wondered briefly whether we still could invite him but rejected the idea. The group was definitely set against him because he had not cooperated in obtaining a turkey.

On the sly, Dave told me a funny story about the chickens. He had taken out three of them to thaw on the kitchen counter, only to have one fall prey to Dingleberry, the cat who had such a gourmet tooth for frozen meat. Before Dave caught on to the feline's enterprise, Dingleberry had devoured half of the bird, undeterred by its frozen state. We agreed we would cook the remnant anyway since the oven heat would destroy any bad microbes.

So the group and our guests—two Filipinos, including Lillibeth, my younger daughter Patricia's former babysitter, and a few Arab friends—sat down to eat two and a half roasted chickens. Nothing was said about the fact that one of the chickens was half-size.

Imad—who by this time had assumed the mantle of leadership in most of the group's operations because of his ability to move around freely and become privy to so much outside information—was not a fan of American cooking and only dabbled at the various vegetables and pies.

Since I was the instigator of the meal and the leading proponent of the Thanksgiving feast, I was permitted to say a few words before we began to eat. Instead of saying grace, I opted to read a poem by the German Jesuit, Rupert Mayer:

"Lord, what you will, let it be so;
Where you will lead, there we will go;
What is your will, help us to know,
Time and eternity are yours:
You give the years, the weeks, the hours—
Our time to learn from your will ours.
To share your burden brings no pain;
To forfeit all for you is gain:
Enough should we your own remain.
Because you will it, it is best;
Because you will it, we are blessed
Till in your hands our hearts find rest."

I'll have to admit it is one of those touching poems, and I became teary-eyed thinking of past holidays that I had spent with my family as a boy and a youth in Boston and the later ones with Jill and the children.

Cliff, the crusty publican, who usually had a steady glow on throughout the day, commented that I was "the sentimental type. Being British, I still don't know why this day is so important to you."

The focus of both family and food on Thanksgiving Day reminded me of the time Dave and I had set out 12 eggplants to be heated up and served to the group. Dingleberry had sniffed at them and, then to show his disdain, had urinated all over the tray. Since food was a critical item, Dave and I shrugged, rewashed them, and slipped the tray of eggplants into the oven. We figured what the members didn't know, wouldn't hurt them. "A little piss never hurt anyone."

Another time, good old Imad went foraging and came up with a great buy—40 kilos of cucumbers. I served those cucumbers every which way, even trying to make a pie of sorts out of them. People gingerly ate one slice but refused all attempts to get them to have a second serving.

When the cucumbers looked like they were beginning to turn and not wanting them to go to waste, we had the brilliant idea of pickling the remainder. The only problem was that we didn't quite know how to do it and actually didn't have the proper ingredients to carry it out nor the seal-proof bottles needed to store them. The result was that the newly-made pickles were digestible, but they generated a tremendous amount of flatulence. You get five to nine people breaking wind from such a source in a sealed room, and the result could be incredibly noisome and distressing.

Even through Thanksgiving Day, there was no let-up in the looting. It was months after the Iraqis had invaded the country, and the hard-line thieves were still finding stuff to steal. Day after day, we observed from our windows the trucks, averaging about 100 daily, headed for the Sheraton Roundabout and the road north to Basra. Not one of them ever left without being filled to the roof with loot. It was quite obvious that the Iraqis were then ransacking the thousands of deserted houses and offices in the city.

Quixotically, no army was immune from officialdom. The civilian thieves had to get clearance papers for their loot at the police station, off to the left along Al-Hilali Street, which was guarded by a 60-mm machine gun. The bastards would be out there first thing in the morning to begin lining up. Their empty vehicles, ready for looting, stretched along the right side of the street past our building and down to Fahd Al-Salim Street. This activity would continue throughout the day, not even ceasing on Friday, the Sabbath.

I had to wonder whether there was anything left of value in Kuwait after observing on many occasions how efficiently the Iraqis and their cohorts performed their thievery.

Chapter 25

Up to Baghdad

Immediately after Thanksgiving, Paul Kennedy and his assistant warden, known to me only as Brian, exerted tremendous pressure on anyone in Kuwait City with an Irish *laissez-passer* to get up to Baghdad as quickly as possible to register for an exit visa.

Kennedy pointed out that while he himself had obtained an exit visa to leave Iraq on his Irish passport, two others had been granted the visas with the same Irish documentation that I possessed. He informed me flat out that the Irish diplomats wanted me to get up to Baghdad no later than the first of the month.

"You've got to get up to Baghdad, Rob," he said over the phone, "to get the visa. No one here in Kuwait is ever going to get one. I know the Irish document will work for you. Everybody's getting out with the *laissez-passer* from the Poles, Germans, French, Spanish, and Indians."

Reluctantly, I had to agree with Kennedy that there seemed to be no other recourse. John Levins had earlier confirmed the same report on his return from Baghdad. Moreover, he said the UN *laissez-passer* would only be made available from the UN office in Baghdad.

Chris Chambers and I discussed the situation and agreed that we should chance the Irish papers in an effort to get out. We determined we would remain in Baghdad for two weeks. If the exit visas weren't forthcoming by then, we would return to the security of the group in the Al-Muthanna complex under Imad's leadership. It would be safer by then in Kuwait City if the Coalition forces began their assault. We reasoned they were far more likely to bomb the hell out of Baghdad than to inflict further damage on ravaged Kuwait City.

After informing Kennedy and Brian that we were set to go, they urged us to move into a so-called safe house in Kuwait City in the few remaining days before December 1st. The idea was for us to get away from our surroundings of the past four months and to unwind and relax in a secluded and secure apartment in the outlying Mishrif district.

We opted though to remain in our building until our departure because we felt we would be safer there under Imad's protection. He seemed to have the security of the building completely in hand. The secret police officers had even left the Hoyles' apartment. Imad had moved quickly to change the locks and remove the doorknobs to prevent their returning.

During the next few days, I telephoned about eight to ten friends to tell them of my plans so they wouldn't hear it later and think I had abandoned them. Among them were my oldest friends in Kuwait, George Daher and Jawad Behbehani. Both expressed their appreciation for letting them know I was "signing off" and wished me good luck. At this point I had been in daily contact with George for over 100 days.

I told George I was not going to inform the U.S. Embassy in Kuwait City that I was leaving. I felt that the remaining personnel could not have cared less, and the phone could be tapped. I did say I would contact the U.S. Embassy in Baghdad on my arrival there. I was a bit emotional in saying goodbye to George because of our long and warm relationship, but I assured him I felt we soon would be playing tennis together again somewhere.

It was just about this same time that I received a message via the embassy from Philip Balmforth, Jill's godson, that he was still in Baghdad. Even with his new Canadian passport, he had yet to get an exit visa. He wanted to be sure I contacted him if and when I made it to Baghdad.

For some three days, I pushed, stacked, and stored everything of value that would fit into the air vents and ducts in the ceiling of my apartment. Just about anything valuable and capable of fitting through the openings went up into the air conditioning system, including the kids' toys, Nintendo games, albums, photographs, and silverware. I had convinced myself that any looters would not think to look overhead.

Otherwise, I left the rest of the rooms, including the girls' bedrooms, just as they were in case I returned. If I did, I wanted to find myself in familiar surroundings so I could quickly adapt to the group's deeply hidden way of life again. I had also concluded that it would be better for my mental health to find everything intact—hopefully. I arranged with various members of the group to redistribute my food supplies and provided Imad, the young Brits, and Cliff with keys to my apartment.

On December 1st, it was time to say goodbye to Imad and the others. Cliff, the publican, came by momentarily and shared the last of our booze. One of the Filipinos dropped in to thank me again for supporting her people. I had also talked with Lillibeth earlier.

While I was bidding the group farewell, Imad had reconnoitered the building and the immediate area for any signs of potential trouble. He was assisted by Fred Skolberg, who would drive us to Brian's place. Brian would also travel with us to Baghdad on Irish documentation.

We had a final cocktail together, one that Chris didn't need as he was already enjoying a warm glow induced by his hidden supply of liquor. Fred reported that "everything looked good."

I whispered to Imad once again that he was a "saint" and that we all had him to thank for our lives. We shook hands one last time, and he vowed he would soon follow us to Baghdad. (1)

Taking our small suitcases, we followed Fred into the elevator and went down to the garage. In thinking back, I figured it was the first time I had been out of the building since about August 15th. The garage was like a junkyard with trashed vehicles left behind. It was deadly quiet—absent of the hundreds of noisy looters.

Chris piled into the rear seat, and I sat in front with Fred. As Fred drove up the ramp, we came upon the length of heavy chain that Imad had strung to prevent the Iraqis from driving out of the garage. I quickly got out of the car and used a key Fred handed me to remove the thick lock holding the chain taut across the driveway. After Fred drove over the chain, I went back to secure it to a steel post. Several Arab voices shattered the stillness of the garage and gave me a terrible fright. I looked about and pinpointed a small darkened shed as the source of the noise.

I figured the shed held several Iraqi soldiers, who were yelling at me. What to do? Not waiting to find out, I dropped the chain and the lock and jumped back into the car, bellowing at Fred to get the hell out of there. Fred spun the wheels and we drove away. Looking back, I never did see anyone come out of the shed. Probably too drunk to move, I thought whatever. They had scared the daylights out of me. It would have busted my backside to have been nabbed by the Iraqis on the first day I had emerged from the building in three and a half months. And the first day, too, of my intended escape attempt.

We headed for the Sixth Ring Road and turned right to get to the Mishrif Section where Brian had an apartment. As we approached each major intersection Fred had to drive off the road to stop at the Iraqi roadblocks. They were strung along like a row of blackbirds on a telephone line. The Irish *laissez-passer* we each had got us through the roadblocks.

It was about 3 p.m. when we arrived at Brian's place and were inside for drinks and an early dinner. Paul Kennedy, whom I had not personally seen since he had been to Baghdad and tried to blackmail me on his return, was present. I acted coolly toward him figuring I had only one more night to spend in the city before flying to Baghdad.

Not too long after our arrival, John Levins showed up. He and Kennedy immediately began hassling each other with verbal attacks. John's latest complaint was that Kennedy had screwed up a new underground mail pick-up system, leading to the arrest of eight Brits and two Americans just the night before.

"You insisted on using the effing Palestinians, Kennedy, just like always," John charged in his angry, stuttering voice. "When are you going to learn that they're in bed with the Iraqis and get paid off every time they pick up our mates?"

Kennedy was absolutely contemptuous of John, regarding him as though he were a piece of dog shit on the floor. Typically, he threatened to kneecap John if he didn't let off with his foolishness. Once again, we had to step in to keep the two of them from squaring off in a brawl that could only end badly for John.

To me, they only showed themselves to be two "paper tigers" with ridiculous ideas of glory. John was just a buffoon, a well-intentioned one. However, Kennedy with all his secret dealings, machinations vis-a-vis the Palestinians, and endless plottings with other shady groups was malicious.

When we had separated them again, Kennedy ripped into John for always taking stupid risks. I found it a case of "deja vu" and suggested to John that he ought to get out and leave us in peace. Kennedy was not about to let up and recited a litany of John's foolish actions like the time he had filled the petrol gas canisters with drinking water—not even bothering to empty the remaining gas from the canisters first.

"And all the stupid things you wanted to do to ingratiate yourself with the Yanks in the embassy. Telling them you were going to get them water when they had a swimming pool full of water, to supply them with food when they had rice and staples by the barrels, and to hook up their electricity."

Kennedy laughed. "How were you going to do that, you Aussie creep? Stick one finger in the embassy plug and the other in an Iraqi generator? Or maybe in your ass?"

Kennedy asked whether we had heard how John had called the embassy and asked to speak with a CIA agent, only to be informed there were no CIA people assigned to the embassy. We joked that John was looking for "Catholics in America" to make a substantial contribution to his new fund.

"Silly bugger," Kennedy spat. "When he was in Baghdad, he went around the city looking for the Holy See because he wanted to get a Baptist minister out of Kuwait City. Didn't have the slightest sense that the Holy See is in Rome."

Brian asked the big question. "Why did he want to see someone at the Holy See?"

Kennedy looked triumphantly at John and explained how the Aussie believed the Holy See was a Protestant organization, which would act swiftly to expedite the escape of the minister in Kuwait City because he was a Baptist.

"You're a dumb shit, John. That's all I can say," Kennedy sneered. "Absolutely the dumbest shit Aussie I've ever met."

Not one to be deterred by the truth, John retorted, "You can't achieve anything in this world without taking risks. I've been the first in that department from the beginning. You all know it, and I know it, and there's no denying it."

With that said, he indicated he was off, and I walked him out to his car for a final goodbye. The December weather was just magnificent. The air was cool, the skies were filled with stars, but the trees and bushes had died from lack of water.

Knowing that John had been receiving money from the U.S. Embassy in Baghdad to distribute among Americans hiding in the city, I asked him for some. Incredibly, the bastard told me, "You're not an American, and you're not in hiding. You're going to Baghdad."

I stared at him incredulously for a few moments. "Of course, I'm a goddamned American. What do you think I am? The Irish papers don't change anything. I'm still more in deep hiding than you ever were. Now, give me the hundred bucks."

Getting a final rise out of me, John quickly counted out the hundred U.S. dollars and handed them over. I thanked him, and we shook hands and parted with his wishing me "good luck."

I walked back into the apartment with dichotomous feelings about John. I knew that in his mind and heart he was always trying to do his best for many people trapped in dire circumstances, but his incompetence and foolhardiness usually left him spinning his wheels.

I was no sooner back inside when Brian showed himself to be another hard man and critic in the mould of Paul Kennedy.

Right off, he started on my accent. I had to clean it up. I had to sound more Irish—as though an Iraqi, who had trouble trying to understand a little English, could spot the difference between a Yank, Aussie, Welsh, Scots, or Irish accent.

"And you have to stop all the talk about America and all that Yank shit about the troops in Saudi Arabia and the rest of it," he insisted.

I think just about then I had had a bellyful of people telling me what I could do and what I could say and what I could think. I lit into Brian with both barrels.

"Listen, my friend, I'll damn well have my say about anything, and I'll do just what I want to do—as long as I don't jeopardize you or anyone else. And talking about the war and the way it's being handled isn't putting anyone in jeopardy. Now get off my case!"

Surprisingly, Brian shut up. I figured he had this idea that because it was his "safe house" we were beholden to him and he could dictate everyone's behavior. Frankly, I was fed up by then with officious, pompous Irish having so much to say about the U.S., its armed forces, and its wars when neither the Irishmen nor the Republic had been in anything resembling even a cock fight in decades.

Kennedy had left at some point after announcing he would not be using his exit visa right away because he still had so many "missions" to carry out in Kuwait. I just looked away and yawned.

After we awoke the next morning and had breakfast, Brian called a taxi to take us to the Kuwait International Airport. I couldn't help noticing that his refrigerator was bulging with food, much of it rotting, and that he had made no plans to leave it to anyone on our departure. So much for memories of the "great famine."

When we were within a mile of the airport, the driver halted and told us we had to get out and take a different cab. His fare was equivalent to $30 U.S. His Palestinian friend, who drove us the last 500 yards, charged the exact same amount. We kept our mouths shut and paid up. Talk about collusion!

Even at that, Brian, Chris, Ray (a newcomer), and I were short of the main entrance. To get there, we had to board a small bus which took us to the old Terminal Number One I knew from previous flights in and out of Kuwait. Just in front of the entrance, there was a brand new Mercedes luxury bus with all its tires removed. It was so typical of the Iraqis to steal the tires and then abandon the expensive bus. What a waste!

Passing inside, we encountered two Iraqi guards, who waved us through. Brian urged us to be cool and keep quiet. He would do all the talking. With our documents from the Irish Embassy in hand, he went to the check-in desk to get our tickets for the flight to Baghdad.

We collectively held our breaths as we watched with outward indifference while he handed over the papers for inspection by the airport personnel. I said a little prayer, urging God to just get us on that airplane up to Baghdad.

I winked at Chris when I saw Brian receive the documents back along with a handful of flight tickets. Rejoining us, he directed us to another line where we had to obtain our boarding passes. Our fellow passengers were mostly Iraqi civilians, businessmen, and traders, trying to make a fast buck off the occupation. Mixed in with them were some Kuwaitis. Everyone was very sociable and waited courteously for their boarding passes. Next, we had to get into another line to have our luggage inspected. The Iraqis only took a cursory look at the belongings in my small bag.

While in the terminal, we tried to make use of the toilets, but they had been hopelessly trashed, the fixtures broken, and the water shut off. Feces filled the toilet bowls, urinals, and sinks. I was sickened by the sight, remembering how pristine clean the Kuwaitis had kept all their public rooms before the occupation. I never found them to be anything but spotless at all times.

As Brian had explained, we would not fly out of Kuwait International Airport. The Iraqis had closed the field down and shifted their flight operations to a military airfield some 70 miles away toward the Iraqi border.

So once again, after a 45-minute wait, we had to clamber aboard one bus while our luggage was stored aboard a second one for the last portion of our trip. Soon we were back on the Sixth Ring Road, which took us to Al-Jahra Road and the ride north to the military airfield.

I thought I would make good use of the time by taking mental notes of any military activity along the way. Surprisingly, I saw very little in the way of Iraqi equipment. I was sure I would spot many tanks buried up to their turrets in the sand, but I didn't see one. The only military vehicle I spotted was an armored personnel carrier parked under a highway overpass

We passed the sprawling Chevrolet sales lot, and I had to chuckle on again seeing the hundreds of Caprices still abandoned in the open. Every vehicle had been stripped of its battery and tires, and the hoods remained up as though saluting us as we passed. Seeing them made me think of Max and Mary—of blessed memory.

Farther along the highway, we saw hundreds of Iraqi soldiers sitting or standing about with only a few of their numbers marching desultorily southward. To my eyes, they were a sorry looking lot of fighting men, poorly dressed and equipped. I put them down to conscripts with very little military training. (2)

Upon our arrival at the airfield, two jerk-looking Iraqis—obviously secret police types—drove up to the bus in a stolen 1990 silver-colored Audi to check our documents. Frankly, I was surprised they weren't driving my BMW. Brian took our papers in hand again and warned us to stay cool. We didn't need any reminding because those two dudes, dressed in blue jeans with the bottoms rolled up about six inches, were carrying wicked looking pistols in holsters belted around their waists.

In truth, I don't think they had very much interest in either the duty they were assigned to or us. They no doubt would much rather have been raising hell with the locals down in Kuwait City than stuck in the backwaters of the occupation at a military airfield. We were waved through the gate and informed there would be a wait of an hour and a half. Once again, we sought out the toilets only to be rebuffed by their miserable state and stench.

While hanging around in the heat and humidity of the hangar, the Iraqis announced that we were to carry our luggage to the runway and stand by our individual pieces. In turn, each of us had to identify our personal bag for a member of the flight crew. Only the luggage so identified would be permitted on board.

In my mind, all was going well. I was convinced we would soon be on our way when an Iraqi guard pulled me aside. I looked about bewildered. I was the only one singled out. Why only me? What is the bastard up to?

The guard motioned me to follow him back to the check-in line where I was turned over to a second Iraqi. By then, I was imagining the worst. My head was filled with visions of every cruelty man could wreak on another.

"Dr. Morris?" the Iraqi asked.

I looked at him, nodding my head affirmatively.

"Just a formality. Nothing else," He went on in excellent English. "You are Irish, yes?"

"Yes, I am," I managed to say, wondering whether Brian would approve of my Irish accent. Actually, it was more a Boston-West Indies accent than Irish because of my years of association with the UN in the West Indies. Would he discern the difference?

"A very lovely country. So green and cool compared to our part of the world, yes?"

I just nodded, not certain whether I could trust my own voice.

"And St. Patrick's Cathedral in Dublin is a truly magnificent Roman church. I am a Christian Iraqi, you know. Some ten percent of Iraqis are Christians, yes?"

I smiled slightly, unsure as to whether I was to answer or not. I decided I best say something because he looked at me with his head cocked.

"I think I had heard that at one time. I think it always comes as a surprise to Westerners. We think of Arab countries and their inhabitants as being strictly Muslim in faith."

While I spoke quietly and slowly to maintain my relaxed demeanor, I watched his chiseled features for any sign of a positive or negative reaction. He gave nothing away with his expression.

"And St. Patrick's. Have you attended services there?"

My heart bumped upward. Was the Iraqi trying to trap me? It was a loaded question, but had he intended it that way? I decided to give him a straight answer.

"No, I don't. I'm a Roman Catholic, and St. Patrick's, as you know, is Church of Ireland, a Protestant church."

He let a slight smile play around his lips. "Yes, of course, I think I had heard that at one time or another."

With that remark and a final scrutiny of my papers, he bid me a pleasant journey to Baghdad and expressed the hope that I would soon be back in Ireland. I smiled in grateful appreciation turned around, and let loose a long, silent breath full of anxiety. I sensed, as I walked back toward my traveling companions, that his eyes were fixed on my back.

Brian looked at my quizzically. I nodded that everything was fine. Moments later, we were lined up to board the plane but only after a thorough search of our bodies by two plainclothes policemen. We maintained our silence as we went aboard and claimed our seats. I was seated next to Chris.

On the flight to Baghdad, none of us spoke to one another—although our fellow Iraqi and Kuwaiti passengers were jabbering away incessantly. We just didn't want to attract any attention by speaking English, with whatever kind of an accent. We obviously were westerners, but we decided we would let the Arabs try to figure out our nationalities. In truth, they probably could not have cared less.

Left to my own thoughts, I reviewed the past four months in my mind and wondered anew how I had managed to elude the Iraqis and their stool pigeons for so long. There had been some close calls, but I was still free and on the run. Thank God, I thought.

I was also free at last of John Levins and Paul Kennedy and their interminable squabbling and foolishness. I pushed thoughts of them from my mind and filled it with flickering images of Jill and the girls. It had been so long since I had last seen them. Maybe my luck would hold, and I would soon be with them.

Chapter 26

Into the Lion's Lair

After about an hour's flight, we landed without incident in Baghdad, picked up our bags, and strolled from the airport terminal without interference. There were only a few Iraqi soldiers and security types about, and they didn't evince any interest in us.

Once outside, we hailed a cab driver who said he would take the four of us to the Al Rashid Hotel, a five-star property, for $30 U.S. We agreed because Brian said it was a long ride. Then the driver said he could only take two of us. The other two would have to go with his friend, who naturally was right behind him.

Out of the blue, Brian blew his stack. "The bloody bastard's out to screw us over." He whirled on the cab driver and berated him for trying to cheat us.

I was taken aback by Brian's outburst because all along we had been cautioning each other not to do anything that would draw attention to our quartet. Now Brian was raising his voice to the sky and doing exactly what we had tried to avoid.

In his defense, the Iraqi kicked his tires, arguing, "They are not good. Not good to carry four passengers. Two of you have to go with Mustafa there."

I urged Brian to cool it before the Iraqis took us all into custody. Pay the goddamn money. What difference did it make at this stage of the game? Were we going to forfeit our chance to escape over a lousy 60 dollars—money given to us by various embassies? Money they probably would never come looking for?

We swept out of the airport and sped along a lovely boulevard lined with date and palm trees. I had never been to Baghdad before and was quickly impressed by the attractive buildings and parks we passed on the ride to the hotel. I thought of the Hanging Gardens of Babylon. What most impressed me was the cleanliness of the streets and the walkways in the city, very similar to the way the Kuwaitis maintained their public areas.

I kept a close eye out for any military installations but mostly counted only anti-aircraft guns on many of the rooftops. Other than those batteries, there were few other signs of military activity. I saw an occasional truck or armored personnel carrier and the ubiquitous foot soldiers, strolling about in two's and three's.

We went to the Al-Rashid Hotel because it was the best in the capital, and Westerners, including most of the media people, always stayed there. All our expenses were to be picked up by the Irish embassy.

The Iraqis always strove to get Westerners to register at the Al-Rashid Hotel to facilitate their ability to keep track of them. The talk was that hard-eyed Saddam Hussein's people had the property bugged from top to bottom and that there were surveillance cameras turning and whirring everywhere in the hotel. They even had them on the roofs of adjacent buildings. One of my friends had tremendous interference when he tried to listen to his short-wave radio by his bedside. He unscrewed the top of a bedpost and found a listening device inside.

I had already made up my mind before we reached the hotel that I was going to have little, if any, socializing with old friends or members of the media. I was traveling under false documents and was not about to have my cover blown by some stupid encounter. Once I had my exit visa and was out at the airport and ready to board a flight to the West, maybe then I would have a different frame of mind.

We no sooner had entered the lobby when an Irishman I knew as Dave singled me out and whispered, "Your embassy wants you to check in. They're unhappy with the papers you're carrying." I ignored him, and as I walked by, gave him a dirty look.

One of the first things I did as soon as I had checked in was to carry out a plan to call Jill, via intermediaries in a friendly European country. Our group had established the necessary contacts, people who knew how to get Jill and to maintain secrecy. We had learned that Iraq was not good at quickly tracing incoming calls, which this would be. In Boston, Jill again received the message to hang on and we were connected. We had a wonderful talk. She was overjoyed that I had arrived in Baghdad especially with the US-led attack just on the horizon. She believed I could be home soon—hopefully.

I indicated to her in our code talk that I was now traveling on the "Green Line." I would still try to obtain the UN *laissez-passer* as back-up insurance, and she should also keep up the pressure on the UN from her end.

My next call was to Philip Balmforth. We arranged to meet at the hotel bar later in the day. I still couldn't believe he had been held up in Baghdad. I had thought he was safe in Amman or back home in Canada.

We linked up with more Irish and the "new" Irish, who had come up from Kuwait. A few of them were paranoid over the fact that I was an American moving about on their government's documents. As we drank in the bar they implied very strongly that I was going to blow their cover. I was fed up with them. First, Paul Kennedy and then Brian. Now I had more of them on my back about my accent.

Frankly, I was somewhat disappointed by their attitude. In my mind, the Irish historically had always been brave soldiers, Davids constantly holding their own against Goliaths. This bunch wasn't living up to that image at all. Where was Audie Murphy when I needed him?

When Brian joined in the attacks on me, I counterattacked and told him to bug out. "Just stop telling me what to do, Brian. I'm tired of your telling me that I have to do everything your way. I'll goddamn well do it my way. I'm sick of your self-righteousness and holier-than-thou attitude. This bullshit idea you Europeans have that somehow or another you are superior to Americans. Yet, we have to come over to your corner of the world every 20 or 30 years and save your asses again!"

My outburst was poorly received by Brian. He left the very next day on his exit visa without any farewell. A solid trio in the group declined from that moment on to have anything to do with me. They, in effect, ostracized me, refusing to acknowledge me in any way during the remainder of our time at the Al-Rashid Hotel.

Philip and I had a happy reunion and downed many celebratory drinks to mark the occasion. He looked well to me and reported he had maintained contact with his relatives in Amman. He thought I looked rather pale and drawn—not surprising since I had lost almost 25 pounds in the past four months.

The next day, Chris Chambers and I went to the UN office to meet with Stefan Bodemahr, who was employed as a representative for the UN High Commissioner for Refugees. He smiled warmly and indicated immediately that he knew I was an American.

I was stunned. "How did you find out I was an American?"

"I called the U.S. Embassy."

"Why did you call the U.S. Embassy?"

"Because the UN in New York indicated in our efforts to obtain a *laissez-passer* for you that you were an American. I wanted to check it out."

I was flabbergasted. Here I had been trying to hide my American identity for months, and the U.S. Embassy in Baghdad and the UN in New York were telling anyone who asked that I was a U.S. citizen. Sons-of-bitches! How stupid can you be?

Bodemahr was very gracious in dealing with me and was well aware that I had the Irish *laissez-passer* and was trying to pass myself off as Irish. He had no problem with that vis-a-vis my family's efforts to get me the UN *laissez-passer*.

"You should know that I received a telex only yesterday saying the *laissez-passer* would be issued to you," he said.

I felt one hundred percent better at once. "Great, where is it?"

His face darkened. "I checked when it did not arrive and was informed that it was lost in Frankfurt—perhaps held up there. It was not made clear. I'm still looking into it."

So there it was. More bureaucratic screw-ups. I had really been counting on that UN document as back-up to the Irish papers. In truth, I was terribly upset that after the efforts of so many people—my family, people at the U.S. State Department, Senator John Kerry and his staff—the UN had bungled the project at the very end. My anger was enhanced remembering others who had received the UN *laissez-passer* although they had never had any connection to the world body.

At that point, I pulled out my old UN passport, which must have been 15 years old. It had been legally updated to 1985. I had altered the date to 1992 but had done a terribly amateurish job.

"Think it will pass muster?" I asked.

Bodemahr studied it and smiled. I asked him why he was smiling.

"You've changed the date. That's easy to see."

"It's that obvious?"

"Oh, yes," he replied.

In the end, we agreed he would attempt to get the old passport updated correctly if the new one didn't arrive. To protect himself, he would ask permission from the UN staff in New York.

During the next few days, several of my associates went to the Iraqi authorities to try to obtain exit visas with their Irish papers. At that particular period of time, they had stopped giving out exit visas. I had not made the attempt myself, waiting instead to see how the others fared. Mostly, Philip and I remained fast to the hotel's heated pool, tennis courts, and various bars.

During this time, a U.S. Embassy officer started on me again about which way I intended to leave—as an Irish citizen or as an American? I reiterated again that I had opted much earlier to go out with Irish papers—due me because of my grandfather's birth in Ireland. Yes, I said, as requested, I would meet secretly with the American military attaché in the Irish Embassy.

From the very beginning, I considered such a meeting farcical. It was held in the Irish Embassy and could hardly be secret because most of the secretaries were Iraqis. The American officer was a nice enough young fellow, but I quickly put him down as naive when he said he could take me to a "safe house."

When I inquired what "safe house," he said the American Embassy. I thought "safe house" for what? Once I took refuge in the embassy, I could be stuck there for months. Any male who took refuge in the U.S. Embassy in Kuwait was still there. Americans were not being allowed to leave. With my Irish papers, I had a chance to get out when the Iraqis began issuing the exit visas again. He probably thought I was crazy—passing up the comforts, good food, and booze at the embassy. I thanked him, and we parted graciously.

I went back to see Bodemahr to determine the status of the UN *laissez-passer* and was informed it was "stuck" in Frankfurt, whatever that meant. Ultimately, the Irish got wind of this activity and wanted to know why I needed both Irish and UN papers. They were concerned that the UN document would state my nationality as American. I pointed out that UN documents do not indicate the nationality of the bearer.

One Irish official was very persistent and truly felt that I should give back the Irish *laissez-passer* if I was going to go out on the UN one. He suggested I let them hold the Irish document until it was determined whether the UN papers would be forthcoming. It was very obvious to me that the Irish were confused and worried about my activities and fearful I was going to queer their patch. In my mind, I wasn't trying to queer anyone's patch. All I wanted to do was cover all bases to get out of Iraq.

In the end, I reluctantly handed over the Irish *laissez-passer*. I don't want to sound hard on the Irish. They were the only ones who provided genuine assistance. They took excellent care of me. In fact, they gave me over $8000 to pay my way. No other country, including my own, came close to matching their generosity.

Chapter 27

Saddam's Surprise

Incredibly, the whole week long, there was a conference of Eastern Orthodox Church bishops from around the Middle East being held in the Al Rashid Hotel. The bishops were striking, handsome, wearing thick black beards, big gold rings, and enormous icons fastened to heavy gold chains.

Iraq is a secular country, but the people are very religious. While most are Muslims, about one out of ten is a practicing Christian. Churches are found throughout the country, and the congregations enjoy religious freedom under the Baathist Party.

On occasion, I would slip into one of the bishops' sessions to hear what they were up to and was appalled to listen to their encomiums of Saddam Hussein and their diatribes against the United States and the UN. Talk about a bunch of bum-kissers, making sure they survived whatever was to come out of the confrontation between Iraq and the Coalition.

At this point I noticed a bearded priest who somehow stood out from the group. When he dined he would sit by himself and ignore the Arab priests. While in the buffet line he greeted me, attempting to make pleasantries. I said hello and asked him where he came from. He replied, "Los Angeles." I asked him if he was a Roman Catholic. "No, I am Assyrian Orthodox," he replied. "My name is Father Bartholomew Fox." He announced that he was trying to evacuate American hostages for a Texas oilman named Bryant. (1) He had come to Baghdad with the former governor of Texas, John Connolly. Connolly's claim to fame was that he had been shot by Lee Harvey Oswald on that fatal day in Dallas in 1963.

If he was trying to take out hostages, I thought, why not me? Yet, who was I? I could not tell him I was American. I dropped the conversation, but immediately established contact with Jill by phone and explained that John Connolly was in the room above mine taking out hostages and I wanted my name on his list. Jill did not understand my coded talk about "1962," "Dallas," "John John's father," "the fatal bullet." I told her that my brother-in-law, Jim McDevitt, would decipher the code. I said that she should go to the top, i.e., the White House, with my request. At the same time I told her of the bishops' conference and asked her to contact the Archbishop of Trinidad to call the Pope to use his influence!!

Unbelievably, I had one answer back in a few hours—the Holy See knew of the conference but had no representative, nor immediate contact with the Orthodox Christians. While I waited from an answer from Jill on the White House request, John Connolly departed with only eighteen hostages on his Boeing 707. I believe they were all oil workers.

There were long periods of boredom while I waited to hear when the Iraqis would make exit visas available again. I passed the time by playing tennis with Philip and was quite pleased when I beat him consistently after being away from the game for months. There was also the heated swimming pool, which I found very relaxing.

I had a lingering touch of tennis elbow and took advantage of the free medical service offered by a team of Irish doctors at Park Hospital. They prescribed several relaxing massages, heat, and whirlpool therapy. Another time, I went to the Sheraton Hotel to have my first genuine haircut in months for only six bucks.

In the evenings, we would treat ourselves to a spartan dinner and drinks in the various bars and lounges. I usually drank with Philip, Ray and Chris and a few Irish, who still acknowledged me. None of us needed all that booze, but it was something to do, a way to forget our predicament, and a means to stop thinking constantly about going home.

Finally, on Friday, we received big news on Iraqi radio. Saddam Hussein announced his rubber-stamp Parliament was to meet the next day to act on an important bill. The media people reacted like someone had given them a collective hotfoot, scurrying around the hotel and back and forth across the lobby like a horde of mad buffalo.

The rumors, of course, started flying like miniature Scud missiles throughout the Al Rashid Hotel:

> Saddam was going to withdraw from Kuwait.
>
> Saddam was going to start executing the hostages.
>
> Saddam was going to let all the hostages go.

You name it, and I am sure I heard it that day. When several of the press people began to interview westerners to get their reaction to the possibilities, I quietly left the lobby and went out to the pool. I was still doing everything possible to avoid the media. To me, they were a royal pain in the backside. I was not about to let one of the eager beavers blow my cover and put the Irish government in hot water with the Iraqis.

Hanging around the pool, I concluded again that Baghdad was a surrealistically beautiful city. The grounds of the hotel were magnificent, lined with royal palms, date trees, and flowering bushes of all kinds. The myriad trees and gardens were wonders to behold.

I wondered how a place of so much color and beauty could be the source of so much hate, oppression, and fear. Here I was, living in the lap of luxury, all my expenses being paid, with nothing to do all day but loll around in the brilliant sunshine by the pool and wait. Yet, there was always the fear that Iraqi soldiers could appear at any moment and take us off to be imprisoned or shot.

I made no effort on Saturday to listen to the radio to learn what the Parliament was up to. Whatever—it was something ordained ahead of time by Saddam Hussein, and we would find out soon enough. Instead, I went out to the pool, and one of the Park Hospital doctors soon came by and said the Parliament had passed the bill.

"What bill is that?" I asked quietly.

He looked at me in disbelief. "The one that's going to get us all out of here. You and me and all the rest of this mob. They're letting us all go. Out. Starting tomorrow. No conditions. They just want us out of here."

I found the news incredible but remained outwardly calm. Was it really true? The sons-of-bitches were really going to let us go home? As the physician walked away, I felt warm tears bathing my eyes and waves of relief and joy wash over me.

Going home at last. After the months of concealment and fear. All the efforts expended to survive. My mind was a kaleidoscope of conflicting thoughts.

Then in alternating fashion, I would shake myself in disbelief. It couldn't be true. There had to be a catch somewhere. The Iraqis wouldn't let us go without expecting something in return.

Obviously, the news we could leave on the morrow was the one and only topic of conversation the rest of that day and night. By the pool, around the dinner table, and over too many cocktails, we dissected the report from every possible angle—one moment with enthusiasm and the next with black fits of disbelief.

All around us throughout the remainder of that day was a crush of people, preying on each other for any further tidbits to help them believe the report. The air shook from excited voices and turned blue from tobacco smoke.

"What bothers me," said Philip in one of his down moods, "is how come nothing seems to be happening? We haven't heard a word about the process involved in getting out. What the hell do we do—just go to the airport tomorrow and get on a flight out?"

We would all jump on that thought and come up with a flurry of possible answers. One of the Irish guys said the process was quite simple. Get an exit visa from the Iraqis, and then check with your embassy to see that you got on a list for a scheduled flight. Nothing to it.

The night became rather blurry as Philip, Chris, Ray, and I turned our discussion into a celebration and drank round after round of toasts to our survival. Philip and I were a bit late in getting started the next morning because of the pounding in our heads. Still, it was a night we will always remember.

I went by the Irish Embassy and picked up my *laissez-passer* without any difficulty, murmuring that I had given up on the UN. After all the running around by so many people at home and in the Mideast, the UN never did provide me with any papers.

Hell, who needs them, I figured, as I hurried to rendezvous with Philip and proceed to the Iraqi Ministry for our exit visas. Philip had the UN *laissez-passer* he had received earlier through his father's efforts. He would use it for travel purposes.

On arriving at the visa office, I was surprised to find a large contingent of Americans there, many of whom I knew quite well. They, of course, were effusive in their greetings, but I had to put them off.

"I can't talk to you. Not now."

"It's okay, Rob," they insisted. "You can talk. It's not a problem."

"No, no. Don't you understand?

In my mind these Americans were telling the Iraqis I was an American. If I were an American, an Iraqi might want to know what I was doing with an Irish *laissez-passer*.

The Americans finally pulled away and went about their own business. They must have thought I was a weirdo, but I didn't care. I wasn't going to have anyone screw it up for me at the last minute.

Even Philip eyed me as though wondering whether I was about to flip out. "Not to worry, Philip," I smiled. "I just don't want anything to happen after coming this far."

We handed over our *laissez-passer's*, and the Iraqi clerk glanced at both. We were waved over to a corner and told to wait. Philip was shortly called back and given his UN *laissez-passer*.

Philip asked what the problem was with his UN *laissez-passer*. The clerk and his boss said they couldn't accept it because they had never seen one like it before. Philip argued almost to the point of tears to get them to accept it but in vain.

He told me he was going to the Canadian Embassy to try to get another passport. He had lost his original one at the Kuwait airport when he had arrived at the end of July. A second one was issued by the Canadian Embassy to replace the lost one, but it too became lost by bureaucrats in the Iraqi Ministry during an exit visa request.

Just then, my name was called out. "Philip, wait here. I'll only be a moment, I hope."

And that's all it took to get my exit visa although there was one small hitch. The Iraqis had run out of the correct stamps to affix to the visa. Instead they wrote the correct authorization onto the visa itself. Would the absence of the stamp cause me to come up a cropper later?

I turned to Philip, who appeared glum-faced and ticked-off, and told him I was all set. He was probably thinking, "What's this shit? I'm up here long before Rob and can't get out. Rob's here only a few days, and everyone's getting out but me."

"C'mon, Philip, snap out of it. We'll go to your embassy and get your passport. It'll all work out."

And that's just the way it happened for him. There was no delay in obtaining his third passport or in getting his exit visa on our return to the Iraqi Ministry. Somehow they even came up with the official stamp for his papers, claiming it was the absolutely the last one.

We asked the Iraqis how we could get on a flight out of the country. We each had to go to our own embassy, they replied. The embassy would provide us with the flight information.

So Philip and I bade farewell, expressing the hope that we would see each other at the Saddam Hussein International Airport (what else would it be named!!) depending on our individual flight times.

"This time, Rob, we're both going to make it," Philip swore. "There's no way we aren't getting out. We'll catch up to each other somewhere in the West in the next few days. You can count on it."

I gave him a final embrace, and we parted. (2)

All I could do as I headed for the embassy was to think about being on my way home soon.

Chapter 28

Free at Last

You can imagine my shock when I arrived at the US Embassy and was informed by a guard that it was closed. I couldn't believe it. The world's going to hell, and the goddamned embassy is taking a holiday. I have a chance to go home, and the embassy is closed.

I dashed past the guard and ran to an open window in the wall where the locals usually lined up trying to get visas to visit the U.S.A. There was a woman at the window. I said she had to help me get on the flight taking the Americans out.

"Are you an American?" she asked coolly.

I looked at her sharply. "Yes, aren't you?"

"No," she said matter-of-factly. "I'm an Iraqi."

I almost dropped dead on the spot. I was claiming I was an American and demanding, in effect, to get on the flight. All I had to show her was the Irish document. She appeared to be a bureaucratic type who would not overlook such a discrepancy—let alone ever get me on the flight—and someone who could readily report me to the Iraqi secret police.

I glanced about wildly, filling up with a sense of both fight or flight, when I spotted a man I knew was a military attaché. I thanked the Iraqi clerk and told her I was going to talk to the American.

He was on the phone. I could hear snatches of his conversation. Coincidentally, he was discussing the possibility of his caller getting on a flight to the States. I smiled broadly. From then on, he was my boy.

He caught my eye and ended his conversation. He was well aware of who I was. He had been among the civilian-dressed Americans who had contacted U.S. hostages as they arrived in Baghdad. At one time, he had sidled up to me in the hotel and asked whether I needed any money from our government. I had declined with thanks and answered a few questions about what I had seen going on inside Kuwait before I had left.

"Boy, I'm glad to see you," I blurted out. "I've got these Irish papers, but I want to go out on a flight with the Americans."

"Not to worry. We know all about you from the senator," he said. "We've got one leaving for Frankfurt, Germany, for our guys, the Brits, and the Irish—so it's no problem."

"How soon is the flight?"

"The flight's scheduled for 1600 hours. Why don't you go out with me at 1500 hours, and I'll confirm you're on the list?"

"You mean you can't get me on the list from here?" I began to get bad vibrations.

"Not to worry, Dr. Morris. The list is at the airport. We'll get you on. Do you want a ride with me?"

I looked at him dubiously. "Will there be any problem about getting me on the list?"

"I know you're not on the list now. One plane is coming in with a bunch of U.S. citizens from Kuwait City. I'm sure there'll be room for you."

"I've got to go back to the hotel and get my bag and check out. If I'm not here by three, don't wait. I may go right to the airport from the hotel."

Of course, the bloody hotel staff had to take a long time to check me out. A lot of foolishness anyway since the Irish Embassy was picking up the tab. Still, I needed the bill for their records and to keep any Iraqi from claiming I was trying to skip without paying.

Can you imagine that in my relatively short time there I had run up a tab for $4000? It had to be padded, but there was no way I was going to argue about the bill.

I hailed a cab outside the hotel and was at the airport in about half an hour. It would have been sooner, but we were stopped at one last military roadblock. I couldn't believe it. The checkpoint was a joke, and we were quickly on our way again.

When I arrived at the terminal entrance, I had to push through a mob of reporters, many of whom addressed questions to me. Who was I? Was I an American who had been used as a human shield? How did I feel about going home? I ignored the lot of them like I was the Prince of Wales and swept into the terminal, where I was quickly taken in tow by the Irish Embassy staffers. I was glad to see their faces, but they had some disappointing news for me.

"We want you to go over there and keep a low profile because they don't have a seat for you yet."

"Tell them I'll sit on the damn floor—in the cockpit, in the pilot's lap. Just get me on that plane," I pleaded. "I can't stay here another minute."

Several of the reporters were attracted by our lively conversation and came gliding up to ask another series of questions. "Scram, you bastards," I muttered. "I can't talk to you now. You'll ruin it for me."

Happily, the media people were distracted as the Americans and others, who had been held as human shields in various sites about Kuwait and Iraq, came streaming into the terminal from their recently arrived aircraft and buses. As the reporters scrambled to interview them, I breathed a sigh of relief.

As always, I remained my own worst enemy. I spotted my old tennis buddy, Clem Hall, from Kuwait City. Without thinking, I grabbed him as he walked by and gave him a big embrace. Suddenly realizing what I had done, I whispered in his ear: "Look Clem, I can't talk to you now. Trust me. There's a good reason. I'll catch up to you on the plane."

A worldly man, he nodded his head and went off without a word. I turned to one of the Irish Embassy staffers, who had attached himself to me. "You guys aren't going to forget me, are you?"

He saw the concern in my face and said, "No, no. Just hold on now. Remain here. Don't be worrying."

One of the Irishmen came by to tell me that Joe Wilson, the *charge´ d'affaires* from the embassy, was well aware of me and would get me on the flight.

"It's a big 747. Plenty of seats for everyone. He's just trying to figure out how many are going to be boarding."

I wasn't convinced. 747 or not, there was an immense mob of humanity filling up the terminal, 9000 hostages in all. I could not stop wondering how we all were going to get aboard. There had to be more of us than seats available. I prayed there was one for me.

Someone up there heard me. One of the Irishmen came hurrying up. "Okay, go for it. Get your bag. Go to the counter. Put your bag on the counter, and they'll give you a boarding pass. It's all set."

I scrambled to stand up, grabbing my bag. I looked at him and smiled and expressed my thanks. "That's all there is to it? Just go to the counter and get my boarding pass?"

"C'mon, Yank, piss off. Move! Get the pass and go into that Iraqi Airways lounge over there." He pointed to the middle of the far wall.

Without another word, I went to the counter, put down my bag, showed my exit visa, and was handed a boarding pass. As simple as that. It was just as easy to clear Immigration shortly thereafter with my visa and pass.

The terminal was jammed with people from many countries. The noise of their myriad conversations—shouting back and forth to each other—and the loudspeaker announcements rang throughout the huge expanse of the modern airline building.

I saw one lounge filled with Vietnamese, waiting to fly out on a chartered Air India. Another lounge was stuffed with Russians set to take an Aeroflot jet. A third lounge was pulsating with excitable Italians and a sprinkling of Brits, who would be sharing an Iraqi Airways flight. The fourth was mine—crammed with Americans and more Brits.

I no sooner walked through the entrance to the lounge when I was overwhelmed by seeing old acquaintances from Kuwait City, mostly squash and tennis partners from the SAS club. All of them expressed surprise at seeing so many familiar faces because more than one of us had lost touch from day one onward.

My joy on being reunited with all these friends was heightened when George Daher and I spotted each other and embraced. George was the landscaper from Pennsylvania, a divorced bachelor, and my best friend whom I had called just before leaving for Baghdad.

I had been concerned since then that he might be upset because I left without him—even though he had blessed my escape attempt. The warmth of his welcome and obvious pleasure in seeing me again dispelled such notions entirely from my mind.

Drinks were on the house so we availed ourselves of a few rounds and talked each other's ears off while we waited for the boarding announcement. People would join us, bring us up to date on their lives during the occupation, and drift away to other groups. Several hours passed.

"I knew it, George. I knew it," I said. "Saddam Hussein's playing effing games with us. It's one last trick by the bastard. Tease us. Keep us waiting, guessing. Delay the flight for hours."

George agreed emphatically, feeling the drinks the same as I was. As though to prove us wrong one last time, the announcement came for us to board the Iraqi Airways 747. We headed for the exit and our waiting plane like a herd of stampeding cattle. George and I stayed close to each other so we wouldn't become separated and be left sitting in different sections of the aircraft.

There was one last check of our exit visas and passes before we entered the plane. Each of us received a pleasant "goodbye" from an "airline employee." We only said "goodbye" in response. Many were tempted to give the Iraqis the finger, but fortunately, no one did. We didn't want to give them any reason to hold us any longer.

We took our seats funereally without a single shout or cry of euphoria. It was not the time. We were still in the Iraqis' clutches. We were flying out aboard one of their aircraft.

It was eight p.m. on Sunday, December 9, 1990, and it was dark outside when the plane roared down the runway and took off—bound for Frankfurt Germany and freedom in the West. The flight would take six hours.

It could have taken sixty as far as I was concerned because I was finally going home to my family and to America.

EPILOGUE

Dr. Morris' flight to Frankfurt, West Germany was uneventful until the very last minutes when he was sure Saddam Hussein was going to get him at last.

The Boeing 747, cleared for landing, was some 100 feet above the runway when it began to shake violently. "The whole plane just shook," he reported. "Most of us were asleep or in a daze from too much drinking when there was an announcement that we were about to land. It was about 2 a.m. on Monday, December 10, 1990.

"Land, my ass. The way that plane began to shake I was convinced we were headed straight into the ground. I was already halfway through my imaginary rosary when I saw the runway. Instead of landing on it, we were cutting right across it."

The Iraqi pilot had apparently come very close to stalling out his aircraft. The 747 could have dropped like a powerless brick to the runway. Fortunately, he gave it full power instantly and ever so slowly the giant plane went around the field, climbing by inches into the sky. Twenty minutes later, the plane landed safely. As it did, the now wide-awake passengers gave the pilot a big cheer and scattered applause. It was no time to hold a grudge.

Happy to be alive and well after the near crash of the 747, Morris was appalled when confronted by U.S. bureaucrats as he attempted to deplane. He and the others were told they had to be processed. While there were hundreds on the plane, there were only a few embassy types to do the work.

"I couldn't believe it," Dr. Morris recalled. "All those months in hiding. The days in Baghdad. It had been hours since I had left the Al-Rashid Hotel. The bastards knew we were coming, and here they had only a few people to handle the paperwork."

When Morris and the others began to harangue the bureaucrats, they were told that most of the embassy's personnel were off for the weekend. Incredible! His opinion of the embassy people sank to an even lower level.

Just inside the terminal, a swarm of reporters and photographers were waiting to interview them. Ignoring the bureaucrats, Morris and several companions wandered over and were quickly interviewed by the media.

"Where did you come in from? Where have you been all these months? How bad was it? Got any recommendations?"

"Yeh, we've got to bomb the . . . . "—he was about to say the great Anglo-Saxon word but caught himself—" . . . hell out of them!"

His sentiments were echoed by almost everyone queried by the press, but Morris' comment was aired on TV news across the United States.

The comedy of errors continued to spin out after the passengers cleared the bureaucratic paper hurdle. First, many of their bags were lost. Others arrived slowly. Many of the containers for family pets had broken open, and dogs and cats were running loose around the airport.

On arrival about 3 a.m. at the Sheraton Hotel, a short walk from the terminal, there were only a few people available to register them. The hotel staff claimed it had never been alerted to their impending arrival. They did keep the check-in process down to a name, room number, and a key.

Happily, the U.S. government was footing all their bills, and the hotel clerks said the group could make long distance calls to their hearts' delight. There was a problem though because only one operator was on duty. She had to be reached to explain how to use the complicated German telephone service.

George Daher and Morris obtained adjoining rooms and began placing calls to home immediately, or almost immediately, depending on when they raised the operator. He and Jill still talked for over a half hour.

She was overjoyed learning he was in Frankfurt and was finally free. He would be flying home later that same day aboard a chartered Pan Am 747. (In Boston, it was 9 p.m. on Sunday, December 9, 1990.) They talked about their daughters, their health, and their abiding love for each other.

After his conversation with Jill, he also called other family members in the Boston area, friends in London, in Washington, D. C, and Australia.

After a few hours of fitful sleep, Morris went for a walk with the hope of finding a bar where he could buy a beer. Nothing was open so he returned to his room to go jogging with George Daher. Despite the near freezing temperature and falling snow, the pair ran around the terminal twice to clear their heads.

They passed the remaining morning hours eating breakfast, "first real western breakfast after 130 days," and shopping for Christmas gifts at the Christmas Fair at Frankfurt Airport. A German shop keeper insisted on giving them extra free gifts after learning they had just arrived from Baghdad. They skipped various meetings scheduled by the embassy to discuss the flight home.

"We'd been under cover for four months, and we didn't want to go to any embassy meetings to listen to those blowhards tell us about security requirements because of terrorists. Most of us had little use for embassy personnel, and we ignored those bureaucrats who were just showboating for the media."

Although they had skipped any involvement with the embassy personnel, the men had no problem picking up their passes to board the Pan Am flight, which was scheduled to depart at 1 p.m. German time. The airline staff attempted to short circuit the security process, but the State Department insisted that every individual be interrogated and every bag carefully examined.

Morris and Daher cleared the security check and went off to have a beer when they spotted a group of press people. The pair decided it would be fun "to give the media a little show," so they became extra exuberant, smiled brightly, and waved their U.S. flags.

The resulting photographs were printed in hundreds of newspapers. One transmitted by the AP appeared in Dr. Morris' hometown newspapers. In his view, "the photo was a perfect picture of true happiness."

Dr. Morris was surprised when a U.S. Embassy staffer called him over and said there was a gentleman looking for him. The gentleman turned out to be Valentine Brendl, a 68-year-old resident of Bad Homberg, a small village outside of Frankfurt. Morris had tried earlier to reach him by phone, leaving a message that he would call him again from Boston.

Despite the distance involved and the fact that he was on crutches from a leg injury, Brendl had taken the subway to the airport to greet Morris and to congratulate him on gaining his freedom. The men were old friends and had not seen one another since Brendl had worked for GTZ (Deutsche Gesellschaft fur Technische Zusammenarbeit GmbH) in Guyana, South America in the early 1980s.

Dr. Morris felt both honored and happy that his old German friend had made the effort to see him at the airport before the 747's departure. They talked for almost an hour before parting, promising to talk at great length by telephone.

Finally, the Pan Am plane, with only 200 passengers aboard, took off for Andrews Air Force Base outside of Washington, D.C., and Dr. Morris finally became convinced he was forever free of Saddam Hussein's clutches.

"There was a great cry of joy when we flew out of Frankfurt airport," he recalled.

Later, after George and he had talked themselves out for a while, Dr. Morris daydreamed how great "it would be if President Bush sent out two Navy jet fighters to contact us over the Atlantic. What a show it would be if the fighters tipped their wings in a welcome home salute and provided an escort to Andrews. We would make one splendid pass over the field to announce our arrival and get everybody set for our appearance. We were so important the President just had to come to meet and greet us."

Neither the aircraft nor the President showed up, but there was a plethora of bureaucrats awaiting the 747's landing—even agriculture, immigration, and currency people.

The passengers were welcomed by a young lady from the Department of Agriculture, who wanted to know whether any of them was "carrying any plants or vegetables." The 747 fuselage reverberated with laughter.

"It was hilarious. Everyone kept asking her, 'Where do you think we're coming from?'" Typical bureaucrat, she dodged, claiming, "I'm just doing my job."

There was a pleasant surprise when a lady from Immigration asked Dr. Morris for his documents and only said, "Welcome home," after he explained he had lost them all, but he was truly from Boston.

After about 20 minutes, they were allowed to clear the 747, only to run immediately into hordes of additional bureaucrats who hustled them onto buses, into a hall, onto other buses, and into a second hall where they were seated in different sections.

"The same bureaucrats got up again and asked us the same questions and made the same announcements. I began to wonder whether President Bush thought our welcome home should be as boring as possible. They offered several services to us in another hall, including aspirins and a few bucks to get home, only if you signed for them."

Finally, the bureaucrats told the people to go into a large adjoining room, where the government officials "messed around" with a bunch of papers while making weird comments with an air of great importance. It was all bullshit, and we all knew it. We knew no one would ever read any of the forms that had been filled out.

When Dr. Morris caught a glimpse of the gymnasium filled with family, friends, and media people—who had been impatiently awaiting their arrival—he broke for the head of the line and was among one of the very first to file into the entranceway.

"We gave our name to some bureaucrat, who then broadcast it very dramatically to the crowd. I blurted out that I was Robert

Morris and dashed forward as I had already caught sight of Jill standing with Tricia, Anna and other family members. The announcer had only gotten out 'Robert . . . ' when I was seizing her in my arms and hugging her wildly. She was holding Tricia, and I grabbed Anna, and we all kissed and hugged and cried with joy in the midst of hundreds of people."

The family became the center of many photographers when little Tricia began to wave her American flag and smile at the crowd. Within moments, the Morrises were surrounded by a crush of relatives and friends. Boston TV news crews recorded the wonderful moment for millions of viewers in New England.

"It was all so wonderful. A beautiful homecoming like I had been imagining for so long. For now, I'm not going to think about all those months in hiding. I know it will live with me—certainly forever. For all of us who lived through that experience, it's going to take a long time to shake free from some awful memories."

CHAPTER NOTES

Chapter 2

Page 34
(1) After being released, Morris learned that Iraqi helicopters had put a missile in the apartment of a good friend who worked for Siemans Germany. Fortunately, the apartment located close to the US Embassy was empty as the friend and his family had missed his flight back to Kuwait.

Chapter 7

Page 86
(1) The Spanish Embassy never forwarded John Levins' list of names to the United States Embassy.

Page 87
(2) I had actually retained my UN diplomatic passport as a souvenir over the years and it was in my apartment.

Page 90
(3) Dr. Morris learned months later that the people held with him in the Sheraton Hotel comprised the first shipment of hostages sent to Iraq.

Page 91
(4) A top U.S. Embassy official disclosed some ten days later that he had never received any information about the seizure of Dr. Morris and John Levins. He suggested the information had been quashed at a lower staff level.

Chapter 8

Page 96
(1) With two companions and his pet dog, John Evelyn fled in a small boat several days later to safety in Saudi territorial waters.

Page 97
(2) During the Iraqi occupation, the rink had to be used as a public morgue for many victims of the Iraqis.

Chapter 10

Page 123
(1) The Hansens decided to abandon their attempt to escape and to return to Kuwait city. Checking on a rumor, the Hansens went to the Holiday Inn near the airport. At the Holiday Inn, they met up with a group of expatriates who were forming a caravan to cross the desert. They left their small car and boarded a bus which managed to make it to freedom in Saudi Arabia.

Chapter 11

Page 127
(1) Ironically, the car still served a purpose. After returning to the United States, Morris received a phone call out of the blue from a US Marine in Iowa. He asked if Morris had ever owned a charcoal gray 635 BMW. Morris cautiously replied yes. The Marine explained on their hike north to Iraq from Kuwait, he and his partners had enjoyed the comfort of the leather seats for a good night's sleep. He added that Morris should forget about retrieving the car as the Marines had riddled it with bullets as target practice the next morning

Chapter 12

Page 133
(1) Dr. Robert Hansen died of a heart attack in Tulsa, Oklahoma on March 16, 1991.

Chapter 14

Page 174
(1) See Addendum, *Boston Globe* Letters

Chapter 15

Page 177
(1) Many journals including the prestigious Atlantic Monthly had long since discounted the possibility of MIA's in Laos. In reality, the Government of Laos had returned more US bodies than the US Government had indicated were in that country.

Chapter 16

Page 189
(1) After the war, Morris learned that indeed a list had been prepared by friends of the Iraqis at the Ministry of Housing targeting Westerners to be handed over to the Iraqi secret police, and as he was one of the few Americans in the Ministry of Health, his name headed the list.

Chapter 17

Page 199
(1) Dr. Morris learned later that the newsman truly was NBC's Tom Brokaw, who used a portion of the interview on his TV news show.

Page 200
(2) Jill Morris had been contacted by a man with an Eastern European accent who described himself as a "messenger of mercy." He said he would be putting a telephone call through to her soon from Rob. Jill waited beside the telephone for fifteen consecutive days, but the call never came.

Page 206
(3) Philip Balmforth was unable to obtain an exit visa on his arrival in Baghdad and was still there when Morris arrived. Indeed, he did not leave Iraq until several days after Dr. Morris had flown to the States.

Chapter 20

Page 228
(1) Dr. Morris was informed after his return to Boston that the Hoyles had returned safely to their home on Cyprus.

Chapter 22

Page 244
(1) Imad informed Morris when they met in United States at a reunion that the Iraqis had put a pistol to his head demanding that he turn over the Americans

Chapter 25

Page 261
(1) Imad was granted a "humanitarian" visa by the American Embassy to enter the United States shortly after Dr. Morris returned home. Some six months later, he was still seeking work as an engineer in the Washington, D.C. area in order to remain in the States.

Page 267
(2) Dr. Morris provided the CIA and military intelligence with these Iraqi army details on his return to Boston.

Chapter 27

Page 277
(1) Bryant was the former toe-sucking lover of Lady Sarah Ferguson

Page 282
(2) Dr. Morris and Philip Balmforth were unable to locate each other at the Baghdad airport. Philip later went in a motor vehicle convoy across country to be reunited with his family in Amman, Jordan. Six months later, the two men still had not seen one another, but they had conversed several times by telephone.

ADDENDUM

The Boston Globe Letters

September 21, 1990.

"We remain deeply depressed as George Bush's diplomacy achieves nothing, and Iraqi soldiers are reported well dug in with some 2,600 tanks in and around Kuwait.

"Our earlier concerns are realized . . . the Americans lost the early initiative, may even now lose the propaganda war. Saddam Hussein may successfully divide the fractious Arab nation with George Bush and the West then having the battle alone.

"We hear of weakness in the American Congress, of doubts that victory can be achieved. We laughed, ready to cry as we despair. The greatest fighting machine in the world—$300 billion a year for arms—cannot fight the rag-tag army of old men and children who pass by our windows, armed mostly with plastic bags filled not with arms but rather with food or a few stolen items of pleasure somehow overlooked in the initial plunder.

"In "American Caesar" William Manchester wrote that Douglas MacArthur lived by the maxim that every mistake in war is excusable except inactivity and the refusal to take risks. George Bush has committed the inexcusable—he failed to take action in good time, he failed to take risks, to bring his hostages home. If ultimately, as seems more certain each day, he fails diplomatically, then he will stand responsible for not preventing the future carnage by early action.

"We hear daily of atrocities and deaths. They are not reported on the international news. Are the reports true? Are the news services paralyzed, unable to obtain any of these stories?

> Six to twelve doctors massacred in Ahmadi Hospital presumably for refusing Iraqi orders
>
> Three young children gunned down and killed in a supermarket for wearing the Kuwaiti flag
>
> Three teenage boys executed in front of their mothers for alleged Resistance activities
>
> Twenty-four Kuwaiti men machine-gunned in a diwaniya (meeting place)
>
> A supermarket manager shot dead for refusing to put up a poster of Saddam Hussein in his shop
>
> The Kuwaiti chief of the Red Crescent disappears when lodging a complaint over treatment of patients at the Amiri Hospital
>
> An Iraqi doctor attempts to disconnect a wounded Kuwaiti from a life-support system in an ICU
>
> Kuwaiti men arrested at the Saudi border and separated from their fleeing families to be presumably turned over to the Iraqi army and conscripted
>
> An entire nurses' hostel sealed off, and every nurse raped by marauding Iraqi soldiers

"These are just some of the stories we hear, and we cannot confirm these. We remain dismayed. Quite possibly all this could have been prevented, but George Bush committed the inexcusable. He failed—and is continuing to fail—to act."

R.E.M.—Kuwait City

October 9, 1990.

"We are in our 69th day of Iraqi occupation of Kuwait. Through the grace of God, we have eluded the enemy and remain in deep hiding. We have increased our food supplies to hold out for another 130 days. Physically and mentally, our group of 13 can survive, although we are demoralized by the approach of my government and other governments to the hostages and the failure to rescue us.

"Less and less is heard each day on the BBC, VOA, Radio Moscow, or other short-wave stations on the Gulf crisis and the hostages. We assume, correctly or not, that we are forgotten, unimportant, and, as Americans, do not fit into the strategic deliberations of George Bush on Kuwait. We think back to Tehran and some 52 hostages; here, there are thousands of hostages with violence on a far greater magnitude.

"Letters from home are nonexistent; information is scant. VOA fails to broadcast any programs directed at us; BBC leads away with its Gulf stories, even doubling program time. In England, there are support groups, welfare assistance, even loans suspensions. We learn nothing of U.S. support to our families. This causes us only more worry, unnecessary if information were only provided. The embassy begrudgingly forwards messages—only one a week allowed. The staff advises some Americans of available food, but not all of us—a very questionable action.

"International reports on local conditions remain vague. Only Amnesty International speaks out on the atrocities. Iraq piously denies all.

"We are visited this week by a Kuwaiti doctor. Three of us have health problems, all of which are controllable. One member has bronchial asthma—an attack might force a visit to the hospital and certain arrest and imprisonment. The doctor updates us on events in the country.

- A young Kuwaiti physician is summarily executed in front of his wife when caught with saline drips in his car—one bullet in the head

- Some four Filipinos are executed for aiding the Resistance

- All nurses in a five-story hostel were raped. A bomb explodes in the Hilton lobby—several injuries are reported

- An Iraqi commercial jet is attacked as it lifts off at Kuwait Airport.

- A top agent of the Iraqi secret police has his head blown off by the Resistance

- Al-Adan Hospital has 100 beds set aside for gas victims

- British, trapped in the oil fields, are down to canned beans

"It is easy to be wise after the event, but our early statements, predictions, and questions vis-a-vis U.S. actions remain valid. The President should have ordered the immediate evacuation of all Americans from Kuwait, covering the operation with helicopter forces, fighter aircraft, and amphibious craft. A relatively simple exercise has become a very difficult exercise with each passing day, and may eventually be paid for in a lot of blood and tears."

R.E.M.—Kuwait City

because a Navy officer and his wife were accosted in the city. In Kuwait—with several thousand western hostages and other hostages of friendly countries—the U.S. fails to act.

"We have taken it upon ourselves to survive each day, hardly holding out hope that our great country will see the wisdom to bring its family home early. Rest assured, the psychological destruction of many hostages has already occurred, and there will be countless more tragedies—the results of Iraq's invasion and the U.S. failure of will in August past."

R.E.M.—Kuwait City

October 25, 1990.

"An eerie silence has come over the city. While Friday is the holy day, it does not account for the absence of activities. Our guards continue to watch the building and ignore us. Our two fellow travelers were taken away almost two weeks ago by the secret police. Since then, we have, if it is possible, increased our silence.

"We had hoped that the two taken—because of age and illness—would travel with ex-PM Heath. They did not get on the plane. Others younger and healthier did; and our group here feels that Heath and the old-boy network came to secure release of friends only—a sad commentary, but apparently true.

"Tank movement is constant out on the Ring Roads. Sixty plus tanks were seen moving north on October 24th; a similar amount on October 23rd. The road south to Saudi is sparsely patrolled, but no westerner will risk it just yet. But we are all thinking and sending out reconnoiter parties.

"The atrocities continue—three Kuwaitis strung up and castrated in front of their families. This happened after a military sweep that caught eight to ten westerners. That is the punishment for protecting westerners!!"

R.E.M.—Kuwait City

October 15, 1990.

We are in our 75th day of deep hiding. Unfortunately, there are those among us with delusions of grandeur, invincibility, invisibility, and immortality. These delusions have led to breaches of security by three of the nine in our immediate group.

"These three, exposing the entire group to danger, are spotted by the barbarians. Two are captured as they return to their unit after a match of bridge at my place. A Jordanian had betrayed the couple, reporting their presence to the officials in Baghdad. We had warned them, even placed them in a safe apartment, but their delusions of invisibility led to their capture. If good is to come of this because of their age and Edward Heath's promised visit, they may soon return to England.

"The third member of our group was spotted departing on foot in the parking lot. He is a loose cannon, unable to think logically. Confronted by friendlies, told that he was seen, he illogically argued that since he saw no one, no one could have seen him. Utilizing our instant communications network, the group comes down hard on him. He had jeopardized all of us.

We intensify our secret patterns, reduce noise and conversation to a minimum, bathe and wash dishes at 2 a.m. presuming the secret police must sleep some time. We know they are only some 100 feet away. Yet they do not approach our units. They are more interested in robbing empty units, we believe It is now eight days since the security breach. We believe we are over another hurdle.

"Daily we collect food. We are well stocked now except the Asians below seem paralyzed. The women won't move. The men won't spend money on food. We have five more mouths to feed. We will face fierce shortages in four weeks if these people fail to act.

"We remain disillusioned. VOA says little of us. Messages and letters are almost nil. Congress speaks not of us. We remember Grenada—the U.S. attacked because of some students in danger at St. George University Medical School; in Panama, we attacked